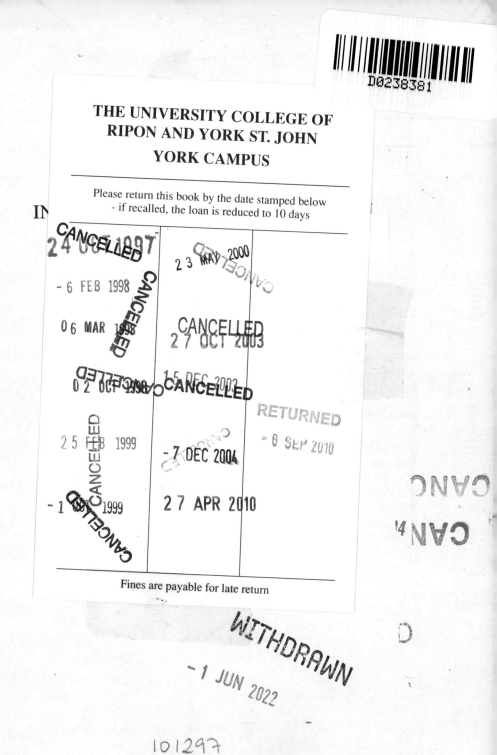

D0238381

101297

Open University Press
Psychotherapy in Britain series
Series Editor: Windy Dryden

TITLES IN THE SERIES

Individual Therapy in Britain
Windy Dryden (ed.)

Family Therapy in Britain
Eddy Street and Windy Dryden (eds.)

Group Therapy in Britain
Mark Aveline and Windy Dryden (eds.)

Sex Therapy in Britain
Martin Cole and Windy Dryden (eds.)

Related titles

Cognitive-Behavioural Approaches to Psychotherapy
Windy Dryden and William Golden

Personal Responsibility Counselling and Therapy
Richard Nelson-Jones

The Presenting Past
Michael Jacobs

Therapist's Dilemmas
Windy Dryden

INNOVATIVE THERAPY IN BRITAIN

Edited by
John Rowan and Windy Dryden

Open University Press
Milton Keynes · Philadelphia

Open University Press
Celtic Court
22 Ballmoor
Buckingham MK18 1XW

and
1900 Frost Road, Suite 101
Bristol, PA 19007, USA

First published 1988
Reprinted 1990

British Library Cataloguing in Publication Data
Innovative therapy in Britain.
  1. Psychotherapy – Great Britain
  I. Rowan, John   II. Dryden, Windy
  616.89′14′0941   RC480

ISBN 0 335 09837 1
ISBN 0 335 09827 4 (pbk)

Typeset by Inforum Ltd, Portsmouth
Printed and bound in Great Britain by
Biddles Ltd, Guildford and King's Lynn

CONTENTS

THE EDITORS

JOHN ROWAN

Starting in 1969, John Rowan has had a wide and deep involvement with the human potential movement, Already qualified as a psychologist, by 1972 he was chairperson of the Association for Humanistic Psychology (AHP) in Britain. In 1978 he became vice-president of the European Association for Humanistic Psychology. In 1980 he helped to found the AHP Practitioners group for raising standards of practice in the field of humanistic psychology (psychotherapy, education, research, management consultancy and so on). In 1981 he co-edited (with Peter Reason) *Human Inquiry: A Sourcebook of New Paradigm Research* (John Wiley). Other books include *Ordinary Ecstasy: Humanistic Psychology in Action* (RKP) and *The Reality Game: A Guide to Humanistic Counselling and Therapy* (RKP). More recently he has been involved with the attempts of the British Association for Counselling to produce a valid accreditation scheme for counsellors. He practises primal integration therapy, trained by the late Dr William Swartley. He teaches at the Institute for Psychotherapy and Social Studies in London.

WINDY DRYDEN

Windy Dryden is senior lecturer in psychology at Goldsmiths' College, University of London. He is the author of *Rational-Emotive Therapy: Fundamentals and Innovations* (Croom Helm, 1984); *Therapists' Dilemmas* (Harper & Row, 1985) and *Counselling Individuals: The Rational-Emotive Approach* (Taylor & Francis, 1987). He is series editor of the *Psychotherapy in Britain* series published by Open University Press and series editor of the forthcoming *Counselling in Action* series to be published by SAGE Publications. He is a Fellow of the British Psychological Society, and serves on the editorial boards of several international journals including the *British Journal of Guidance and Counselling* and is co-editor of the *Journal of Cognitive Psychotherapy: An International Quarterly*. At present he practises part-time as an honorary psychotherapist in the department of psychiatry, St Thomas' Hospital, London, and part-time for the Raphael Counselling Centre in London.

THE CONTRIBUTORS

Ari Badaines trained as a clinical psychologist in the USA, where he received his PhD. He had a fellowship from the National Institute of Health to study psychodrama and group psychotherapy. In 1972 he came to London, where he directed the Richmond Fellowship's training house and was group work adviser to Lambeth Social Services. Ari developed a private practice in individual and family therapy, and did further training at the Institute of Family Therapy in London. During this time he was also involved in running training programmes in psychodrama in the UK and Europe, and in supervising psychotherapists. He is now in Sydney, Australia, where he is engaged in private practice, consulting and psychodrama training. He has presented at professional conferences, and published articles on psychodrama, psychotherapy supervision and therapeutic communities. Ari returns to Europe each summer to continue his training and experiential groups.

David Boadella is the founder-editor of *Energy & Character*, the journal of biosynthesis, founded in 1970. He has worked as an individual therapist at the Gerda Boyesen Institute for Biodynamic Psychology for many years, and was a director of the Institute for the Development of Human Potential, London, from 1977 to 1981. He was the principal of Abbotsbury School in Dorset until 1981, and since then has travelled widely as a visiting group leader to biodynamic and bioenergetic training programmes. In 1982 he created the Centre for Biosynthesis to co-ordinate these programmes. He is the author of eight books on different aspects of somatic psychology.

He can be contacted at BCM CHESIL, London WC1N 3XX.

Jocelyn Chaplin grew up in West Africa and then went to Durham University where she obtained a BA in psychology in 1967. Since then she has held various posts in research and communication. She is also an artist with a particular interest in symbols and myths in psychological growth. Her therapy training was at the Westminster Pastoral Foundation, where she now teaches counselling. She has a private practice as a feminist therapist and runs workshops for the Women's Therapy Centre and courses for the ILEA and City University. Her publications include *The Mass Psychology of Thatcherism* (Socialist Society, 1983). She is a socialist feminist with a spiritual dimension.

Rose Evison says: 'Exploring the universe, human relationships and changing the world have always been important to me. Co-counselling has enabled me to liberate my creative intelligence, my caring for others, my joyful nature from anxiety, alienation and despair. I work as an occupational psychologist, counselling psychologist, management trainer and as a therapist. In these areas I offer co-counselling theory and practice as an effective technology for change, and myself as a guide. In all my life I laugh and love and climb mountains. I write in the hope that conceptualization can form footholds to help others step further into their experience.'

Ian Gordon-Brown is joint founder and director of the Centre for Transpersonal Psychology. In addition he is in private practice as a psychotherapist and consultant psychologist. He read psychology at Cambridge and spent the years 1949–55 on the scientific staff of the National Institute of Industrial Psychology. He was director of the Industrial Participation Association from 1970–76. From 1955 to 1969 he worked with the Lucis Trust, becoming director and an international trustee. In the early 1970s he and Barbara Somers founded the Centre for Transpersonal Psychology. He has had a Jungian analysis and his special interests include ways of expanding individual and group consciousness, esoteric movements and social networks.

Jean Hardy graduated from the Psychosynthesis and Education Trust in 1985. She is a lecturer at Brunel University, teaching political philosophy, political and religious belief and social policies. Her book *A Psychology with a Soul* on the ideas underlying psychosynthesis was published by Routledge & Kegan Paul in 1987. She is a qualified social worker and is now both a teacher and writer.

Richard Horobin says: 'Three strands weave together in my life, distinct but interacting: living with people, doing science and co-counselling. The challenge and support from the people I love form the core of my life. Doing science gives me allies across the world, experiences of transcendence, and the glee of mixing mess-painting with story-telling. Braided through all this, the ideas and activities and skills which make up co-counselling form a marvellous tool kit, helping me love and learn, and leap into the dark. And, lucky me, co-counselling is a tool kit I can hand on to others. The chapter in this book is one way of passing on the tools.'

Eric Robbie, before he became involved in Neuro-Linguistic Programming (NLP) had experienced a range of therapies. He studied groups with the Group Relations Training Association (GRTA), lay on a couch at the Tavistock, tried co-counselling, gestalt, and lots of Transactional Analysis (TA). He also studied postural integration with Curtis Turchin, and did primal re-integration with Janet Lake. In 1981, he decided to switch chairs and become a therapist, and went to train at Cathexis Institute – and discovered Erickson and NLP instead. He now writes, teaches, and has a private practice. He was the first British associate trainer with the Society of Neuro-Linguistic Programming, and is a trainer with NLP International.

Barbara Somers is joint founder and director of training for the Centre for Transpersonal Psychology. She has a private practice as a psychotherapist and trains and supervises counsellors and therapists both within and outside the Centre's network. She also plays a central role in the Centre's pro-gramme of workshops in London. Previously she has worked in personnel, as a literary editor and was for nine years with the Society of Authors. She has had a personal and training analysis (Jungian). Her special interests include dreamwork, symbolism and mythology; the interaction of psyche and soma; and eastern systems of spiritual development, especially Tibetan and Zen.

Clover Southwell was born 1935 in Oxford, obtained her early education in the United States, and then came back to London, Oxford and Cambridge, studying classics and moral sciences. She then spent five years working in Austria with 'hard core' refugees from World War Two, followed by eight years in a London advertising agency. In 1973 she met the work of Gerda Boyesen and her family, with which she has been involved ever since. Following six years at the Gerda Boyesen Institute in London, she now works mainly with training groups in Europe and the United States. Her favourite refreshments are friends, solitude, music and gardening, es-pecially roses.

Geoffrey Whitfield is a group consultant and psychotherapist in Brighton and London. He initiated and co-ordinated the British training programme for bioenergetic analysis between 1976 and 1981. He concluded his own bioenergetic training in Holland in 1982. He has contributed to a wide variety of training programmes and conferences throughout the United Kingdom in bioenergetics and other disciplines. In addition he is course director to the Sussex Diploma Course in Counselling, which trains professionals and other interested persons as counsellors and supervisors. He is also a visiting tutor/supervisor to the Mid Downs Post Graduate Medical Centre of Cuckfield Hospital.

Diana Whitmore is chairperson of the Psychosynthesis and Education Trust and director of its Professional Training Programme. She obtained her BA in mass communications from the University of Minnesota and her MA in confluent education from the University of California, Santa Barbara. From 1969–72 she was a staff member of the Esalen Institute, California, and trained in gestalt and other humanistic psychologies. From 1973–75 she trained with the Psychosynthesis Institute in California and with Dr Roberto Assagioli in Florence. Based in London since 1977, Diana has given many public programmes and professional trainings in the UK and Europe and in 1980 reactivated the Trust for the Furtherance of Psychosynthesis in Education founded by Dr Assagioli. Her book *Psychosynthesis in Education* was published in 1986 by Turnstone Press.

Mike Wibberley has a BA in social sciences and has been involved with therapy and groupwork since 1970. His early work was in mental hospital, remand home and half-way house. He is a former co-director of the Centre for Therapeutic Communication, where he taught family therapy and reality therapy. In 1973 he undertook a two-year training in encounter with Brian Coombe and Eva Chapman, involving some 3,000 directly supervised group hours. He trained in psychotherapy at the Minster Centre, has participated in numerous other short training courses and has recently learned much from the work of Terry Cooper. Mike has worked at the Open Centre for the last six years and does individual therapy in London and in Milton Keynes.

CHAPTER 1

INNOVATIVE THERAPY IN BRITAIN: INTRODUCTION

John Rowan and Windy Dryden

The success of the companion volume *Individual Therapy in Britain* (Dryden, 1984) has led to the emergence of this one. That book dealt with the Freudian, Kleinian and Jungian approaches, person-centred, personal construct, existential, gestalt, rational-emotive and behavioural psychotherapy, and transactional analysis. It also went into the whole question of eclectic approaches to psychotherapy. What we are trying to do here is to fill in certain gaps left open, and also to add new work which was not so easily available then. That is why we call it *innovative* – the therapies decribed here are relatively new.

As in the companion volume, our aim is to produce a book which will specifically refer to Britain, because so much of the writing in this field comes from the USA and is not usually oriented towards the unique cultures of non-American countries. Each therapy has to be naturalized into its adoptive cultures and subcultures if it is to be successful. As in *Individual Therapy in Britain*, each chapter takes the same format: historical context and developments in Britain; theoretical assumptions; practice; and a case example. This permits the reader to make comparisons among the different approaches. The result is a book which stands on its own, but which can also be added to the previous volume to make a two-volume account of the vast majority of all the therapies now available in this country. The main gap still left open is perhaps the cognitive-behavioural therapies, but this is filled by *Cognitive-Behavioural Approaches to Psychotherapy* (Dryden and Golden, 1986) which is not restricted to Britain.

When we come to compare this book with its predecessor, what stands out is the way in which the more innovative therapies seem theoretically thinner than those which are older and better established. They do not have such a thorough underpinning, or so many technical terms. Of course this is obvious in a way – there is just less time for them to have established a whole body of theory and practice and folklore. But in another way it is strange, because everything is so much more technical and fully researched these days and we expect anything new to share in that character. Perhaps psychotherapy is in a way in opposition to the way things are moving in society at the moment. Certainly the more humanistic psychotherapies, which form the majority of those in this book, have a temperamental aversion away from anything which reduces the person to anything less than a whole human being. And many of the existing forms of technicization and objective research do seem to split the person up into a whole host of fragmentary parts, each of which is studied on its own. Perhaps also there is a turning away from the heavy theoretical commitment of psychoanalysis or analytical psychology, just as in sociology there has been a turning away from grand theory.

Certainly there is a marked emphasis on things like spontaneity or intuition, and both of these emphases tend to push out a strong reliance on theory. If you really believe that the best things in therapy go beyond words, perhaps the attempt to tie down a form of therapy in words is more suspect. And yet to say this is to make books like this impossible.

Well, perhaps in a way this is an impossible book. It was certainly very hard to put together. And yet, now that we see it, it seems very necessary. Some of the approaches in this book are difficult or impossible to find elsewhere. There is no book or chapter on primal integration anywhere that we have been able to discover. Books and chapters on feminist therapy are few and far between. Biosynthesis has hardly been written up before. Encounter is notoriously hard to pin down in written form. Transpersonal psychotherapy has very few texts to its name, though this position is improving quite quickly at the moment. So the word *innovative* in our title is really justified.

INNOVATIVE THERAPY IN PERSPECTIVE

In this volume we begin with a chapter on 'Primal Integration'. This was chosen to be the lead chapter because we considered that it is the most comprehensive approach included and alerts readers to issues that are covered in other chapters.

In Chapters 3–5 the approaches are characterized both by their social orientation and by their emphasis on the egalitarian role of the therapist. While there are different theoretical orientations within 'Feminist Therapy' (Chapter 3) as Jocelyn Chaplin notes, this approach is characterized more by its attitude toward therapy than by a shared theoretical basis. Feminist therapists are sensitive to the impact of culturally and socially defined gender roles on clients' psychopathology and a significant number of them are active as social change agents as well as therapists. In addition, they seek to establish and maintain an egalitarian relationship with their clients, viewing non-egalitarian bonds as manifestations of patriarchal attitudes which they see as being at the root of the social oppression of women.

In 'Encounter' (Chapter 4), the therapeutic rationale can be characterized as one where the group (a microcosm of society) is helped to develop an attitude of mutual openness and sharing. This serves to counteract the non-self-disclosing communication that is a feature of general social groups where individuals protect themselves from other people by adopting social roles and wearing public masks. Encounter group facilitators are also egalitarian in that they eschew the role of 'expert'. Their style of participation in these groups is one which emphasizes openness, disclosure of human vulnerability and caring for others. They endeavour to be themselves in the therapeutic process and avoid playing the role of therapist. They show through their democratic participation that they can and should be challenged by other group members. Encounter group leaders who try to be very challenging and charismatic tend to be less good as leaders than those who adopt a more equal stance.

'Co-counselling' (Chapter 5) is perhaps the most democratic of the approaches discussed in this book in that the 'client' and 'counsellor' exchange roles within a given therapeutic contact. The co-counselling movement is also actively involved in social change programmes producing, for example, valuable leaflets for disadvantaged groups.

In Chapter 6, 'Psychodrama' is discussed. This approach has a decided social orientation (the work is carried out in groups, and Moreno was always interested in broader social issues) but here we begin to see the emergence of the therapist as 'expert'; the therapist in psychodrama is usually called the *director*. This theme of therapist as expert continues throughout the rest of the volume culminating in 'Neuro-Linguistic Programming' (Chapter 12) where the therapist is not only an expert but one who seeks to bring about change by methods which are often obscured from the client. In some ways the therapist here is akin to a 'magician' and it is noteworthy that many of the NLP book titles have the word *magic* in their titles, or titles which refer to magical transformations.

In Chapters 7–9 three approaches are presented which have as their prime focus the body. Readers may wonder why we have included three body therapies in this text. We decided to do so because there exists a growing number of therapeutic approaches in Britain which are body-oriented. A recent very slim booklet on humanistic psychology (Rowan, 1987) mentions fifteen of them in a single paragraph!

In Chapters 10 and 11, the therapeutic focus switches away from the body. Both 'Psychosynthesis' and 'Transpersonal Psychotherapy' are concerned more with the interior life of the person and are characterized by an emphasis on spiritual issues. Here the therapist serves as a gentle spiritual guide contrasting sharply, one might argue, with some of the other approaches.

Finally a concluding chapter draws together some important themes and presents our reactions as editors to the material presented in Chapters 2–12.

THE THERAPEUTIC SPACE: LOCATING THE APPROACHES

One of the worst things about psychotherapy is the way in which it tends to be very parochial and very ignorant. Each school tends to know very little about the other schools, and where it does acknowledge their existence, puts them down in very unfair ways. This is probably because each therapist has been through her or his own therapy, and the lessons of this very personal process are more powerful than any theory or clinical experience with clients. This results in books like Joel Kovel's (1978) *A Complete Guide to Psychotherapy*, which purports to be an objective tour round various therapies, but which in fact boosts psychoanalysis and puts down everyone else. In the previous volume, Dryden (1984) did attempt to overcome this by drawing up a set of dimensions on which therapies could be compared and contrasted. This brought about a great deal of clarification, but at the cost of producing a chart at the end which was hard to look at and understand. In this chapter we would like to adopt a different approach, which is to use just two dimensions, and to range all the therapies in the space so created. In Figure 1.1 may be found all the approaches mentioned in this book, plus some other approaches which help to define this space.

The first dimension is arrived at by saying that some therapies work at the level of conscious awareness and rarely or never mention the unconscious, while others are continually referring to that which is unconscious and not present to awareness. This is a fairly obvious one, because one of the main controversies in the field has always been between psychoanalysis and

Figure 1.1   The therapeutic space

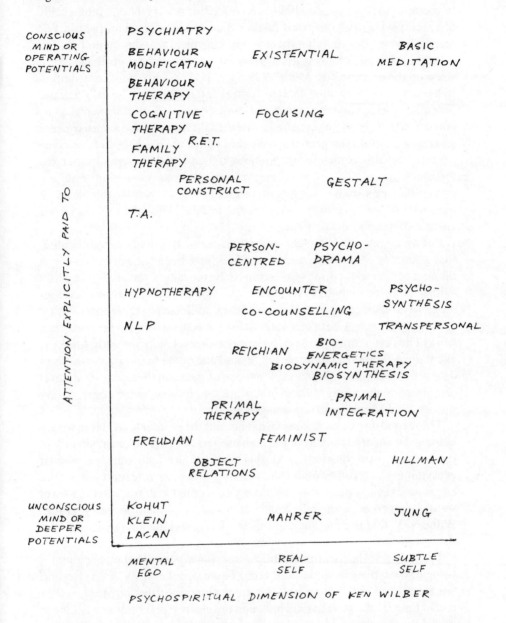

CONSCIOUS
MIND OR
OPERATING
POTENTIALS

PSYCHIATRY

BEHAVIOUR MODIFICATION   EXISTENTIAL   BASIC MEDITATION

BEHAVIOUR THERAPY

COGNITIVE THERAPY   FOCUSING

FAMILY THERAPY   R.E.T.

PERSONAL CONSTRUCT   GESTALT

T.A.

ATTENTION EXPLICITLY PAID TO

PERSON-CENTRED   PSYCHO-DRAMA

HYPNOTHERAPY   ENCOUNTER   PSYCHO-SYNTHESIS

CO-COUNSELLING

NLP   TRANSPERSONAL

REICHIAN   BIO-ENERGETICS
BIODYNAMIC THERAPY
BIOSYNTHESIS

PRIMAL THERAPY   PRIMAL INTEGRATION

FREUDIAN   FEMINIST

OBJECT RELATIONS   HILLMAN

UNCONSCIOUS
MIND OR
DEEPER
POTENTIALS

KOHUT
KLEIN   MAHRER   JUNG
LACAN

MENTAL EGO   REAL SELF   SUBTLE SELF

PSYCHOSPIRITUAL DIMENSION OF KEN WILBER

behaviourism, and this is the main bone of contention between them. But
existential therapy also denies the importance of the unconscious in the way

in which it arises in Freudian theory, and so do some of the other approaches to therapy, so it is not just about behaviourism. And orthodox biologically oriented psychiatry goes even further than modern behaviourism in this respect, almost denying that there is anything mental about mental illness.

At the other end of this scale, it is not only psychoanalysis which lays great stress on the unconscious. Mahrer (1978), in his very important contribution to humanistic theory, also deals in central detail with what he calls 'deeper potentials' occupying very much the same region as Freud's unconscious, and the various approaches to body-oriented therapy also use such a concept a great deal, as do the primal approaches which are close to them in many respects. So this conscious/unconscious dimension does separate out the therapies quite well, though approaches such as encounter and co-counselling are variable, ranging at different times all over the dimension in question, so we have to put them in the middle. This, then, gives us our vertical dimension in the figure.

But what are we to use as the other dimension? It is really very difficult to find a suitable continuum, and many ideas have been tried in the past, but the best answer so far discovered seems to be the dimension outlined by Ken Wilber in his many books. This is a dimension of psychospiritual development. In *No Boundary*, which is specifically addressed to therapists, Wilber (1981) distinguishes between three broad levels on which therapists can work. The first of these, he says, is the *persona* level; here we are helping the client to adjust to his or her role in life, and one of the main tasks in this is to deal with the *shadow*. Wilber says that one of the main therapies at this level is transactional analysis, though others are rational-emotive therapy, reality therapy and of course psychoanalysis itself.

The second one he mentions is what he calls the *centaur* level. Here we are helping the client to find his or her own existential self, and one main task in this is to re-own the body. At this level we have to question almost everything which comes under the heading of ego, or role; and indeed the ego is now seen to be almost exclusively concerned with roles. At this level we are concerned with self-actualization, autonomy and meaning in life. Wilber says that the therapies at this level may include hatha yoga, gestalt therapy, focusing and bioenergetics.

The third level he mentions is the *transpersonal*. Here what we are about is going beyond the existential self, going beyond authenticity, going beyond 'meaning in my life'. Jung was the great pioneer of this territory, but in recent times Roberto Assagioli has been the clearest practitioner working in it. At this level we do not even try to solve our personal problems or distresses – we simply watch them, and let go of them. We move to a state of choiceless awareness. Wilber recommends as therapy at this level Progoff's journal approach, psychosynthesis, vipassana meditation and of course Jungian therapy.

These are discrete levels, but the process of development joining them is a continuous one, so that it is appropriate to regard the dimension as a continuum. This is what has been done in Figure 1.1, and it can be seen from this that the various forms of psychotherapy spread out rather well over the space formed by the two dimensions. This in itself is reassuring, because it seems from many accounts of psychotherapy that there are just two categories – those which are right and those which are wrong. Also the therapies which we intuitively regard as close to one another do come out close to each other on the map, so this tends to assure us that the approach here does make sense.

The only therapy which does not relate very well to this schema is feminist therapy, because here a political dimension comes in which very rarely appears in most other forms of therapy. This makes it very distinctive; it is perhaps as if we should have a third (vertical) dimension, running perhaps from conservatism to radicalism. If we did this, we should see the whole of the middle part of the chart rising into the air, and the edges moving downwards. We should get a sort of arch or tunnel. Co-counselling, encounter, the person-centred approach and gestalt have historically been associated with radical groups and political awareness. Mahrer pays lengthy and explicit attention to social factors. The existentialists have always had a political streak. TA, too, has made some moves in this direction. But feminist therapy goes further than any of them, it seems, in very centrally relating therapy to the social context.

Interpretation

One of the things which joins all the therapies in this book is that they are all very active in their approach; in other words, they all involve engaging the client in some experience initiated by the therapist with the words 'Let's try this.' It is important to recognize that this is a form of *interpretation*.

For those who do not know the term very well, perhaps we should explain that this is one of the hottest controversies in all of psychotherapy. The psychoanalytic schools say that the heart of therapist activity is interpretation, and everyone else says that interpretations are useless or even harmful. In psychoanalysis, an interpretation is a revelation by the therapist to the client of what is *really* going on beneath the surface appearances; making something which was hidden open; making something which was unconscious conscious. The critics say that to try to give the client an insight in this way is much too external and intellectual, and so ineffectual. If this is true, we must avoid all interpretations as basically time-wasting. But what we want to say here is that all the alternatives to interpretation are merely ways of making more effective interpretations. Let's see what could be meant by this.

There are two steps in making an interpretation. The first step is to notice that something is going on, to decide that here is an area worth probing. For example, a young man may refer to his girl friend in very dependent terms, which may make the therapist think 'I wonder if he is seeing his mother in her, and trying to get from her what he couldn't get from his mother?' It is a possibility which is worth exploring, because if it were true, this would go back to very early material in the Freudian oral stage. This is, then, the first essential stage in interpretation – picking out something as worth paying attention to.

Step two is to get the client to pay attention to it too. Unless both parties are paying attention to the same thing, no interpretation is going to be at all effective. So the therapist takes the last thing the client did which was relevant, and holds it up for the person to see in some way. A Rogerian might say 'You're kind of *imploring* her to pay some mind to you.' A gestaltist might say 'On this cushion is sitting your mother. Try saying the same thing to her.' A co-counsellor might say 'Try saying that again a few times, and see what comes up.' A primal therapist might get the young man to lie down and hold up his arms and repeat the last request a few times, such as, 'I want more from you.' And a psychoanalyst might say 'It is as if you were really talking to you mother', or 'I wonder if it is really me you want more attention from?'

Now, it is difficult to say how any of these responses are *not* interpretations. They all put the therapist's guess into the client's mind in some way or other, more or less directly. And sure, there are all sorts of moves one might want to make between steps one and two. One might want to get the client to focus more on the general area before deciding exactly how specific to get. But this is just as true of the psychoanalyst as it is of the humanistic practitioner.

So when we hear a psychotherapist saying that he or she does not interpret, but lets the client be, or lets the client do the work, it is always worth probing to see whether this is really so or not.

Traumas – real or imaginary?

One of the issues which comes out in these pages rather clearly is the question of early trauma. Janet Malcolm (1986) shows how important this controversy has become within psychoanalysis. According to her account, it is rather like a battle in which one side says that early trauma explains everything (what is outside the person causes the neurosis), and the other side says that it is the responsibility of the patient which explains everything (what is inside the person causes the neurosis). This seems to be quite an absurd quarrel, because if early trauma is important, it is still crucial what the client made of it. Why shouldn't both be important?

The example which comes to mind is the case of Sybil (Schreiber, 1975) which was made into a vivid film, shown more than once on television. Here is a case in which both sides of the equation come out with great clarity. The child was abused and maltreated, both sexually and otherwise, by a psychotic mother, supported by a passive father. The defence she chose was splitting, in the form of dissociated personality. Over a period of time she developed and showed sixteen distinct personalities. So this was her form of defence, in response to a very real attack. The very fact that we call these things defences leaves the way open to the consideration that the attack might come from inside or from outside.

This does not mean that we have to say that the child is totally innocent – there is no way of saying that anyone is totally innocent, nor is it necessary to do so; all we have to do is to say that – innocent or not – this person was traumatized. This is the major thing we have to deal with in the first instance, and by doing that we shall get everywhere we need to go.

Of course this is very much Alice Miller territory. It was Alice Miller (1985) who raised in its most acute form the need to deal with the real suffering of the hurt child, and not to dismiss it as fantasy or avoidance. She puts in a very moving way the need to pay attention to the poisonous pedagogy of the majority of parents. Most parents, she says, deal with children in a way which suits them but offends against the integrity of the child, and this results in various ill results in the unfortunate child. The child is then prevented from complaining, because the parents have to be right – that is the system. She is, as it were, on the side of the injured child. And this has made a big impact on the psychoanalytic world, because it seems to argue counter to·the Freudian theory of repression – what Miller calls the *drive* theory – and she even argues that a great deal of what analysts do is just another form of the same poisonous pedagogy that the patient suffered from in the first place. Analysts, too, prevent the child from complaining, by turning it all back on to the patient, and having to be right.

Now Janov has always said much the same thing. In his 1977 book he is very clear that trauma really is important, and he too is on the side of the child. In general, most of the humanistic psychotherapists go with the idea that infantile trauma is real and has to be worked with as such. Grof (1985) and Lake (1980) are of course prime examples, Lake having outlined four levels of trauma which may be experienced, and showing how each level has different implications. Recently John Southgate and Liz Whiting (1987) have been pointing out many ramifications of the whole thing, and showing that it affects all psychotherapists, because they too may be practising poisonous pedagogy in their own way. Zelda Hall (1987) too has said a good deal about 'soul murder', quoting the work of Schatzman (1973) and Shengold (1975) to show that there is much more to be said in this area than even Alice Miller has supposed. But there is probably not one contributor to this book who would practise poisonous pedagogy in the therapy session – that is, taking up a parental position, siding with the parents, or having to be right.

But it also needs to be said that therapy does not stop with anger against the parents. Sybil (Schreiber, 1975) eventually got down to the anger, but then when her symptoms had disappeared she was able to forgive her mother, and forgive herself, and see her mother as a psychotic sufferer, and feel sorry for her. If you can let go of your symptoms, you can let go of your hate too. You can take responsibility for your part in the events, without it turning into self-blame.

This does not mean that everyone has won, and everyone must have prizes. It means that we have to beware of overlooking poisonous pedagogy, whether perpetrated by parents or by therapists. It means that we have to go with the client into the client's world, and see it through the client's eyes, before doing anything else, and maybe instead of doing anything else. It is a pity in a way that we could not have had a chapter on the approach of Mahrer (1986), because he takes up this position more thoroughly than anyone else we know. However, his method is not practised much, or perhaps at all in its pure form, in Britain, at least as of the moment of writing.

Of course, some therapies do not give much importance to early trauma, and for them this whole controversy is rather lacking in interest. To them we can only say that an awareness of these matters is very valuable, simply because many clients will bring it up in some form or other, whether they are supposed to or not. It is even true, apparently, that a student of Zen meditation came up to the *roshi* and said 'I expected to get enlightenment, but all I am getting is all this childhood stuff.'

REFERENCES

Dryden, W. (ed.) (1984) *Individual Therapy in Britain*, Harper & Row, London.
Dryden, W. and Golden, W. (eds.) (1986) *Cognitive-Behavioural Approaches to Psychotherapy*, Harper & Row, London.

Grof, S. (1985) *Beyond the Brain*, State University of New York, New York.

Hall, Z. M. (1987) Soul murder *Changes*, Vol. 5, No. 5, pp. 303–6.

Janov, A. (1977) *The Feeling Child*, Abacus, London.

Kovel, J. (1978) *A Complete Guide to Psychotherapy*, Penguin, Harmondsworth.

Lake, F. (1980) *Studies in Constricted Confusion*, CTA, Oxford.

Mahrer, A. R. (1978) *Experiencing*, Brunner/Mazel, New York.

Mahrer, A. R. (1986) *Therapeutic Experiencing*, W. W. Norton, New York.

Malcolm, J. (1986) *In the Freud Archives*, Fontana, London.

Miller, A. (1985) *Thou Shalt Not Be Aware: Society's Betrayal of the Child*, Pluto Press, London.

Rowan, J. (1987) *A Guide to Humanistic Psychology*, Association for Humanistic Psychology in Britain, London.

Schatzman, M. (1973) *Soul Murder: Persecution in the Family*, Penguin, Harmondsworth.

Schreiber, F. R. (1975) *Sybil*, Penguin, Harmondsworth.

Shengold, L. (1975) *An Attempt at Soul Murder: Rudyard Kipling's Early Life and Work*, Psychoanalytic Study of the Child, Vol. 3.

Southgate, J. and Whiting, L. (1987) *Journal of the Institute for Self-Analysis*, Vol. 1, No. 1.

Wilber, K. (1981) *No Boundary*, Routledge & Kegan Paul, London.

CHAPTER 2

PRIMAL INTEGRATION THERAPY

John Rowan

HISTORICAL CONTEXT AND DEVELOPMENTS IN BRITAIN

Primal integration is a form of therapy brought over to Britain by Bill Swartley, although it was also pioneered here by Frank Lake. It lays the major emphasis upon early trauma as the basic cause of neurosis, and enables people to regress back to the point in time when the trouble began, and to relive it there. This often involves a cathartic experience called *a primal*. But some people using this approach do not like this language, and instead call what they do regression-integration, or re-integration, or holonomic integration, or intensive feeling therapy. It is strongly influenced by the research of Stanislav Grof (1975), who points particularly to the deep traumas often associated with the experience of birth.

Historical context

Historically, this approach is close to early Freud, early Reich and Janov. But all of those adopted a medical model of mental illness, which primal integration therapists reject. As Szasz (1961) pointed out long ago, neurosis is only a metaphorical sickness. Rather do we stand with those who say that we are less concerned with cure than with growth.

As soon as one gets down into the early roots of mental distress, deep and strong feelings come up, because the emotions of early life are less inhibited, less qualified and less differentiated than they later become. And so the whole question of the importance of catharsis in psychotherapy arises here. As Kaufman (1974) reminds us:

> It was Reich and Perls, not Janov, who discovered the techniques for deep emotional release that are utilised to produce primals . .,. the Reichian-oriented therapist Charles Kelley (1971) used the term 'an intensive' years before Janov to describe experiences identical to primals. (p. 54)

One can go further back and say that catharsis is found in prehistoric shamanism, Greek tragedy, the work of Mesmer and throughout world literature. Nichols and Zax (1977) have a very full discussion of this long history, where they say

> catharsis has two related but separate components: one is relatively intellectual – the recall of forgotten material; the second is physical – the discharge of emotion in tears, laughter or angry yelling. (p. 8)

But in the kind of work which is done in therapy it seems better to be more specific, and to say with Pierce *et al.* (1983) that catharsis is the vigorous expression of feelings about experiences which had been previously unavailable to consciousness. This lays more emphasis upon the necessity for the emergence of unconscious material.

What Swartley, Lake, Grof and others did was to bring together the idea of catharsis and the emphasis on getting down to the origins of disturbance with another important question – the transpersonal and the whole area of spirituality. (These terms are explained very well elsewhere in this book, particularly in the chapters by Hardy and Whitmore and Gordon-Brown and Somers.) This means that primal integration therapy can deal with the major part of the whole psychospiritual spectrum mapped out by Ken Wilber (1980). I believe it is unique in this, except possibly for the holotropic approach recently described by Grof (1985).

In 1973 about a hundred people met in Montreal to form the International Primal Association (IPA), founded by Bill Swartley, David Freundlich, William Smukler and others. In an attempt to get Janov to admit that he was part of a wider movement, he was offered the position of first president, but declined. In 1974 a journal was produced, called *Primal Community*, and Janov proceeded to sue for infringement of his registered service mark *Primal Therapy*. After a court case (the high expense of which meant that *Primal Community* could no longer be produced), the IPA won on the grounds that the word *primal* had been used by many other people (including Freud) over the years, and could not be taken out of the public domain in the way required for Janov to win the case.

Swartley travelled round the world starting up primal integration centres of one kind and another, and in Italy a very good one of these still exists, run by Michele Festa, who is very active in Rome in the whole field of humanistic psychology, and who has now also extended to Zurich.

Developments in Britain

Frank Lake started to work with LSD at Scalebor Park Hospital in 1954. He discovered, as Grof (1975) was also finding at about the same time in Czechoslovakia, that getting in touch with perinatal (round about birth) experiences could be very important in the process of psychotherapy. Around 1970 he discovered bioenergetics (see Chapter 7) and the Reichian and neo-Reichian work of Boadella and others (see Chapter 8), which showed that LSD was not necessary to get into the reliving of early traumas – all that was needed was permission and possibly some help with breathing. This connected with the earlier work of Rank (1934), Fodor (1949) and Mott (1948) who had been unjustly neglected, mainly perhaps because they did not have any technique to offer other than the very slow and tortuous analysis of dreams. It also connected with the work of Donald Winnicott (1958) and the rest of the object relations school, who stressed the import-ance of pre-Oedipal problems.

Lake started calling his work primal integration only in the 1970s, after meeting Swartley. He then went on to further discoveries about fetal life (compare Verny, 1982), and later produced some of the most exciting work yet done on fetal traumas (Lake, 1980; 1981). His death in 1982 robbed us of much more exciting work. Recently his major work has been published in abridged form (Lake, 1986), making it much more accessible.

Another pioneer was William Emerson, another member of the IPA who spent a good deal of time in Europe. He had been trained as a clinician, and worked for some time in hospitals, but got more and more involved with regression and integration therapy. He also started calling his work primal integration, and was a quite separate source of influence in Britain. He pioneered the idea of actually working in a primal way with children, and produced a pamphlet on *Infant and Child Birth Re-facilitation* (Emerson, 1984) and a video film of his work with them.

Also in the mid-1970s Stan Grof came to Britain several times; he had met primal integration people at the second IPA conference and had found there the way of carrying on his work without the use of drugs.

I came across primal integration in 1977, and worked closely with Bill Swartley until his unfortunate death in 1979. We who had been involved with Swartley carried on for a while as the *Whole Person Cooperative*, but this no longer exists. At present Richard Mowbray and Juliana Brown are doing excellent work at the Open Centre in London. I am doing individual therapy, and a few training workshops. The CTA carries on teaching Lake's approach, and many of Emerson's pupils are now working. An important centre is *Amethyst* in Ireland, where Alison Hunter and Shirley Ward work themselves, and also bring over Emerson and others to develop the work.

THEORETICAL ASSUMPTIONS

It will be clear from what has been said that primal integration is a syncretic approach which brings together the extremes of therapy: it goes far back into what Wilber (1983) calls the prepersonal realm and deeply into the internal conflicts of the individual; and it goes far into the transpersonal realms of symbols, intuition and the deeper self. It is this combination of extremes which makes it so flexible in practice.

Image of the person

The person is at bottom human and trustworthy. Deep down underneath all the layers and the roles and the defences and the masks is the real self, which is always OK. This belief gives great confidence in going down into those areas of the client which he or she finds the deepest and darkest. Here we are very much in agreement with Mahrer (1986), although the language is different.

The person starts early. Memory can go back before language is acquired. People can often remember their own births. The fetus is conscious. All these statements are empirically checkable, and in recent years more and more evidence has been appearing about them. Much of this material is now written up and easily available in Verny (1982) – this Canadian therapist was actually one of the founders of the IPA. More evidence about consciousness at birth is given by Chamberlain (1984).

This means that Swartley (1977) can write about eight major categories of trauma which may occur and be important in later life, all located in time between conception and the end of the first hour of life: conception trauma (Peerbolte, 1975); Fallopian tube trauma; implantation trauma (Laing, 1976); embryological traumas; uterine traumas (Lake, 1980; Feher, 1980; Demause, 1982); birth traumas (Grof, 1975; Janov, 1983; Albery, 1985); and bonding traumas (Klaus and Kennell, 1976). Of these, the birth, uterine and implantation traumas are the ones which come up most frequently in therapy, though Shirley Ward believes that conception trauma may come up more often if we allow it do so.

So to sum up, our image of the person is essentially of a healthy consciousness which may become visible as an ego at any point between conception and about three years old.

Some primal integration practitioners are prepared to work with the notion of previous lives (Netherton and Shiffrin, 1979; Grof, 1985), and this is done at the Amethyst centre in Ireland, but I have little experience of this myself and prefer not to talk about it until my understanding is greater.

Concepts of psychological health and disturbance

We are naturally healthy mentally, just as we are naturally healthy physically. We have basic needs to exist, for protection against danger, for contact comfort, for love, for sustenance, for exploration, for communication, for respect, and so on. As long as these needs are satisfied, we will stay healthy and grow, as Maslow (1970) more than anyone else has insisted. But if we get poison instead of food, isolation instead of contact, exposure to danger instead of protection, hate or indifference instead of love, insecurity instead of security, emotional withdrawal instead of support, mystification or double-bind instead of learning, then those basic needs will remain unmet or unfulfilled.

When such primal needs are unmet by parents or other caregivers, or seem to be from the infant's point of view, the child will experience primal pain. And needs do not go away – they still remain – so the child has primal pain and unmet needs, too. This is what is meant by trauma.

This primal pain can be too much to bear. Lake (1980) describes four levels of experience. Level 1 is totally need-satisfying – everything is all right. Level 2 is coping: there are some unmet needs but they are bearable, still within the realm of the 'good enough'. Level 3 is opposition: pain of this order cannot remain connected up within the organism; it is repressed, and many aspects of the matter are pushed into the unconscious, in the manner suggested by Freud. Defences are then set up to preserve this solution, and to make sure that it stays forgotten. Level 4 is transmarginal stress (this term is taken from Pavlov's work) and here the pain is so great that the much more drastic defence of splitting has to be used. The whole self is split into two, and only one part (the *false self* as described by Winnicott [1958] and others) is adapted to the new situation, while the other part (Winnicott's *true self*) is hidden away as too small, too weak and too vulnerable. The self is then defined as not-OK or bad (this is now the false self, which is all that is present in awareness) and can even turn against itself, willing its own death and destruction. In this area Reich, Balint, Winnicott, Janov, Grof and Laing are in substantial agreement, emphasizing that Level 4 is not an unusual response. The earlier the trauma, the fewer resources the infant has for dealing with it, and the more likely it is that the more drastic defence will be used. In this context, health is staying with the true self (real self) and disturbance is whatever leads to the setting up of a false self (unreal self). So in adult life many people, not just a few, cultivate their false selves (persona, self-image, role, mask) rather than keeping or retaining touch with their true selves.

Alice Miller (1985) has attracted a good deal of attention recently by her criticisms of many psychoanalysts for ignoring early trauma, and has specifically said that the primal approach has a much better record in this respect. But she shares with Janov a tendency to blame the parents and leave it at that, which we in primal integration do not do, Freundlich (1973) makes it clear that this is not a criticism of parents in general, or mothers in particular:

> Thus primal pain will occur no matter how loving and caring parents are, and how diligently they attempt to fulfil the child's primal needs. Since the child is helpless and dependent and cannot understand much of what occurs in his world which is beyond his control, he experiences pain even though the intent of those around him may be loving.   (p. 2)

What we are saying, therefore, is that most people have some degree of disturbance rather than being totally healthy. If this is so, we shall expect to see neurosis on a vast scale. And according to Mahrer (1978), Demause (1982), Wasdell (1983) and Miller (1985) this is indeed the case. They have brought out social analyses which demonstrate in great detail just how much our whole society is subject to projections, denials and other defences on an enormous canvas.

Acquisition of psychological disturbance

We have already said that neurosis is acquired through traumatic experience. The same is true of psychosis and borderline or narcissistic conditions, except that here the trauma is earlier in time. The most adequate account of this is to be found in Wilber (1984), who develops the notion of a fulcrum. A *fulcrum*, in his terms, is a point where a developmental step has to be made by the individual. There are three things which we can do when faced with such a developmental moment: we can retreat and resist altogether (this is most likely to be when the previous step was so traumatic that defences were raised which placed the utmost emphasis on safety and security); we can go halfway and then get stuck (this will be mostly when a trauma hits the person during the process of that particular developmental moment); or we can go all the way and thus ready ourselves for the taking of the next developmental step. Wilber (1984) distinguishes nine such developmental fulcrums, though he says much more about some of them than about others.

Janov (1975) has his own simpler version of this idea, and describes three broad stages of development, which correspond to different traditions in psychotherapy, and also to three different areas in the brain.

Third-line traumas are those which occur when we have access to speech. These are the events which the classical Freudian analyst is most commonly working with – the Oedipus complex may be involved in some form. They are registered in the cerebral cortex – the newest part of the brain – and language and meaning are very important. Often three people are involved in such late traumas – the child and the rival parents.

Second-line traumas are much more primitive, going back to the time before speech came on the scene, but where emotions were developed and deeply felt, often involving dramatic fantasies. Language is not important in these cases, and may be altogether absent. And this is usually a pre-Oedipal two-person relationship, which the object relations school are very happy working with (also Kohut and Lacan). Such traumas are involved with the limbic system of the brain – this is the area where tranquillizers are aimed at, and where they have their main effect.

First-line traumas are more primitive still, going back to the time before any differentiation of the emotions took place, and where survival is the main issue. This involves the reptilian brain or R-complex – the most basic and oldest part of the brain, which we share with most of the animal realm. There is hardly even much sense of two-ness here – just deep fundamental feelings of positive or negative.

Where we would differ from Janov, however, is that we do not believe that experience is reducible to brain function. It seems clear now from all the research on the near-death experience (Grey, 1985) that the brain can be completely knocked out while experiencing continues. Similarly in fetal experience, as Mowbray (1985) points out:

> Certainly there are more physical and survival traumas in the early stages, however there is also a *being* there experiencing the meaning of these, and the splitting-off of the memory is not necessarily an event in the brain alone. Thus we find aspects of these very early experiences that are expressible in words.
>
> (Personal communication)

Even when the earlier traumas are not expressed in words, it often takes many words to work through the experience of reliving such a trauma and to integrate such a breakthrough into current daily life.

What we find is that third-line traumas tend to produce neurotic defences, while first-line traumas tend to produce psychotic defences. (Second-line traumas may go one way or the other, or produce borderline or narcissistic conditions, as Kohut [1971;1977] has suggested.) And again, this suggests that psychosis is more common and more ordinary than we thought. Some of us now talk about the 'normal psychotic' just as a few years ago we used to talk about the 'normal neurotic'.

This means that we are apt to regard as screen memories (that is, memories which purport to be basic but which are actually hiding something more fundamental) the material which many other therapists are quite willing to treat as bedrock. Swartley (1977) gives the analogy of tearing down a rotten building: you tear it down until you get to something solid, and then you build up from there:

> Or you might have to go further back again. In one case this woman was dying of tuberculosis, knew she was dying, and when she knew she was pregnant she didn't want to know, she rejected the baby right from the start, and that was transmitted to the child *in utero*. And there was no good motherhood to look back to, the mother had never been a good mother. So this person had to go further back, we took her back to Jung's archetypal level and she found inside herself the archetype of the Great Mother. And that is somehow inherited as part of the racial heritage, and she went back to Ireland and nourished herself with the Great Mother inside of herself. And that was 'solid' for her.   (p. 168)

It can be seen here how the transpersonal comes in as an integral part of the process of therapy, as Grof (1985) also emphasizes.

But of course traumas are seldom as dramatic as this. The commonest causes of neurosis are simply the common experiences of childhood – all the ways in which our child needs are unmet or frustrated. Hoffman (1979) speaks eloquently about the problem of negative love. Because of the prevalence of neurosis and psychosis vast numbers of parents are unable to give love to their children. Hoffman says:

> When one adopts the negative traits, moods or admonitions (silent or overt) of either or both parents, one relates to them in negative love. It is illogical logic, nonsensical sense and insane sanity, yet the pursuit of the love they never received in childhood is the reason people persist in behaving in these destructive patterns. 'See, Mom and Dad, if I am just like you, will you love me?' is the ongoing subliminal query.   (p. 20)

This is not necessarily a single trauma, in the sense of a one-off event – that is much too simplistic a view. Rather would we say with Balint (1968) that the trauma may come from a situation of some duration, where the same painful lack of 'fit' between needs and supplies is continued.

Perpetuation of psychological disturbance

We have many, many ways of maintaining our neurosis. Our defences have been built up over years, and they are designed to keep the system going – painful as it may be. Losing them feels very dangerous.

If we study ourselves as we go around our world, we find that we are talking to ourselves the whole time. This is a very old observation, which Buddhism and Yoga noted and commented on centuries ago. There is a sort of chatter which proceeds independently of our will or control. Recently the cognitive therapists such as Beck and Ellis have been spelling this out at length. And with neurotic people, the talk is usually negative (though it can also sometimes be grandiose), consisting of statements like: 'you'll get it wrong'; 'you don't deserve to have any pleasure'; 'they will all reject you'; 'you aren't worth anything'; every possible self put-down.

This is part of the defensive system, and part of the negative love system, and the whole object of it is to keep us safe. But of course it doesn't keep us safe at all. Whether the actual content be good or bad, it is compulsive. And it is our character.

This is a radical position, close to that of Reich, who said somewhere that character *is* neurosis. What this means is that all our rigidities, *and particularly the good ones*, are holding us back and stopping us from developing any further. But they are not under our conscious control because they have their roots in our defensive system, which has its roots in our primal traumas. So the self-talk, whether negative or positive, actually keeps us away from the deeper parts of ourselves – what Mahrer (1978) calls the deeper potentials. And in fact the object of the self-talk is precisely to do this, in just the same way that the muscular defences described by Whitfield and Boadella (Chapters 7 and 8) are there to keep us away from our deeper feelings.

And because much of the self-talk comes from injunctions given to us by our early caretakers, it is really the opinions of others which we are using to avoid our own deeper selves. We see ourselves through the eyes of others, instead of looking out through our own eyes. We are alienated from our own selves and our own freedom. We are, in a word, inauthentic.

Society, of course, helps us to stay that way. It is very convenient for those who run the world to have working under them a great mass of people who only want to play roles and who have no desire to know who they really are. Our whole social system acts in such a way as to support our inauthenticity, our role-playing, our false selves. It continually tells us that the self-image is very important, the self not important at all. It even throws doubt on the notion that there is a real self.

This whole effort is strongest in the area of sex roles. We tell ourselves, and are told by others, that there is a right masculine way for men to be (Reynaud, 1983), and a right feminine way for women to be (Condor, 1986).

This again is a socially sanctioned inauthenticity which enables us to hide behind a role and not know who we really are. If men are schizoid or psychopathic or rigid, this is partly because these things fit all too well with the masculine image; if women are masochistic or depressed or hysterical, this is partly because these things fit all too well with the feminine image.

That is why we lay so much stress on integration. *Integration* is the process by which our insights and breakthroughs in therapy can be translated into action in the everyday world – what we sometimes call the unreal world. It is only in the nitty-gritty details of everyday life that we can stop the perpetuation of disturbance.

PRACTICE

Goals of therapy

The goal of primal integration is very simple and straightforward, and can be stated in one sentence. It is to contact and release the real self. Once that has been done, enormously useful work can be done in enabling the person to work through the implications of that, and to support the person through any life-changes that may result. But until the real self has been contacted, the process of working to release it will continue (see Rowan, 1983a, chapter 5). This is actually a very common notion in the whole field of psychotherapy, as Table 2.1. shows.

Table 2.1 Goals of therapy

Writer	Peripheral	Central
Adler	Guiding fiction	Creative self
Assagioli	Subpersonalities	I
Janov	Unreal self	Real self
Jung	Persona	Self
Laing	False self	Real self
Mahrer	Operating potentials	Deeper potentials
Moreno	Conserved roles	Spontaneity
Perls	Self-image	Self
Winnicott	False self	True self

Many other writers could be cited, particularly Reich, who however did not have any such neat statement of the matter as that given by those in Table 2.1. What they are all saying, in their various ways, is that in therapy we have to encourage the person to move from exclusive concern with what is peripheral in the personality towards what is central in it. Unless this move is made the person will continue to go round in the same circles.

What primal integration says is that this process carries on by the integration of splits in the personality, the most important splits being those which are due to unconscious processes of defence. When we get beneath the defensive layers, we very often find primal pain due to early trauma; and we believe that unless and until the primal pain is experienced and dealt with, the split cannot be healed. However, we say that primal joy is important too. An experience of real love can be just as powerful, and just as primal, as anything else. This point is made very powerfully by Lonsbury (1978), who quotes a case where Tom deeply cries out to his grandfather – 'You really cared, Pop.' This was actually very important and very primal, but it was not an experience of Pain with a capital P: 'The deep crying for his grandfather was that of purest love. I can be explicit on these matters because I am Tom' (p. 25). And Lonsbury quotes another case history where love and joy were the key primal feelings for the individual concerned.

So primal integration keeps on coming back to the central value of reality, truth, authenticity, whatever you may like to call it – the main existentialist concern. Friedenberg (1973) sums up this position thus:

> The purpose of therapeutic intervention is to support and re-establish a sense of self and personal authenticity. Not a mastery of the objective environment; not effective functioning within social institutions; not freedom from the suffering caused by anxiety – though any or all of these may be concomitant outcomes of successful therapy – but personal awareness, depth of real feeling, and, above all, the conviction that one can use one's full powers, that one has the courage to be and use all one's essence in the praxis of being.   (p. 94)

In recent years, the whole subject of the real self (existential self, integrated body-mind self) has been clarified and illuminated by the work of Ken Wilber (1979;1980). What we are talking about here as central is what he calls the *centaur* stage of psychospiritual development. It lies between the mental ego and the subtle self, and represents from one point of view the highest development of the individual personality, from another point of view the foothills of spiritual development. To put the centaur stage within this context makes contacting the real self more of an objective reality and enables us to see it as quite a modest and achievable aim.

Freundlich (1974a) suggests that there are four phases we have to work through as clients involved in this process of moving from what is peripheral to what is central within the person: first, reliving primal experiences; second, connecting up those experiences with present-day existence; third, action in the present where we keep our feelings open instead of being shut down; and fourth, taking responsibility for our own lives and changing what needs to change. Freundlich holds that these phases are not sequential, but simultaneous processes which re-inforce each other.

We would now go further and say that contacting the real self now makes it easier to go on and contact the transpersonal self. This can be conceptualized as going deeper into the centre – in other words, the centre is itself a series of concentric circles (Rowan, 1983a).

The 'person' of the therapist

Probably the best discussion of the whole question of the person of the therapist comes from Alvin Mahrer (1983). He suggests that there are four basic paradigms of the therapist–client relationship: a parent and a child, where the parent knows more than the child and controls the child; a saint and a supplicant, where the saint is holier than the supplicant, who tries to live up to the standard set; a scientist and a subject, where the scientist knows just what to do to transform the subject; and his own form of therapy, where the therapist identifies with the client.

While we cannot discuss this in full here, in terms of these paradigms Janov's work seems closest to the scientist-and-subject model. It is quite technique-based and results-oriented, as can be seen in Albery (1985). And although primal integration therapy is quite different from Janov's work, and even has some different roots (as for example the encounter group background of Swartley and the LSD research background of Lake and Grof) it does still share something of this approach, even though considerably softened and modified. We do not usually assign homework (which is one of the hallmarks of the scientist/subject approach, according to Mahrer), but we do use methods quite freely taken from gestalt, psychodrama, encounter, body work, art therapy and so on, as well as of course the basic regression approach. It often does not seem to the client that we are very technique-oriented, because we can be so flexible in following the client's own experience and needs moment by moment. I once heard a good therapist say that her attitude towards clients was one of tough loving, and that has always struck me as one of the best descriptions of what the primal integration therapist is aiming at. It is the loving which lets the therapist stay so close to the client's experience, and it is the toughness which lets the therapist notice and act when clients are avoiding, contradicting or otherwise defending themselves against themselves.

But there is one aspect which is missed out in Mahrer's account, and which is crucially important. This is that the primal integration therapist feels it very important to be authentic. If the aim of the therapy is that the client should be enabled to contact the real self, as we have said above, then it is important for the therapist to model that, and to be a living example of a real human being.

So this gives us the paradox of primal integration therapy relying at one and the same time on authenticity and tricks. At first sight these two things seem simply contradictory. How can I be real and at the same time be using techniques, which by definition must be artificial? I think Bergantino (1981) puts his finger on the answer when he says:

> Being tricky and authentic can be two sides of the same coin. Being an authentic trickster will not destroy the patient's confidence if the therapist's heart is in the right place. (p. 53)

A similar point is made by Alan Watts (1951), who tells us that in Eastern religious disciplines the learner is often tricked by the teacher into some insight or breakthrough or awakening. The tricks (*upaya*) which are used are an expression of spiritual truth. In primal integration, we may use deep breathing, massage, painting, guided fantasy, hitting cushions or reliving birth, all in the interests of enabling reality to dawn.

Therapeutic style

The style of the primal integration therapist varies greatly among individual practitioners. In Lake's groups there was often a procedure of taking turns to work. In Swartley's groups there was a formal go-round at the beginning, where people had to state what piece of work they wanted to do, and who they wanted to do it with. Emerson's groups are different again, and he does a lot of work with children. Grof does more individual therapy and so do I. In individual work the therapist will often use a similar approach, educating the client to the point where one can say at the start of a session 'What would you like to work on today?' But this is even more variable, in line with the needs of the client, the personality and experience of the therapist, and the interaction between the two.

We do tend to get clients every so often who may or may not have read Janov but in any case somehow expect to get into primals at once. If they find, as many do, that in fact they are nowhere near ready for that because their defences are much stronger than they thought, they become disappointed. People too often abandon the here-and-now and shoot for the deep cosmic experience. This can sometimes produce the phenomenon of the pseudo-primal, where a client tries to make a primal happen by sheer effort of will. But feelings cannot be forced, and primals cannot be manufactured.

Again we are sometimes faced with clients who expect to get immediate entry into the world of deep feelings, which up to now they have been avoiding. When such a client says 'I'm not feeling anything', or 'I can't get in touch with my feelings', it is usually due to not paying attention to gentler feelings, such as relaxation or mild restlessness, because of trying so hard to feel something else. The thing we do is not to get the person out of this, but simply to encourage focusing on this itself. Go into the lack of feeling, really experience it, focus on it, sink into it, be it. In that way it can lead us to whatever is really there.

People often expect the primal integration therapist to encourage them to scream, but in fact we do not do that. Nor do we think that screaming is essential; it can be very important for certain clients, but quite often it is not. Experience has taught us that primal experiences vary tremendously from one person to another, and even within one person over time. In any case, the process is much more important than simply having cathartic primal experiences. Indeed, it is even possible to get addicted to 'primalling', at the expense of any proper integration.

So the style of the primal integration therapist is very broad and sensitive, and places a good deal of emphasis on listening at all levels: body, sexual, emotional, imaginative, intellectual, spiritual, social, cultural, political. We also place emphasis on countertransference, recognizing that in primal work it is very easy for the therapist to avoid the deepest levels of experience, because these can be so painful. As Freundlich (1974b) says, we have to be aware of our inner feelings as therapists and then decide what to do with them. And because of our more active approach, this may mean taking risks. For example, he says:

> In a group session I revealed, with embarrassment, that I was having sadistic punitive fantasies toward Marianne, and this was a reaction to her passive, pouty and uncooperative efforts in the group. My interaction with her was an opening to explore how she had expressed anger toward her mother in a withholding, obstructionistic manner. (p. 7)

I don't like the tone of this example, but it does show how the therapist was able to get the client into some very important material by using his own countertransference. And it does show the mixture of authenticity and trickiness which was mentioned earlier. In sum, the therapeutic style is essentially one of spontaneity, which allows intuition and a creative flow.

Major therapeutic techniques

Obviously the main therapeutic technique is regression – that is, taking the person back to the trauma on which their neurosis is based. Laing (1983) argues that we should also talk about recession – the move from the outer to the inner world. And Mahrer (1986) makes a similar point. Going back is no

Figure 2.1   The affect tree

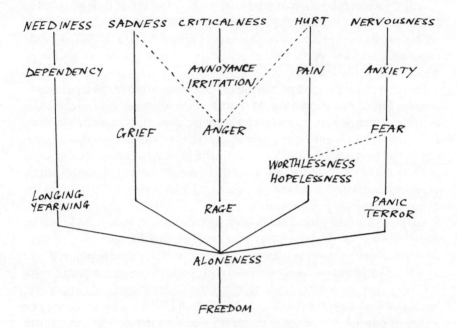

use unless at the same time we are going deeper into our own experience. We agree with this, and find that recession and regression go very well together. One of the clearest statements of the case for doing this comes from Grof (1975) when he talks about the COEX system. A COEX is a syndrome of experiences which hang together emotionally for a particular person. It is a pattern of feelings, meanings and other mental and physical experiences which keeps on reappearing in the person's life.

This gives us one clear way of working with a client. I might take an experience in the present and say something like 'Get in touch with that whole experience. What does it feel like? How does it affect your body and your breathing? What are the thoughts and meanings tied up with it? (Pause) Now see if you can allow a memory to come up of another time when you had that same sort of experience. Don't search for it, just focus on the feelings and let them float you back to an earlier time when you had those same feelings.' When a memory comes up, I encourage the person to go into it and concretize it as much as possible – relive it in some detail, getting right inside it, express whatever needs to be expressed there, deal with any unfinished business from that time. Then we go back further, in the same way, and do the same thing with an earlier memory. Then again, and again, as often as necessary. In this way we descend, as it were, the rungs of the

COEX ladder which leads us into deeper and deeper feelings, further down on the affect tree (see Figure 2.1).

As we do this, I go into the experience with the client, much in the way which Mahrer (1986) calls 'carrying forward experience' – that is, entering into the experience and co-feeling it with the client. In this way I can say things which make the experience fuller and richer for the client, and which take the client closer to the heart of that experience.

Often it also helps if the client breathes more deeply and more quickly than usual. There is a very good discussion of the whole question of hyperventilation in Albery (1985), where he examines the medical evidence in some detail. It does seem to all of us who work in this area that deep breathing is very helpful in allowing access to deep emotional layers, going deeper both in regression and recession.

Now it is obvious that a procedure like this takes time, and it is really best to go all the way with a particular COEX in one session, rather than trying to take up the tail of one session at the head of the next, which usually does not work. This means that the primal integration therapist tends to prefer long sessions, which also enable the client to take a break or breather if need be during the session. I personally conduct some 1-hour sessions, but I also have some 1½-hour, 2-hour and 3-hour sessions; some people working in this area have used up to 10-hour sessions. One situation we like is the group experience over several days, where each piece of work can be as long as it needs to, because we often have two or three pieces of work going on at the same time in the group, either in the same room or in different rooms. We often have two leaders and one or two assistants to make this way of working possible.

In this process people open themselves up to deeper feelings, and thus become more vulnerable. So a high degree of trust has to be built up between client and therapist. But in reality, trust is not a feeling, it's a decision. Nobody can ever prove, in any final or decisive way, that they are worthy of this trust, so the client just has to take the decision at some time, and it may as well be sooner as later.

In this and other ways we lay a lot of stress on the self-responsibility of the client to do the work and make the necessary internal decisions. For example, in a group where the person may need to go back to a situation when they were being physically squashed or hurt in some way, and where they may need to say all sorts of things about getting away, stopping it, not being able to stand it and so on, we have a rule that if a client says 'Stop! I mean it!', everyone immediately stops what they are doing without question or delay. We trust the person to have enough ego outside the regressive experience – vivid though it may be – to know when things are going too far, for any reason. It is the client who decides about readiness to proceed with any approach or method.

It is useful to know where the person has got to in the process of regression. Body movements can be very helpful in enabling the therapist to assess this, particularly in the preverbal area. Swartley (1978) gives some guidelines in the matter:

> *Conception trauma*   Hands at sides, feet move like a tail, most of the physical activity is focused at the top of the head. (Sometimes the client will identify with the egg.)
> *Implantation trauma*   In most cases, the psychosomatic energy is focused in the forehead, which searches for the right spot of skin on another person on which to attach.
> *Birth trauma*   Here the energy is directed toward breaking out of mother's womb. Pushing with legs very characteristic. Pain in head, which wants to be held tight.

Emerson also has some unpublished work on the typical movements associated with the first trimester in the womb.

If the body gets stuck – that is, there are signs of tension but the body is not moving – we may do some primal massage. We look for the tense spots and very gently move into them with our hands. This very often releases more feelings and more movements. Or sometimes it is pressure which is needed, on the head or on some other part of the body. We encourage the person to make sounds of any kind, as this helps to mobilize energy and keep things moving. If we can just keep the client still moving, still active, still breathing, more regression is likely to occur.

But there are other ways of enabling the client to get in touch with inner experience. A useful approach is simply to get the client to talk to a person, rather than talking about them. For example:

Client	My father never paid any attention to me. He always . . .
Therapist	Try putting your father on this cushion and talking directly to him.
Client	That's ridiculous. He's dead.
Therapist	He may be dead out there, but the father inside is still just as much alive as ever. Just imagine him sitting there on the cushion, and say whatever comes. It may be telling him something, asking him a question, making some demand on him, anything at all.
Client	That won't do any good: he never listened anyway. He always ignored me by . . .
Therapist	That's the point: he won't listen to you. Just see him

| | sitting there and tell him that. |
| Client | Daddy, daddy, please pay attention to me. Please put down the newspaper and talk to me. Daddy, please look at me . . . |

Doing it this way triggers far more feelings and memories than talking *about* the father or hearing interpretations *about* the therapist being the father. And because the therapist is outside the action and facilitating it, it can be pushed further and further into deep unconscious material. Like the psychoanalyst the primal integration therapist is very interested in working with the fantasies and primary process thinking of the unconscious, but prefers to work directly with them rather than refracting them through the transference. Again here our work is close to that of Grof (1985) and Mahrer (1986).

When memories come up, the primal integration therapist likes to make them as full and detailed as possible. A dim light often seems to facilitate this, by cutting down the distractions of the environment, so usually we will work in a room with a dimmer switch and heavy curtains or blinds. If the client wanders away from a scene which seems to be important, we often re-establish it by picking on some vivid detail already mentioned, and pulling the client back with it. We always use the present tense in this work. Freundlich (1974c) says 'To support the emerging feelings and to work through the defences I encourage the person to repeat the key words and phrases which contain the feeling.' (p. 5)

The repetition of key phrases is a favourite move in most cathartic forms of therapy, for example co-counselling and gestalt therapy, and as Mahrer (1986) points out, it is one way of amplifying bodily sensations. The repetition of the primal words in a louder voice helps to intensify the feeling as the defence recedes. The person's throat opens up, the voice comes out more clearly, and the person is able to say the words which were held back for years. The hurt and need are finally felt and experienced. If the original splitting was severe enough, the original emotions may hardly have been experienced at all, so they may now be felt for what is virtually the first time. The person is then freer to make current needs known because the fear of rejection, for example, is finally connected to where it belonged in the past.

Music is a potent way of increasing an emotional charge, as Grof (1985) points out, and primal integration therapists often use music for this purpose.

Bill Swartley suggested the principle of opposites: If something doesn't work, try the exact opposite. When a person will not express the feeling, perhaps it is more possible to express the defence against it. Many times, when a person has said that he or she seems to have a block against doing something, I have asked the person to draw a picture of the block, or put the block on a cushion and talk to it, or to speak for the block. This often results in a strong and effective piece of work, where the block is perhaps a parental voice, or some other important subpersonality or deeper potential.

In my own work, I have found the notion of subpersonalities extremely useful. Very often a person's defences have got into such a convoluted tangle that they are very hard to sort out by following any one single line. But by eliciting the subpersonalities I can then see exactly how the internal games are constructed and played out (Vargiu, 1974; Rowan, 1983b). The idea of subpersonalities was developed most fully in psychosynthesis (Ferrucci, 1983), and we have found these ideas very useful in understanding what goes on at the level of the higher unconscious or superconscious.

One of the things that happen in primal work, as Adzema (1985) has recently pointed out, is that the deeper people go in recession and regression, the more likely they are to have spiritual experiences too. Shirley Ward believes this is because the psychic centres open up. However, in this area there is one very common error we have to guard against. Grof (1980) points out that blissful womb states, which primal clients sometimes get into, are very similar to peak experiences (Maslow, 1973) and to the cosmic unity which mystics speak of as contact with God. This has led some people – Wasdell for example – into saying that all mystical experiences are nothing but reminiscences of the ideal or idealized womb. This is an example of Wilber's (1983) pre/trans fallacy. Grof himself does not fall for this error, and has a good discussion of some different forms of transpersonal experiences. I have tried to be even more specific in discussing the various types of mystical experiences (Rowan, 1983c). The whole point is that we repress not only dark or painful material in the lower unconscious, but also embarrassingly good material in the higher unconscious (Assagioli, 1975).

This can come out in guided fantasies, in drawing or painting, or in dreams. I like working with dreams, as they can always be interpreted, understood or simply appreciated on so many different levels (Wilber, 1984). If we want to do justice to the whole person, then we have to be prepared to deal with the superconscious as well as the lower unconscious. This seems to me part of the general listening process (Rowan, 1985) which is absolutely basic to all forms of therapy and counselling.

The change process in therapy

A pioneering piece of research (Marina, 1982) has brought out a number of interesting points about the change process in primal integration therapy. What we are essentially talking about, it suggests, is a very fundamental cognitive-affective restructuring or personality change. This can happen because the personality is a system such that each part depends on each other part. A change in one part of the system affects the whole of the rest of the system.

For example, one woman in the research study had four main issues which all re-inforced one another: *feeling suicidal; feeling worthless; being jealous and full of rage;* and *feeling like an intruder*. During therapy, a new element came in on the scene: *feeling myself more loving*. This started to affect the whole balance of the other elements. After a time *feeling like an intruder* was replaced by *feeling that I've got the right to be here*, and other similar changes later took place in the other elements.

We do not know the details of the events which led to the incoming construct *feeling myself more loving*. Since the person was in primal integration therapy, this may have been responsible. On the other hand, it may have been due to other life events, and the therapy perhaps merely made it easier for the change to work its way through the system. One of the things which most plague any kind of a decent outcome study is that the client has a life outside the therapy sessions, and that most of the things which happen to the client happen there.

If we believe, as Michael Broder (1976) suggests, that the primal process consists of five phases: commitment; abreaction (catharsis); insight (cognitive-affective restructuring); counteraction (fresh behaviour in the world); and proaction (making real changes); then it must be the case that the later phases are just as important as the earlier ones. In other words, working through is just as significant as breaking through. The glamorous part, and the controversial part, of our work is the 'primal', the cathartic breakthrough; but in reality the process of integration is necessary and equally exciting in its quieter way. For example, it is a great thing to get to the cathartic point of forgiving one's mother; it is another thing to start treating women decently in daily life, as a result of this.

But if we also believe in the importance of the transpersonal, we can go further, and say that the contacting and releasing of the real self is just one stage in a process which, as Wilber (1980) points out, goes much further. As Adzema (1985) suggests: 'A primaller also can be viewed as open to subtler energies after having reached a "cleared out" relaxed state via primalling . . . and thereby to gain access to subtler energies still' (p. 91). In other words, dealing in this very full and deep way with the psychological realm enables us to go on and get in touch with the spiritual realm. But if this is the case, why have not more people working in the primal area noticed this? Adzema (1985) suggests that it is because prejudice gets in the way of it being reported, and creates a myth that nothing of this kind happens. But, on the contrary:

Some long-term primallers with whom I have contact have talked of receiving love, helping, strength or bliss that seemed to be coming from a place beyond the scope of their current physical existence, to be emanating from a 'higher power' of some sort. Their descriptions have many parallels to some descriptions of spiritual experience.

(p. 95)

If this is so – and certainly this agrees with my own experience – then we can eliminate all the projections which come from unconscious material to plague spiritual life, and have for the first time a clean mysticism, not cluttered up with womb stuff, birth stuff, oral-sadistic stuff, Oedipal stuff and all the other unconscious bases for phoney spirituality.

As Adzema (1985) says: 'it becomes obvious that the "demons", the "monsters" and the resulting fear are not "real" (in terms of being rooted in transpersonal or "objective" reality). Rather, they are personal elements invading the perception of transpersonal reality' (p. 104). Not only this, but primal integration therapy also teaches us one of the prime lessons of all spiritual development – the ability to let go of the ego. There are times in our therapy when we have to take our courage in both hands and just go ahead, taking the risk, as it seems, of losing everything in the process. Many times the image of stepping off a cliff comes up in primal work. And of course this ability to let go, to step off into the seeming void, is crucial for spiritual commitment, as Adzema (1985) reminds us:

Likewise, an important benefit of primal is that it can teach us an attitude of surrender to process. That we can throw ourselves, time and again, into the maelstrom of catharsis and still, somehow, be upheld and even embraced, despite ourselves, gives us confidence in a beneficent universe and allows us to foster surrender in our attitudes to the pushes and pulls of process as it makes itself known to us in our daily life.

(pp. 111–12)

Through primal work we learn how to open up to our inner process. Through spiritual development going on from there, we can learn how to carry on with that same process, into the deepest depths of all.

CASE EXAMPLE

This is the case of Heidi, a 40-year-old school teacher. She came to me complaining of having such severe depression that she had had to give up work. Her doctor had given her a certificate and some tablets. She was crying a great deal, and also had a lot of anger with her sexual partner, with whom she was also breaking up at the same time.

At first all I had to do was to let her cry. She needed nurturing and mothering, and I just listened to her and at times held her in my arms. What came out was that she had been taking on more and more duties at work – it seemed that she was a very good and well-liked teacher, who found it hard to say No when interesting projects came up. She had ignored her own needs and thought only of doing a good job and making people happy.

At the same time she had been having for some years a sexual relationship with a man, which had been a great strain. He had another woman, and when choices had to be made it seemed that the other woman took priority. At various times he had talked about leaving the other woman, but Heidi had now come to the conclusion that he was never going to do so, and that this was an unsatisfactory relationship for her, even though she could not help still being attracted to him. She had spent a lot of time trying to work out a three-way relationship. They had all wanted to be 'alternative', and she had not, as it were, wished them bad weather; she often thought they had agreed to something, but then had felt betrayed by some new action of theirs. She had desperately wanted to do justice to both people, but as of now she had run out of energy for it. So she was deeply disappointed about that, too. Every time she thought about making a final break with him she would look round her house and see all the things he had helped to make – he had been of such practical help to her. A whole lot more very complex feelings, too, which came out later.

It seemed that the combination of these two strains had just become too much for her. It was made worse by the fact that both her lover and the other woman were teachers in the same school, so that she had to see him quite frequently, and her a bit less often, in the normal course of the day.

She became extremely sensitive to any suggestion that she might go back to work. Her self-esteem had sunk to a very low ebb. The school policy was to give generous sick leave to senior teachers, so in a way this was an ideal opportunity to do some deep work on herself.

We started off with two-hour sessions once a week, and after two months moved to one-hour sessions twice a week, and after another month to one hour once a week; this latter lasted for a month. The rationale for this was that at first there was a great deal of distress, and the two-hour sessions were very good for dealing with this, giving time for the client to come up from the very deep levels she was getting into. Later there was less distress, and so we could proceed in a more considered and chosen fashion, deciding what needed to be done and doing it as expeditiously as possible. Later again it was more a question of just tidying up the remaining loose ends and working through any new problems quite quickly.

After the first few meetings, the energy seemed to settle mainly around her father. He had died before she was born, at the end of the Second World War, but her mother had not known this for sure until she was two years old.

During that time her mother had been distressed, anxious and impatient, and seemed to have passed on to her in some way the feeling 'Is he or isn't he?' (This was very similar to the feeling she had about her lover – is he or isn't he with me?) Her grandfather had stepped in and allowed the two of them to stay with him until Heidi's mother remarried, when Heidi was six years old. This grandfather was sensitive, intelligent, worldly wise but in some ways innocent, and very devoted to the two of them. He taught her many things and spoiled her, telling her she was wonderful and very clever.

But her father, though absent, had been more important for her. She had idealized him as a child, and thought of him as a hero. She had to live up to his expectations and do him credit. She did do well at school, and passed all her examinations with flying colours, first at school and then at the university. In her present job she had always had the feeling of doing well, and had been given special projects and extra responsibility.

It was then we discovered one of the points I mention in the earlier part of this chapter – it is the things we like which stop us developing, much more than the things we dislike. As we went deeper and deeper into Heidi's memories about her father, we found that she had taken on board as an absolute injunction that she *must* live up to his expectations. Even when she fought against this, and did things she knew he would not have approved of, she had to do them *perfectly*, so as to be able to face him. It would be too much to do something of her own and then find that she had to face his disappointment. So her job had become a challenge to him – a challenge which she could never meet, because he could always raise the standard in a way which left her powerless.

It was clear at this point that her father had turned into an internal persecutor. She had turned him into an implacable and impossible figure, very close to what Freud called the superego, Perls called the topdog, Jung called the father complex, and so on.

As she became more and more aware of this, so her emotions started to become deeper and more engaged. I encouraged her to stay with these feelings and really experience them, rather in the manner which Mahrer (1986) calls 'carrying forward the potentials for experiencing'. The emotions became more and more primal in their intensity. Suddenly, when she was talking directly to her father on the other cushion, a wave of primal rage came over her, and she said 'I don't have to please you any more!!!' I encouraged her to repeat this phrase with more and more intensity, until she went into a powerful catharsis, and then collapsed. I covered her up and watched over her until she recovered enough to leave.

In the following session a great weight seemed to have fallen off her shoulders. She came in smiling, and said 'I didn't really believe in all that therapy stuff, but now you've convinced me.' She was able to talk about visiting her parents abroad for a holiday, and getting a new job, and having a friend over to visit, and going on a psychosynthesis weekend.

She found it much easier now to express her anger towards her ex-lover, whom she had definitely parted with now. Although she was still attracted to him, and found the whole issue a painful one, the degree of pain was now much more bearable. Getting clear in one area made it much easier to get clear in the other.

It is important not to lay too much stress on this one incident, of course. There were at least four other factors which had made this breakthrough possible: the previous course of the therapy, which prepared the way for this act and made it seem natural; a change in medication which meant that she was less drowsy, more alert than before; some autogenic training (involving full relaxation), which made her better able to be present in the here and now; and a stay with a friend who had looked after her with a lot of care.

Heidi began to talk about going back to work, but still genuinely could not face the twin threat of the work and the lover. So the therapy turned more on to the problems around him, which turned out to be very complex. But in the end, Heidi was able to breathe more easily and take back nearly all of her illusions and projections that she had placed on him.

This case was very suitable for a book like this, even though it does not bring out the full holonomic process, because it was quite short and concentrated, so that the main lines are not lost in a mass of detail. We have the initial presenting problem, quite a complex mixture of work and private life; we have the gradual focusing upon one issue, always going by the client's energy and directions; we have the resolution of that issue in a cathartic experience; we have the working out of the complex relationship with her lover; and we have the progressive working out of the practical matters which then emerged.

A number of factors helped to make this case a success. First Heidi had a good friend called Victoria, who spent a lot of time with her, simply listening to her and comforting her and telling her she was OK. We find that the support network of a person can be quite crucial in allowing the client to get the most out of the therapy. In fact, Swartley often said that the 'second-chance family' which is often found in intensive primal integration groups could be a highly significant element in the process of therapy. The fact that Victoria could provide just such a second-chance family, allowing Heidi to regress almost to a baby stage and then grow up, was in my opinion of inestimable benefit.

Second, the fact that Heidi had very good employers, who were willing to support her for three months while she worked out her problems, and who were then prepared to lose her without any criticism, was also of great value. She did not take this for granted, but appreciated it very much as a gift.

Third, the fact that the man she had been with did not pester her or burden her or make life difficult was very helpful. There were certainly occasions when he did suggest coming round or going out with her again, but not in a way which put great pressure on her.

Fourth, her mother and stepfather held open house and were very supportive when she wanted to take a holiday with them. The fact that they lived in another country probably helped to make the holiday she took even more refreshing and different for her.

It is very important to recognize these factors and the part they played. Therapists sometimes write as if therapy sessions were the whole of life, or at least most of it, and of course this is never so. The everday life of the client can be immensely influential in helping or hindering the kind of work which a client needs to do in therapy. And it is everyday life which lasts when therapy is over.

REFERENCES

Adzema, M. V. (1985) A primal perspective on spirituality, *Journal of Humanistic Psychology*, Vol. 25, No. 3, pp. 83–116.

Albery, N. (1985) *How To Feel Reborn?* Regeneration Press, London.

Assagioli, R. (1975) *Psychosynthesis: A Manual of Principles and Techniques*, Turnstone Books, London.

Balint, M. (1968) *The Basic Fault*, Tavistock Publications, London.

Bergantino, L. (1981) *Psychotherapy, Insight and Style*, Allyn & Bacon, Boston.

Broder, M. (1976) An eclectic approach to primal integration, *Primal Integration Monographs*, Vol. 1, No. 1.

Chamberlain, D. B. (1984) *Consciousness at Birth: A Review of the Empirical Evidence*, Chamberlain Communications, San Diego, CA.

Condor, S. (1986) Sex role beliefs and traditional women: feminist and intergroup perspectives, in S. Wilkinson (ed.) *Feminist Social Psychology: Developing Theory and Practice*, Open University Press, Milton Keynes.

Demause, L. (1982) *Foundations of Psychohistory*, Psychohistory Press, London.

Emerson, W. (1984) *Infant and Child Birth Re-facilitation*, Institute for Holistic Education, Guildford.

Feher, L. (1980) *The Psychology of Birth*, Souvenir Press, London.

Ferrucci, P. (1983) *What We May Be*, Turnstone Press, Wellingborough.

Fodor, N. (1949) *The Search for the Beloved*, University Books, New York.

Freundlich, D. (1973) Janov's primal theory of neurosis and therapy, *Primal Experience Monographs*, June.

Freundlich, D. (1974a) Four phases of primal, *Primal Experience Monographs*, July.

Freundlich, D. (1974b) Countertransference in individual and group therapy, *Primal Experience Monographs*, June.

Freundlich, D. (1974c) Methods for reliving primal experiences, *Primal Experience Monographs*, October.

Friedenberg, E. Z. (1973) *Laing*, Fontana/Collins, London.

Grey, M. (1985) *Return from Death: An Exploration of the Near-Death Experience*, Arkana, London.

Grof, S. (1975) *Realms of the Human Unconscious*, Viking Press, New York.

Grof, S. (1980) *LSD Psychotherapy*, Hunter House, Pomona, CA.

Grof, S. (1985) *Beyond the Brain: Birth, Death and Transcendence in Psychotherapy*, State University of New York Press, Albany, NY.

Hoffman, B. (1979) *No One Is To Blame*, Science & Behavior, Palo Alto, CA.

Janov, A. (1975) *Primal Man*, Crowell, New York.

Janov, A. (1983) *Imprints: The Lifelong Effects of the Birth Experience*, Coward McCann, New York.

Kaufman, W. (1974) An anatomy of the primal revolution, *Journal of Humanistic Psychology*, Vol. 14, No. 4. pp. 49–62.

Kelley, C. (1971) Primal scream and genital character, *Energy & Character*, Vol. 2, No. 3.

Klaus, M. H. and Kennell, J. H. (1976) *Maternal-Infant Bonding*, C. V. Mosby, St Louis.

Kohut, H. (1971) *The Analysis of the Self*, International University Press, New York.

Kohut, H. (1977) *The Restoration of the Self*, International University Press, New York.

Laing, R. D. (1976) *The Facts of Life*, Penguin, Harmondsworth.

Laing, R. D. (1983) *The Voice of Experience*, Penguin, Harmondsworth.

Lake, F. (1980) *Constricted Confusion*, CTA, Oxford.

Lake, F. (1981) *Tight Corners in Pastoral Counselling*, Darton, Longman & Todd, London.

Lake, F. (1986) *Clinical Theology: A Theological and Psychological Basis to Clinical Pastoral Care* (abridged by Martin H. Yeomans), Darton, Longman & Todd, London.

Lonsbury, J. (1978) Inside primal therapy, *Journal of Humanistic Psychology*, Vol. 14, No. 4, pp. 19–28.

Mahrer, A. R. (1978) *Experiencing: A Humanistic Theory of Psychology and Psychiatry*, Brunner/Mazel, New York.

Mahrer, A. R. (1983) *Experiential Psychotherapy: Basic Practices*, Brunner/Mazel, New York.

Mahrer, A. R. (1986) *Therapeutic Experiencing: The Process of Change*, W. W. Norton, New York.

Marina, N. (1982) Restructuring of cognitive-affective structure: a central point of change after psychotherapy, Unpublished PhD thesis, Brunel University.

Maslow, A. H. (1970) *Motivation and Personality* (2nd edn), Harper & Row, New York.

Maslow, A. H. (1973) *The Farther Reaches of Human Nature*. Penguin, Harmondsworth.

Miller, A. (1985) *Thou Shalt Not be Aware: Society's Betrayal of the Child*, Pluto Press, London.

Mott, F. (1948) *The Universal Design of Birth*, David McKay, Philadelphia.

Mowbray, R. (1985) Letter dated 2 November.

Netherton, M. and Shiffrin, N. (1979) *Past Lives Therapy*, Ace Books, New York.

Nichols, M. P. and Zax, M. (1977) *Catharsis in Psychotherapy*, Gardner Press, New York.

Peerbolte, L. (1975) *Psychic Energy in Prenatal Dynamics*, Servire, Wassenaar.

Pierce, R. A., Nichols, M. P. and Dubrin, J. R. (1983) *Emotional Expression in Psychotherapy*, Gardner Press, New York.

Rank, O. (1934) *The Trauma of Birth*, Harper & Row, New York.

Reynaud, E. (1983) *Holy Virility: The Social Construction of Masculinity*, Pluto Press, London.

Rowan, J. (1983a) *The Reality Game*, RKP, London.

Rowan, J. (1983b) Person as group, in H. H. Blumberg *et al.* (eds.) *Small Groups and Social Interaction*, Vol. 2, John Wiley & Sons, Chichester.

Rowan, J. (1983c) The real self and mystical experiences, *Journal of Humanistic Psychology*, Vol. 23, No. 2, pp. 9–27.

Rowan, J. (1985) Listening as a four-level activity, *British Journal of Psychotherapy*, Vol. 1, No. 4. pp. 274–85.

Swartley, W. (1977) Interviewed by John Rowan, *Self & Society*, Vol. 5, No. 6, pp. 167–73.

Swartley, W. (1978) Major categories of early psychosomatic traumas, in J. Rowan (ed.) *The Undivided Self*, Centre for the Whole Person, London.

Szasz, T. (1961) *The Myth of Mental Illness*, Harper & Row, New York.

Vargiu, R. (1974) Psychosynthesis workbook: Subpersonalities, *Synthesis* Vol. 1, No. 1, p. 74.

Verny, T. (1982) *The Secret Life of the Unborn Child*, Sphere, London.

Wasdell, D. (1983) Foundations of psycho-social analysis, *Energy & Character*, Vol. 14, No. 2.

Watts, A. (1951) *Psychotherapy East and West*, Penguin, Harmondsworth.

Wilber, K. (1979) *No Boundary*, Shambhala, Boulder, CO.

Wilber, K. (1980) *The Atman Project*, Theosophical Publishing House, Wheaton, Illinois.

Wilber, K. (1983) *Eye to Eye*, Anchor/Doubleday, Garden City, NY.

Wilber, K. (1984) The developmental spectrum and psychopathology, *Journal of Transpersonal Psychology*, Part 1, Vol. 16, No. 1, pp. 75–118; Part 2, Vol. 16, No. 2, pp. 137–66.

Winnicott, D. (1958) *Collected Papers*, Tavistock, London.

Suggested further reading

Albery, N. (1985) *How To Feel Reborn?* Regeneration Press, London.

Grof, S. (1985) *Beyond the Brain*, State University of New York Press, Albany, NY.

Lake, F. (1980) *Constricted Confusion*, Clinical Theology Association, Oxford.

Pierce, R. A., Nichols, M. P. and Dubrin, J. R. (1983) *Emotional Expression in Psychotherapy*, Gardner Press, New York.

Verny, T. (1982) *The Secret Life of the Unborn Child*, Sphere, London.

CHAPTER 3

FEMINIST THERAPY

Jocelyn Chaplin

HISTORICAL CONTEXT AND DEVELOPMENTS IN BRITAIN

This chapter is written in a particularly personal way because it is about *feminist* therapy, and one vital feature of feminist belief is that even the most theoretical or academic concepts and methods are strongly affected by our personal experiences, feelings and assumptions about the world.

I can write as only one particular feminist therapist, not as a representative of an organized school of feminist therapy. There is no such 'school' of unified thought or method. Indeed we vary considerably in our styles of therapy and in the ways we apply our various feminist ideologies to our therapy work. Some of us, at the Women's Therapy Centre for example, work within a psychoanalytic framework. Others, from the Pellin Centre for example, work in a more humanistic way. Many feminist therapists are now working in a cognitive-behavioural way, for example through Assertion Training courses. While an increasing number stress a more 'spiritual' approach often using a Jungian framework or even astrology.

We also vary in our feminist ideology. Some of us are socialist feminists. Others are radical feminists who see woman as the first oppressed class. There are also humanistic feminists, 'green' feminists and spiritual feminists. However these differences can and often are used creatively to develop new connections, new networks and a great richness of approach to human change and growth.

What I have tried to do in this chapter is to describe what we have in common, rather than stressing our differences. In other sections I have attempted to express the main elements of feminist therapy by describing the way I work, as one person's particular way of putting those elements into practice.

1. The first feature we have in common is a recognition that feminist therapy is more like a way of seeing or an *attitude* towards people, towards the world and towards therapy, than it is a specific technique. As Laura Brown and Nechama Liss-Levinson (1981) said, it is more like a philosophy or set of values that can be integrated with almost any other style of therapy. Indeed Sheila Ernst and Lucy Goodison (1981) describe a wide range of therapies from a feminist perspective.
2. Feminist therapy recognizes the interconnectedness of the 'inner' psychological and 'outer' social and material worlds. Joanna Ryan (1983) said 'What is specific to feminist therapy is its concern to understand internal and external reality together' (p. 9).
3. All feminist therapists are aware of the fact that women's 'inner' psychologies have been deeply affected by society's demands on us to play *female roles* and by the gender hierarchy that even today makes us 'second-class citizens'. This hierarchy also renders most of us relatively powerless, which contributes to the depression so many of us suffer from (Nairn and Smith, 1984).
4. Feminist therapists also have in common a commitment to non-hierarchical, *egalitarian relationships*. For some of us this involves having an equal relationship in the therapy. Laura Brown and Nechama Liss-Levinson (1981) describe this relationship as one in which the therapist is not the expert or the doctor and the client is not a patient. Rather they are two people using 'clues' to discover more about one of them.

   For other feminist therapists it means working towards more egalitarian relationships in general but may involve some degree of hierarchy in the therapy itself. This is especially likely where therapists are working in a mainly 'parent–child' way in order for the 'child' inside the client to work through old feelings about parents. The therapist has to 'play' the parent, which in our society usually means being unequal.

   However working and organizing in a *non-hierarchical way* has been a vital feature of most strands of feminism, including feminist therapy. Hierarchies are often seen as patriarchal social structures and ways of thinking, created by men for the benefit of men. And yet they have been with all of us for thousands of years dominating our lives even at an unconscious level.

5. Feminist therapy aims to transform these rigid 'inner' hierarchies and release repressed energies allowing us to express more fully our complex female selves.

Historical context

Modern feminist therapy emerged at the beginning of the twentieth century. As early as 1908 Adler (1964) was arguing that power inequality affected women psychologically just as much as sexual repression. In 1924 Karen Horney (1924) published a paper 'On the genesis of the castration complex in women', in which she argues that Freud's 'penis envy' was just as much about girls' envy of the superior power and status of boys as it was of their physical attributes. Since then there have been many challenges to Freud's more phallocentric assumptions from male and female psychoanalysts.

However, when the most recent women's movement developed, psychoanalysis was rejected by many of the new feminists such as Shulamith Firestone (1979) and Phyllis Chesler (1972). It seemed more concerned to socialize women into their roles as wives and mothers than to encourage them to take control of their own lives in their own way. Many practitioners were still unconsciously biased against women.

It was partly in reaction to the elitism of psychoanalysis that the new therapies, often called 'humanistic', grew up in the 1950s and 1960s. Using methods such as encounter, transactional analysis (TA) and gestalt they demystified therapy for thousands of people. And many feminists preferred to work humanistically (Forisha, 1981).

For example, in California Hogie Wyckoff worked with Claude Steiner (Steiner and Wyckoff, 1975) in the Radical Psychiatry Group which used methods such as TA to look at connections between social oppression and internal repression. Hogie Wyckoff started working with women's groups using TA and problem-solving techniques.

There were also a number of feminist psychologists in the USA who studied the early development of little girls in a sexist society. Jean Baker Miller (1978) and Nancy Chodorow (1978) show how our second-class status affects our deepest feelings about ourselves, often devaluing everything that we are and do. Giannini Berlotti (1977) traces the detailed daily life of little girls in Italy to show how early we are conditioned. In 1971, The Association of Women Psychologists set up the first national register of feminist therapists in the USA. Psychologists and therapists from all kinds of different traditions were beginning to take feminist insights seriously.

Developments in Britain

Like so many other women in Britain in the 1970s, I developed much of my feminist understanding through consciousness-raising groups. In these we met together to share our common experiences as women. But consciousness raising did not always bring about the 'deep' changes we expected. So many women became interested in therapy.

My first experience of therapy was with humanistic self-help groups. And yet, as a woman, I was aware that such groups were often led by 'charismatic' males. These men sometimes used their power to make us feel even worse about ourselves. For example, saying No to sex was often seen as a sign of serious repression!!

Many of the first feminist therapists in Britain started off in self-help groups such as the Red Therapy Group. This was a broadly humanistic, mixed group which shared a socialist perspective and concern with the effect of socioeconomic factors on our 'inner' psychologies. The group did, however, split into a men's and a women's group when some of the women realized that, unconsciously, even there, men had been taking more powerful roles.

In the mid 1970s some women felt that the self-help groups and humanistic methods did not go 'deep' enough. And while many women continued to work and have therapy within a humanistic framework stressing equal relationships and self-help, others returned to psychoanalysis and to an emphasis on the transference relationship between 'parent' therapist and 'child' client. It was felt that only psychoanalysis could deal with the powerful dependency needs that were still experienced even after consciousness-raising and expressing feelings. I should note here that many humanistic therapists are aware of and use the transference and child feelings in their work. Also some psychoanalysts now use humanistic methods too.

This change may have been encouraged by the publication of Juliet Mitchell's (1975) book called *Psychoanalysis and Feminism*, which re-examined Freud in the light of feminist ideas. She criticized feminist writers such as Shulamith Firestone for not considering the 'deep' unconscious factors that keep us oppressed even when we change on the surface.

Feminist psychoanalysts were also encouraged at the 29th International Psychoanalytic Congress held in London in 1975 in which feminist approaches were accepted and debated. Many were influenced by the French neo-Freudian Lacan. He argued that we are all essentially social constructions. As soon as we start to learn language we also learn the social frames of reference of our culture. These include concepts of gender right

from the start. Little girls learn that they are second-class citizens, as
they learn to communicate and become fully human members of
Gender categorization is built in very early on. The male is seen as the norm.
So our very sense of identity depends on our 'sub-normality'.

However there is one place where all these different strands of feminist
therapy meet and interact. That is the Womens Therapy Centre (WTC) in
North London. It is the best known and most influential centre for feminist
therapy in Britain. It was set up as a collective in 1976 by Luise Eichenbaum
and Susie Orbach.

Orbach and Eichenbaum (1982; 1983; 1985) have developed their own
theories through their practice at the WTC. They have used a psychoanalytic
framework based on Winnicott and object-relations theory to look at the
early relationship of the baby girl to her mother. They argue that this
relationship is of a different quality from the one between boy babies and
their mothers. They explore the many complex reasons for the differences,
and in particular look at women's unmet needs for dependency and nurturing.

Recently a number of feminist therapists, including myself, developed an
interest in Jungian therapy. At one time Jungians were dismissed by most
feminists in Britain as being too mystical. But today the 'spiritual' dimension
in many strands of feminism is growing. We do not split spirit from matter,
and use images such as the ancient goddesses as *symbols* of female power not
as transcendental beings to be worshipped. We can use the images to help us
grow and get in touch with our own power.

In the rest of this chapter I use my own approach to provide one *example*
of feminist therapy; it is not a rigid dogma of what we are all supposed to do
and think.

THEORETICAL ASSUMPTIONS

Image of the person

Both women and men are as much the products of society as of their
biological make up. And yet we are not 'things', as the word *product* implies.
We are processes. We are in a state of constant change and transformation.
And we are not isolated subjects. Our being is formed through relationships
with others, with the world, with parts of ourselves. *We are our relationships*.
And the structures of those relationships are strongly influenced by the
structures of social and economic relationships in society.

Where most relationships are hierarchical so are our internalized relationships between parts of ourselves. For example, we think of our minds as superior to and 'in control' of our bodies. Our strong side is seen as superior to our vulnerable side. The splits within us echo the splits in society.

One woman saw her rational side as cold and calculating. She wanted to get rid of it. Yet the opposite, her feeling side, was seen as all good. Another woman was so afraid of her body and its apparently insatiable desires, that she lived almost entirely in her head. Every feeling had to be controlled with careful rationalization. Both these women had rigidly hierarchical inner worlds partly because they live as we all do, in a hierarchical society. There are still 'superior' controlling groups and 'inferior' powerless groups. Being part of an 'inferior' group with second-class status leads directly to deep, often unconscious, inferiority feelings.

Yet society's structures also affect us in more indirect and complex ways. For example, acceptable gender roles such as 'the caring woman' limit our development. They keep us stuck in just one side of ourselves, unable to express our own needs for fear of being *self*ish, that is, concentrating on the self.

By caring for others we are also being strong and denying our weak and vulnerable side, while men often expect their needy sides to be automatically taken care of by women. These women may be mothers, girlfriends or wives. Then the man can go out into the world and be *all* strong. In our society weakness is seen as inferior to strength, failure is seen as inferior to success. We do not recognize that weakness and vulnerability are a vital part of us. It may be the side that is sensitive and creative or the side that needs love and nurturing. Failure is the other side of the coin to success. One could not exist without the other. But today we feel we must be *totally* successful, almost perfect *or* else we must be *completely* useless. These splits are wide and the opposites are pushed to extremes.

Each person is made up of many sets of opposites, each with their unique expression. Everyone has so called 'masculine' characteristics such as aggression, and everyone has so called 'feminine' characteristics such as sensitivity. We may vary in how these are combined, but we are all capable of expressing something of all our sides.

We are wholes who have been split, partly as a necessary phase in our development, in order to make sense of the world. But rather than reconnecting these opposites in a 'healthy' rhythm, social influences have kept us split. The splits, especially between males and females, suit the present order of society.

It is often useful to distinguish between *objective* and *subjective* conditioning. Objective conditions include the social factors such as second-class status and material factors such as poor housing. Subjective conditions include the inner unconscious defences built up through early experiences of a particular family. It is important for many of us to acknowledge the objective conditions as a background to therapy, even though in the therapy itself we are concentrating on the subjective side.

Concepts of psychological health and disturbance

The psychologically 'healthy' person is rhythmic not stuck and rigidly split. She recognizes and understands all the opposites within herself. She is reasonably comfortable with *both* her strong and weak sides, her 'masculine' and 'feminine' sides, her rational and emotional sides, and her 'parent' and 'child' sides. There may be conflict between them. But at least there is a dialogue. They can respect each other. Neither side is completely denied. Sometimes they fight and sometimes they dance together. Everyone has her own dance, her own rhythms. One day she may be strong and bossy and another day gentle and vulnerable. She alternates between them, when it is appropriate.

In Jungian terms she is in touch with her shadow side or those parts of her she fears, and maybe at first wants to reject. When the shadow is accepted it is not so easily projected on to other people. She does not need to fear someone on to whom she had projected her own hidden powerfulness. She can face her own powerfulness even when it seems scary and even potentially destructive. Many women fear their own power and prefer to project it on to others, often men. Patriarchal societies have been afraid of female power for thousands of years.*

The healthy woman also recognizes her opposite needs for *both* dependence and independence. She can allow herself to depend on others when it is appropriate, such as when she is being driven in someone's car or when she feels ill. But she can also be independent when it is appropriate. She can both care for others *and* be cared for. She can be both parent and child at different times. She can move from one state to another because they are *both* hers. She is not only one *or* the other.

We grow and change in more of a spiral than in a straight line. We go backwards as well as forwards. Perhaps we can only go forwards if we go backwards and regress into childlike feelings first. Growth is working with the rhythms, not proceeding from some depressing reality to a perfect harmonious self in the future.

One pair of opposites that are frequently split into extremes, are those of the *real* and the *ideal* selves. As these two sides get to know each other

---

* In the middle ages they burnt thousands of witches, whose crime was often simply having the power to heal.

better, they tend to come closer. Perhaps the ideal is brought 'down' and the real is brought 'up'. As we change ourselves so we change the environment. And as we change the environment so we change inside.

The disturbed woman is someone whose rhythms have got stuck. Her opposites are split, either by being pushed to extremes or by one side being completely repressed or by a battle in which the woman is stuck in the middle.

A woman was being pulled in two opposite directions, one towards complete independence from the man she lived with, and the other towards complete dependence on him. She felt trapped in the middle, immobilized and stuck. Her energies were all being used up in 'keeping in the middle'.

Another woman was stuck in the one-sided role of strong mother figure. She had never allowed her 'child' side needs to surface. She became depressed, exhausted through pushing down her 'child' energies. Social roles and expectations keep so many of us stuck.

Our responses to these social expectations are often neurotic patterns of withdrawal, attack or the desire to lose ourselves or merge completely with the other. Yet many of these patterns can be quite rational survival mechanisms in a society that demands splitting. As Jean Baker Miller (1978) puts it in *Towards a New Psychology of Women*, rather than blame ourselves we need to respect our ingenuity in developing these survival patterns in the first place. At the same time we need to work at changing them, without being too hard on ourselves if we do not change overnight. It is difficult to be healthy in an unhealthy society.

Acquisition of psychological disturbance

Society affects us psychologically in a number of complex ways. First, we are affected by *early relationships in the family*. Because our own mothers are so often stuck and split themselves due to social pressures their neurotic patterns can be enacted with the children. For example, as Susie Orbach (1982) shows, a mother who has had her own 'little girl' within denied is likely to overidentify with her own daughter. A particularly intense relationship can develop which makes it hard for the girl to separate from her mother when it is necessary. There can be a pull/push relationship in which the mother indulges the girl as she would have liked herself to be indulged, but then pushes her away as she has learned that girls and women must not expect to get their dependency needs met. So the girl may grow up with no real sense of her separate self, always seeking the perfect mother to merge with.

The general *social repression* of female sexuality is usually conveyed to the little girl early on in life. She is told not to express her body, not to fight or get messy. So when later she feels desire or excitement, guilt and anxiety result. For many women it is our fear of our own sexuality and of our bodies that keeps us stuck. For many men it is their fear of women. Women have for centuries been seen as the carriers of all the feelings that are unacceptable to society. Female power unlike male power is seen as destructive, changeable, unsafe, sexual and even animal. One woman drew for me her feelings about her female power as a bloody kitchen knife while her male power was a gleaming bejewelled sword. These cultural splits are conveyed to us from early childhood in stories and images such as wicked witches.

Second, as we develop *constructs about the world* our models are usually hierarchical. There are always superior and inferior groups. Just being a child is enough to make us feel inferior to apparently superior grown ups. So as Adler (1964) showed, we start life with inferiority complexes. Then as we grow up we are likely to face other hierarchies of class, colour and, of course, gender. Most people are at the 'lower' end of one hierarchy or another. Most people feel not good enough in at least one area of life. Most people have a feeling of inferiority. In my experience this is the single most important factor in all psychological disturbance. I see clients from a variety of class backgrounds, men as well as women, and everyone seems to be deeply affected by the social hierarchies in which they grew up. These hierarchies continue to affect us throughout life. As Dale Spender (1980) shows, our very language is constructed in a way that implies women's second-class status. The norm is seen as masculine. *Man* is used to denote both men and women. This affects us unconsciously all the time even when on a conscious level we are supposed to be equal.

Perpetuation of psychological disturbance

Feelings of inferiority and the neurotic patterns we develop to deal with them are perpetuated by the *hierarchic organization of the society we live in*, at school, in the office, at home. We continue the patterns because we are still often in the environment that requires them.

However for many people the patterns can take over our lives so that we respond inappropriately to every situation with our habitual pattern. For example, we always withdraw until we become more and more depressed. Or we are always ready for attack, to defend ourselves from what we perceive as a constantly hostile world. These responses may lead us to the doctor's surgery or even into hospital. And all too often these *patterns are seen as illnesses* to be treated with drugs. New dependencies are set up, on drugs, on doctors, social workers, therapists. Society's response is frequently to increase its control over us and make us feel even more inferior and powerless. This is not to deny that there are times when a short course of drugs may be necessary to bring a patient to the point where the causes of her problem are able to be explored.

People often get labelled *sick, nervous, mad* etc. They are often carrying the 'madness' of a whole family or even of society which is split into those who are OK and those who are not OK or even into those who are 'normal' and those who are 'mad'. Women are especially likely to be put into this role. The 'neurotic wife' or the 'depressed mum' are familiar cultural stereotypes. Sometimes when a wife who has been depressed changes and takes her life into her own control her husband goes to pieces. There is often a see-saw effect between couples. When one is up the other is down and vice versa. Many men only feel strong if their wives can be seen as weak.

There are also *cultural expectations* that affect how different groups of people respond to stress. Men will often go to the pub and get drunk. Women who often find that they are not taken seriously when they say how they feel may have to go to extremes of self-expression in order to get attention. They may have to attempt suicide or run naked down the street. Resorting to such extremes in our culture is likely to result in the woman being put in a mental hospital. And all too often, once in such a place, people become institutionalized and may stay for unnecessarily long periods of time.

On the other hand many women who do not reach that point are isolated in the home, perhaps, looking after young children. And it can be their very isolation that leads to deeper and deeper depression. In Brown and Harris's (1978) study on depression, it was found not only that almost 1 in 3 women suffers from some form of depression but that factors such as lack of a job outside the home, more than three children and no intimate relationship for expressing deep feelings are likely to encourage depression.

PRACTICE

Goals of therapy

One of the primary goals of feminist therapy is to increase the client's sense of self-worth. For many people, especially women, having a whole 50 minutes in which all attention is focused on them is a new experience. This in itself can be very therapeutic. The kind of unconditional positive regard that Rogers (1961) talks of is very important. They are being taken seriously, fully listened to and not judged, sometimes for the first time. The whole of them – unacceptable sides, shadow side, angry side – is being accepted and understood.

Being understood is a second vital feature of the therapy. For many people have never been really understood, friends can often put their own projections or needs for identification on them and perhaps partners choose not to understand because it does not suit them. For example, a wife who wants to get out to work because she needs to be somebody in her own right, to express her potential, may be misunderstood by a husband who thinks it is only for the money. His need to be in control may make him insist that they do not need the money. He may even make her feel guilty for wanting to go to work.

So the development of empathy is vital, and many women feel that we can only get that empathy with another woman who also has first-hand experience of being a woman in a sexist society. This might be especially important in the early stages of a woman's personal development. While it could perhaps be useful to see a male therapist later to work through relationships with father and with men in general, this varies from person to person.

This understanding and empathy can include a recognition of the so-called objective conditions of the society that the person is in. It can also mean respecting the way that they experience and interpret their world. Even if it is different from my own way of seeing, I need to as it were 'get inside their heads' to see it from where they are. Many women, for example, will not have a feminist perspective at all. But it is important to start from where they are and not to push my own interpretation or analysis on them too soon, or indeed at all. It is part of another vital aim in therapy which is to build up trust and mutual respect. For me as a therapist, respecting my client means respecting her or his way of seeing and coping with the world in the present, as well as recognizing the problems that usually lie within the client's perceptions and behaviours.

It may also involve helping clients to define their own goals in therapy. Many clients need to have defined goals and I usually do this near the beginning. But these usually change over the weeks or months. For example, one woman came because she wanted to stop crying so easily and over the months we realized together that underneath her tears was a lot of anger. Her goals gradually changed to be more related to her overall development and expression of her considerable potential that she was so angry about being repressed. Another woman came initially to be helped through a crisis, but it turned out that her hidden goal was actually to check out with an 'expert' whether her own self-analysis was 'correct' or not. So by looking at these goals we discovered patterns which had been giving her problems.

The *general goals* of feminist therapy could be summed up as helping clients to accept and feel OK about all sides of themselves and to allow their own growth processes to move. The emphasis is always on them and on the idea that life *is* change and process. If we have the right conditions we will all grow, develop and change all the time, throughout our lives. Therapy can be seen as a small guiding input into that process. It may be needed when the process has got stuck or in times of crisis and particularly dramatic transformations. For many people come into therapy as a part of a 'growing up' process that they perhaps did not go through when society expected it.

This raises the question of what we mean by being grown up or mature. Our society has its own definitions which I would question. And I do *not* see my goal in therapy to help people become 'mature' in our present society's terms. For many women this might, for example, imply finding a permanent male partner and having children. However I do think that it is important that people feel able to choose their lifestyle, sexual orientation, whether or not to have children, career, etc. And it is difficult to make a clear, conscious, comfortable choice when we are driven by neurotic patterns or rigid one-sided social expectations.

More detailed goals could be described in three main categories.

1. Cognitive – changing ways of thinking and perceiving, developing new models.
2. Emotional – being in touch with wide range of emotions.
3. Behavioural – acting differently towards the world, e.g., assertion training etc.

Cognitive

Clients usually come believing that one side or other of themselves is unacceptable. They often come with a view of the world and themselves that is split between OK and not OK, good and bad. This has a profound effect on their sense of self-worth.

For example, one very successful woman came feeling very bad about herself despite her achievements at work. It turned out that only her 'superwoman side' was good and acceptable, while her 'little girl' side was bad, ragged, over demanding and very sad. By working with both sides it became clear that the little girl was also sensitive and creative and the superwoman could be ruthlessly demanding and hard on the little girl. In other words there was *both* positive and negative on both sides. And they actually needed each other.

Another woman had a good school prefect side and a naughty sexual side. We eventually found that she was both and could be in both sides at different times.

So one of the main goals for me is to help clients see that *we can be both* and it is not a matter of either/or which is the main model that society teaches us. This *both/and* model I sometimes draw as a spiral or rhythm to show how we can move between them. At a certain stage in the therapy such a model can be made quite explicit.

Emotional

In the same way that different subpersonalities are a part of us so are our different emotions. For many people some emotions are seen as good and others as bad. For example, it is good to be happy but bad to feel sad. It can be useful to see that sadness is the other side of the coin from happiness and that in the rhythms and cycles of life we need to move between them. But the emotion that is unacceptable does not only need to be accepted but also to be expressed. This is where discharge of emotion is so important.

Therapy can provide a safe place for emotions to be expressed. And much of the work is on allowing and even encouraging unacceptable emotions such as anger to be expressed by the client in a place where they will not be rejected because of it. Sometimes I suggest that clients draw things because visual images can be a more direct route to feelings. Or relaxation and fantasy work can help. Working with memories of childhood experience can be vital in bringing up deep and forgotten feelings. And when appropriate I encourage them to express feelings towards me too.

Behavioural

Changing our perceptions and being in touch with feelings is rarely enough unless some actual changes in behaviour take place. Each client will have different goals about behaviour change in detail. One man came to see me with a very specific list of situations in which he was overwhelmed by embarrassment and started sweating. So each week he had homework to do relating to this list. We started with the easier ones first. This was in addition to working on and exploring the causes of this embarrassment which included social expectations of male roles and behaviour. I also often encourage clients to keep a diary during the week, of times when the behaviour they want to change occurs.

Frequently this is to do with not being assertive or not saying No when they want to. Sometimes we role-play situations in which they want to be more assertive. One of the goals for most clients certainly seems to be having more assertive relationships. And for me the essence of assertive relating is that rather than dominating the other or being a passive victim she is acting as an equal.

In an assertive relationship she respects and acknowledges the other but at the same time expresses her own needs clearly and makes specific demands even if these are not immediately met. It may involve negotiation, but always from a position of equality in terms of valuing self and the other. This goal reflects the theoretical position mentioned earlier about changing relationships from hierarchical ones to more egalitarian and rhythmic ones. This is a goal in terms of the client's relationship with others, but also helps her to feel more self-worth. And it does seem that if people behave assertively it affects their feelings about themselves and their perceptions of the world and in turn, experiencing more inner worth changes behaviour.

The 'person' of the therapist

Just as I encourage the client to develop new kinds of inner and outer relationships, so I am concerned to develop different relationships between client and therapist. So my starting point is always from a position of equal valuing and respecting. Inside myself I am aware of my own problems, weaknesses, vulnerabilities. At another time I could be sitting in her chair telling her *my* troubles. But at this particular time we have a contract for me to be in the role of therapist and for her to be in the role of the client. And I certainly do *not* start pouring out my problems to her. This 50 minutes is *her* time.

Among feminist therapists there is considerable variation as to how much we disclose about ourselves to clients or women in workshops. I generally do not offer information apart from an initial self-description on a handout I send to prospective clients. But I do always answer questions honestly, as that is for me part of respecting the other. I use the question and their fantasies about me as part of the therapy, but I am no blank screen. I also work at home, and the physical environment in which one works is important and reveals much about the therapist's values. I do not pretend to be value free; indeed my use of the model of *both/and* rather than either/or in therapy is a value.

I find that every client I have seen has brought something which feels like a part of me, some conflict I too have had, even the men. Partly I think that this is because of our common humanity and the similarity of the themes that we all grapple with through life. But I also think that people find each other at the right time in their lives. And when I have been particularly open to, for example my own sadness, then I find that the clients can be too. I often feel that I have been through similar stages that they are now going through only a few years ago. And I, like them, am still growing and changing. It is vital that as therapists, we continue to 'work' on ourselves all the time and it is also important that we have support and 'mothering' for ourselves. For an important role for the therapist is that of providing good enough mothering which is something that many clients have never had.

The therapist is both the container *and* the supporter. She is there to provide a safe place in which the client can explore or even just be. My simply *being there* is often enough. One client described me as the gymnasium, while she was the gymnast. I was the floor, the walls and sometimes a rope ladder or an obstacle to climb over, but she was the active person.

For much of the time the relationship of therapist to client is one of mother to child. But what I think is especially important for me in feminist therapy is that I can also be her or his sister. We can have an adult-to-adult relationship as well as a parent–child one. In the course of one 50-minute session I can move backwards and forwards from being mother to sister and sometimes even child, as when we laugh together. So even though she is being a child much of the time she also knows that I respect her as an equal adult as well. When it is appropriate I will put on my adult-to-adult 'hat' and talk on a rational level about, for example, her two sides 'making friends' or about something being especially difficult for women. And at certain stages in the therapy such sisterly talk is more appropriate than at others. For some women it may be at the beginning to make them feel comfortable and not put down. For others it may be towards the end when they have worked through more of their child feelings.

Therapeutic style

My therapeutic style also moves between opposites. It is both *directive* and *non-directive* at different times and in different amounts depending on clients' needs. Some clients either ask for or seem to need quite directive therapy. This might involve fairly precise goals, the use of exercises and definite tasks perhaps to do at home during the week. Other clients either ask for or seem to need relatively undirected therapy, in which they talk most of the time and I simply feed back to them what they have said in a more 'structured' way. It may involve summarizing what the client has said. But I also use the model of opposites. For example, 'It sounds as though you have two opposite sides, a superwoman and a timid little girl.' Or, 'You seem to be saying that one part of you wants to get married while the opposite side doesn't want to get married but wants to please yourself.' This could lead to more directive work as when the client is asked to have a dialogue between the two sides.

For some women non-directive therapy can feel unsafe or strange, especially if this is their first experience of therapy. The one-sided nature of the relationship can feel very odd at first. There may be a hidden anxiety about the relatively powerful position I am in by being only the listener and not talking about myself. Women desire equality, but we also crave safety and parenting. I find that it helps to acknowledge any inequalities when they arise or at the beginning explain how I see therapy.

Women often wonder what they are 'supposed to do in therapy'. This questioning can be used to show women that they may go through life behaving in ways expected of them rather than from their own needs. Yet there are also genuine questions about the 'therapy culture' which I feel should be responded to with respect and not assumed to be 'resistance' or 'defence'.

The limits and boundaries of the relationship are vital too. Women often have problems with boundaries as we tend to merge too easily with others. Although the therapy relationship can be intense, deeply caring, it is only for 50 minutes once a week. We have to 'hold' the contradiction of passionate involvement and complete detachment. This too is a rhythm.

We can also be joint detectives piecing together bits of the person's past into a whole picture. This can involve directing clients to look at childhood experiences or remember forgotten incidents. Asking questions is directive but often necessary, especially in short-term therapy. Indeed it is usually important in the first session to acquire information about clients that might be relevant such as whether they have brothers and sisters. But it can also make the first session feel safer to have a clear structure. After this the techniques I use may vary considerably.

Major therapeutic techniques

I have already mentioned the great variety of techniques used by feminist therapists. And like many of the others I work in an eclectic way and do not stick to one major technique. Flexibility is as important for therapeutic method as it is for the client's own growth. I do not believe that one technique or style is better than any other. It depends on the client.

However it also depends on the therapist and some practitioners seem to feel more comfortable with certain techniques rather than others in that these may suit their personality better. For me the Rogerian technique feels especially comfortable, but I also feel OK using certain directive techniques such as gestalt, TA fantasy work, relaxation, art therapy and assertion training role-playing etc. Gestalt relates especially to the model of the opposites. And putting two opposite sides of a client's self on to two separate cushions is a very powerful and dramatic way of working with these opposites.

Most of the techniques used by feminist therapists will have been described elsewhere in this volume or in Dryden (1984). But one technique that is increasingly popular with feminists is assertion training (AT). It is basically a form of honest, clear and direct communication between equals. It involves learning skills that help us to be clear about what we want, to ask for it firmly while still respecting the other and to negotiate an outcome. It sounds simple, but for many women assertiveness has been labelled *aggressiveness*. And indeed after being passive in a large number of situations we do sometimes explode. Through assertion training we 'unlearn' patterns of behaviour that we learned to fit our female roles such as passivity or manipulation. And through lots of practice and role-playing we learn new behaviour patterns. This approach is described in a popular way by Ann Dickson (1982) in *Woman in Your Own Right*. AT is usually done in groups. But the theory and techniques can also be useful in individual therapy.

The change process in therapy

One of the central points of feminist therapy is that it is difficult to be healthy in an unhealthy society. And that changes within us are not enough. We need to change society too. As Joanna Ryan (1983) put it,

> Our desires for both individual and social change, and our need to operate on both internal and external reality do not need to be posted as false and antagonistic choices, but can be expressed together as they enhance and support each other.
> (p. 24).

Even in small ways we can try and reorganize our workplaces, for example to make them more co-operative. But at the same time, the more individual people that relate assertively the more easily the structures and cultures of workplaces etc. will change. And even where they do not, we feel better about ourselves for having stated our needs clearly.

It is however important to work on external changes as well as internal. Many feminist therapists are also involved in political activity of one kind or another, and it can be argued that we are more effective in our attempts to change aspects of society if we have sorted out most of our own inner conflicts. We can choose which campaigns we want to be our priority rather than hitting out at all authority because we are still rebelling against our fathers. We can use the energies of the rationally rebellious child in a constructive way, when appropriate. Yet feminist therapy begins with the inner world of the client.

I personally, usually start with a six-week contract to give the sessions an initial structure. In this time we look at the main patterns and build up a relationship. While for some clients this has been enough, most continue. The second stage is often about delving into their shadow sides, getting to know and accept them, a process which can take years. This acceptance has to be from the heart as well as from the head and it generally includes a lot of emotional discharge and may involve seeing the negative sides of me and of therapy.

Clients usually start by thinking that the therapist is wonderful, then come the disappointments. Whilst some may leave at this stage, many go on to a third stage which is more rhythmic and involves an acceptance and use of all their own opposites but also seeing the opposites in me and in therapy. Both have their limitations. It may mean that the client wants to mother me in some way. But it can also be the development of a more equal kind of relationship. During this stage it becomes important to change behaviour too, which is where assertion training can come in. Or it might mean making changes to their lifestyles or future plans.

In a sense the *first stage is more cognitive*, the *second more emotional* and the *third more behavioural*. But all three can be used at any point of the therapy. And clients often go backwards and forwards between stages. There may also be periods when a client is stuck and does not seem to be changing at all. Change and no change are after all also two interrelated sides of the same coin. Periods of rest, even absence from therapy for a while to let the new awareness sink in, can be very useful. The client has to go at her own pace. She may not be ready for dramatic changes, or she may need a long period of mothering before she is able to trust enough to allow the shadow side to surface.

The process of change is a life-long journey and the therapist is just a guide for short stretches at a time. Sometimes insights gained in therapy take years to really sink in. Also it may be useful to do other specific forms of therapy as a complement to individual work. Some of my clients have done psycho-drama, attended workshops, been to body-work groups during as well as after their individual therapy. One man that I saw for over a year joined a man's group after he finished therapy with me. I often give clients information about these kinds of possibilities.

One of the most important changes is an increase in self-worth, being able to trust their own process of development, not only during therapy but when it ends too. Sometimes clients come back for one or more sessions when they feel the need. And I often give them drawings or diagrams of the main patterns, themes we had been working with so that they have a structure to relate new life experiences to. Parting and separating is often difficult for people and the ending of therapy is one way of learning to do it comfortably.

Hopefully most of them will have internalized the 'good enough therapist' to take away with them.

CASE EXAMPLE

Mary was referred to me by a friend of hers who had been in therapy with me previously. Forty-one years old, she was feeling confused and unhappy. She arrived smiling brightly, holding herself rather stiffly. She struck me as an attractive and strong woman, tall with dark hair and wide anxious eyes. She told me that she cried too much and did not seem to have any direction in her life. Her goal was to stop crying so much and to 'sort out her life'. She sounded quite impatient with herself. Mary had always been artistic and when she left school she went to art college in London.

While at college she met John who was also a student of fine art. They fell in love and before finishing her course Mary got pregnant and married John. After she had a second child Mary did a secretarial course and began working part-time, John did have some success as a painter but he was difficult to live with at times. He used to tease her all the time and she always felt inadequate and inferior to him. He was the genius. He also had some private means, so they lived quite well and had a full social life which Mary enjoyed.

Then when she was 38 John went off with another woman and Mary was devastated. But she coped and took a full-time secretarial job which she was still in when she came to see me.

On the surface Mary was very rational and reasonable about her situation but when she talked about John leaving, tears welled up in her eyes which she quickly wiped away saying 'There I go again, how silly of me.' Yet she was very vulnerable too, so during the first few sessions I encouraged her to keep hold of her strengths and showed respect for the way she managed. Always the strong side had to be acknowledged to allow her to admit the vulnerability.

It was also clear right from the start that part of her problem lay in social roles and expectations of her as a woman. Like so many women she had been 'holding the family together' so admitting weakness was all the more scary. I did not myself say anything about her roles as wife and mother. But by the second session she herself was commenting on the way women often seem to give up their lives for their men. She saw a new goal as one that involved creating her own self. And we began to get a picture of the two sides – one a strong, wise heroine and the other a frightened little girl.

The next few sessions were mainly concerned with getting to know these two sides better. The tearful little girl was more and more acceptable and she described a house near where she lived that symbolized the little girl. It was a quaint but sad house, that Mary felt could be interesting if it was in another setting. I asked her to relax, and to imagine going inside it. 'The interior was rather dark and scary, but it was interesting and creative,' she said.

The strong side was also repressed in a way, although Mary coped on the surface with life. Her voice was often high-pitched, like that of a little girl. Mary had great difficulty in expressing anger, so I would encourage her to repeat any slightly resentful remarks loudly. Her voice changed and it became strong and angry. After one of these sessions she had a dream that she was driving a car with a Zulu warrior in the back and it was on a wide open plain and it felt very good. We explored the meaning of the warrior. He seemed to represent her strong, hidden, heroine self and the car represented her power.

By about the tenth session her different sides and separate emotions had become clearer. Mary had often talked about being in a muddle and not knowing what she felt. I drew a diagram for her with her tears at the top which were the symptom she came with. Then it seemed that her fear of acknowledging the little girl welled up and made her confused. With this confusion came a feeling of complete powerlessness that stopped her getting in touch with the complex and painful feelings underneath. These painful feelings turned out to be a fear of not getting her needs met and a sadness about being alone and separate. We then looked at the opposites of the needs themselves and the fear of not getting them met. The needs were described by Mary as the need both to give and receive love, the need for respect and the need for connectedness with others. By acknowledging these needs the muddle began to disappear, but underneath there also turned out to be anger at not getting needs met. This anger Mary had turned on herself, blaming herself for not 'getting on with life' etc. Turning the anger outwards was an important part of the next stage in therapy.

At this point we looked at her fears about not getting needs met in therapy and her anger at me about that. This was hard to express and still the tears would come up instead of the anger that lay beneath them. It is culturally more acceptable for women to cry than to be angry. This was acknowledged and helped Mary actually be angry in an outside situation that involved her ex-husband. She felt pleased with herself for having stood up to him more firmly. We did some assertion-training work at this time, which was more directive than most of the work we had done previously.

By this time too she was able to separate out and get in touch with the conflicting feelings towards her ex-husband. She wrote a letter (not to send) to him expressing her rage and then another one with her rational, reasonable side. They are both sides of her. The reasonable side had kept her in control and it was still scary not to be always in control. The tears were her only way of expressing the out-of-control side. As the oldest child with no father she had always had to feel 'in control'. And after about nine months she began talking more about her mother and her resentments towards her because she had not met Mary's needs and yet had expected her always to be strong. At this time Mary also began to see the limitations of therapy and of me. We started having a much more sisterly relationship and talked quite openly about feminist ideas. Mary started going to a woman's consciousness-raising group and was reading feminist books. She also bought a house and moved in.

Then after almost a year she gave up her job and worked part-time while she started painting again. She told me that her artistic side was her 'masculine' side that she had not dared express for fear of harming her husband. It was powerful, too powerful. It was her sun, it was also the Zulu warrior and the car. It was exciting to be in touch with it, but then one day she came feeling very shaky and said she was afraid of slipping back into 'powerlessness and muddle'. We acknowledged that it had been safer and easier to be passive and muddled. Being the sun meant being outside, showing oneself to the world. We talked about the rhythm of life between energies going outward and energies going inwards, the sun and the moon and the need for both. Her growth was not a straight line. And then although we were sometimes sisters together I also continued to be 'mother'. Her need to separate and be on the outside was however increasing and her fear of it seemed to be decreasing. By this time Mary had achieved considerable changes in her life situation and we concentrated for a while on those achievements and on her strengths. Since then I have had a very positive letter from Mary and she seems to be 'moving on'. She has an exhibition with two other women coming up soon. Mary still attends her woman's group.

REFERENCES

Adler, A. (1964) *Individual Psychology*, Harper Torch, New York.
Baker Miller, J. (1978) *Towards a New Psychology of Women*, Penguin, Harmondsworth.
Berlotti, E. G. (1977) *Little Girls*, Readers and Writers Co-operative, London.
Brown, G. and Harris, T. (1978) *Social Origins of Depression*, Tavistock, London.
Brown, L. and Liss-Levinson, N. (1981) *Feminist Therapy I*, in R. Corsini (ed.) *Handbook of Innovative Psychotherapies*, Wiley, New York.
Chodorow, N. (1978) *The Reproduction of Mothering: Psychoanalysis and the Sociology of Gender*, University of California Press, Berkeley.
Dickson, A. (1982) *Woman in Your Own Right*, Quartet, London.

Dryden, W. (ed) (1984) *Individual Therapy in Britain*, Harper & Row, London.

Ernst, S. and Goodison, L. (1981). *In Our Own Hands*, The Women's Press, London.

Firestone, S. (1979) *The Dialectic of Sex*, The Women's Press, London.

Forisha, B. (1981) Feminist therapy II, in R. Corsini (ed.) *Handbook of Innovative Psychotherapies*, Wiley, New York.

Horney, K. (1924) On the genesis of the castration complex in women, *International Journal of Psychoanalysis*, Vol. 5, pp. 50–65.

Mitchell, J. (1975) *Psychoanalysis and Feminism*, Pelican, Harmondsworth.

Nairn, K. and Smith, G. (1984) *Dealing with Depression*, The Women's Press, London.

Orbach, S. and Eichenbaum, L. (1982) *Outside In, Inside Out*, Penguin, Harmondsworth.

Orbach, S. and Eichenbaum, L. (1983) *What Do Women Want?* Pelican, Harmondsworth.

Orbach, S. and Eichenbaum, L. (1985) *Understanding Women*, Pelican, Harmondsworth.

Rogers, C. (1961) *On Becoming a Person*, Constable, London.

Ryan, J. (1983) *Feminism and Therapy*, The Polytechnic of North London Publications, London.

Spender, D. (1980) *Man Made Language*, Routledge & Kegan Paul, London.

Wyckoff, H. (1975) Solving women's problems, in C. Steiner and H. Wyckoff (eds.) *Readings in Radical Psychiatry*, Grove Press, New York.

Suggested further reading

Baker Miller, J. (1978) *Towards a New Psychology of Women*, Penguin, Harmondsworth.

Chesler, P. (1972) *Women and Madness*, Doubleday, New York.

De Beauvoir, S. (1960) *The Second Sex*, Jonathan Cape, London.

Ernst, S. and Goodison, L. (1981) *In Our Own Hands*, The Women's Press, London.

Orbach, S. and Eichenbaum, L. (1985) *Understanding Women*, Pelican, Harmondsworth.

CHAPTER 4

ENCOUNTER

Mike Wibberley

HISTORICAL CONTEXT AND DEVELOPMENTS IN BRITAIN

Historical context

Encounter is less capable of being tightly defined than most other approaches and this has resulted in a fair amount of confusion about what encounter is and where it comes from. Will Schutz (1973), one of the most prominent figures in encounter, lists a number of historical antecedents going back to Ancient Greece, and a number of more modern and more direct influences on the growth of encounter, including psychodrama, gestalt, group analysis, body-work approaches, and T-groups. There is no one source of origin for encounter, as analysis had its Freud, psychodrama its Moreno, or gestalt its Perls. Thus there was no authority to define what was and was not encounter. Shaffer and Galinsky (1974) describe encounter as having 'grass-roots origins'. It evolved from a wide range of sources rather than being invented, and encounter group leaders came from a variety of backgrounds including analysis, medicine, social work, and organizational training as well as the more unorthodox styles of growth work. Many brought influences from their former fields with them and consequently there have been wide variations in the types of group called encounter. The term *encounter* has also been used as a generic term to cover non-traditional growth groups. Lieberman, Yalom and Miles (1973) in their research, for instance, use the term to include ten different types of group, including gestalt, psychodrama, TA groups, analytic groups, Rogerian groups, Synanon groups, non-verbal groups, and two groups led by a tape-recorder!

Despite this confusion it is clear that encounter groups have been characterized by their emphasis on the importance of honest, emotional here-and-now relating, and distinguished from group analysis by the overt emotional involvement of the leader(s). It is also clear that there have been landmarks in the development of encounter, and that four main streams have emerged.

Some writers (e.g. Blank *et al.*, 1971; and Elliot, 1976) place the beginnings of encounter with the National Training Laboratories in 1946, on a course set up to train community leaders in ways of handling intergroup and interracial conflicts. They used role-playing and psychodramatic techniques in the daytime sessions, and the staff met in the evenings to discuss the day's events. One evening, three of the participants were allowed to observe a staff meeting at which it happened that the behaviour of one of them was discussed. She became quite excited, and the interactions quickly focused on here-and-now conflicts. One of the trainers, Kurt Lewin was impressed by the learning potential in the proceedings. Other participants were allowed into subsequent staff meetings, and they soon became the highlight of the week. By the next year Lewin was running courses specifically set up to learn from here-and-now, face-to-face interactions, known as T-groups. Whilst these groups started off as a tool of organizational development, participants also achieved personal growth and learning. Some leaders became increasingly oriented towards personal growth as an end in itself, rather than a tool of organizational development, and they became an important factor in the burgeoning of encounter in the United States.

Second, at about the same time, Carl Rogers was using similar here-and-now, face-to-face methods in the training of counsellors, and went on to develop his own style of encounter as a way of helping people to explore more personally satisfying ways of communicating with each other. He emphasized *congruence* (that what you say and how you look, sound and act match up together) and emotionality. He saw such groups as an antidote to increasing alienation in society.

Third, in 1958, a residential therapeutic community for drug addicts, called Synanon was started (Yablonsky, 1965). Synanon developed the use of encounter groups, though of a quite different style from those led by Rogers. Rogers's groups tended to be encouraging, supportive, and focused on self-disclosure. Outbursts of irritation were not discouraged, but tended to be brief. Synanon groups, on the other hand, were based on loud, hostile confrontations, frequently with the whole group confronting one person. Expressions of support were rare, and usually discouraged as rescuing the person from the truth. Whilst these groups were developed for drug addicts in a residential setting, they also had an influence on encounter groups in general, and many non-addicted members of the general public participated in such groups. (For a critique of the 'attack approach' see Eugene Walder's article, 1971).

A fourth major influence was Will Schutz. He is the most famous representative of what has been called *open encounter*. These groups put more emphasis on the body, movement, structured group exercises, and non-verbal ways of communicating and relating. They strongly emphasized experience rather than 'talking about experience'.

Developments in Britain

In Britain, the beginnings of encounter were in the late 1960s in the two major growth centres of the time, Quaesitor and Community, led by Paul and Patricia Lowe, Mike Barnet, Jerome Liss and others. In 1970, Denny and Leida Yuson were brought to England by the Home Office to start a Synanon-derived drug-treatment programme called Phoenix House. After running into internal political difficulties, Denny and Leida resigned and started running encounter groups for non-drug-addicted members of the general public at Quaesitor. They specialized in 48-hour marathons and long-term intensive groups (six to nine months). They trained Brian Dempsey, Brian Coombe and Eva Coombe (now Eva Chapman), and I was trained by Brian Coombe and Eva. This type of encounter became the mainstream in Britain throughout the 1970s.

Reflecting an aspect of the social climate of the time, encounter groups in the late 1960s to mid-1970s had a very fresh, if naïve, quality about them. The growth movement then was rather like a free child with lots of new things to explore. Boundaries and rules were there to be broken – and they were, with energy and enthusiasm. Many people at this time saw in encounter the promise of new freedom from parental restrictions, social constraints and personal limitations. Whilst there was much excitement, and undoubtedly many people made creative changes in their lives, with hind-sight these groups had an unrealistic quality about them. They were too divorced from people's real lives. There was too much use of group pressure, too much emphasis on emotional expression, and not enough emphasis on integration. As the social climate changed and the growth movement grew up, encounter became rather unfashionable and attracted some valid criticism from some quarters. This situation was not helped by a growing number of untrained leaders, and a small minority of leaders (though none in Britain that I know of) who allowed or encouraged violence in their groups (for a critique see David Boadella, 1980). By the late 1970s it was time for a rethink.

The late 1970s and 1980s have seen the emergence of a different kind of encounter group in Britain. Whilst retaining much of the excitement that goes with personal exploration, encounter groups are now more realistic and more connected to real life. Participants, I have found, come with more mature attitudes and more sense of responsibility. There is more emphasis on the meaning of the experience and how people can use what they learn in their daily lives. There is less use of group pressure, and emotional expression tends to be less extreme and more connected for much of the time. Encounter in Britain seems a much healthier approach in the 1980s. Groups at the Open Centre, at Spectrum with Terry Cooper, and those led by Brian Coombe are responsibly led, and can be recommended. Anyone wishing to do a group with someone else is well advised to contact the leader beforehand and check out their training and their attitudes and practices in groups.

THEORETICAL ASSUMPTIONS

Image of the person

Encounter sees people as a unity of mind, body and spirit (see Schutz, 1973) and seeks to provide a place where people can explore, become more aware, and grow in each of these three areas. Schutz maintains that we are more effective as human individuals when we are in touch with all three aspects of self.

A central concept in encounter is that of *identity*. This has two aspects; an inward aspect of experience, and an outward aspect of expression. The inner aspect of experience has both conscious and unconscious elements. It is quite common in groups and therapy to see people who continually 'put themselves down' – define themselves as unworthy – and are scarcely aware of doing it. This inner aspect also contains our rules for ourselves – what we allow ourselves to do, say, and express, and what we do not allow ourselves. We can incorporate into this view of identity concepts from other branches of humanistic psychology, for example Perls's concept of topdog/bottom dog (Perls, 1969), Berne's parent/adult/child, drivers, and scripts (Berne, 1968; 1973), and Assagioli's concept of subpersonalities (Assagioli, 1971).

The other side of the identity coin is *expression*. This is how we actually relate to others and to the world around us. Our expression of identity also has both conscious and unconscious aspects, and includes our behaviour, speech, vocalization, movement etc.

Our experience of identity and expression of identity are accurate reflections of each other, and are capable of modifying each other. A change in how we experience ourselves, as a result of insight, can lead to changes in our behaviour. Similarly, changes in our behaviour can lead to a different experience of ourselves. Supposing, for instance, a man identifies himself as someone who has little impact or influence with others. This may have come about early in his life – others did not take much notice of him, so he developed a view of himself as someone who was not able to influence others. In a situation where something is happening that he does not like, he *expects* to have no influence and so he withdraws, or says what he thinks in a lifeless, unenergetic way. The result is that he has very little influence in the situation, and so re-inforces that part of his identity. If the person learns to act in a different way, for example to say what he thinks with more energy, a different tone of voice and more direct eye contact, he may well be taken more notice of. If he *is*, this calls into question his previous experience of himself. If he does this a number of times, he may have to change that part of his identity, and re-interpret some of his past experience. This idea is central to the emphasis on here-and-now relating in encounter.

In encounter, each person is seen as responsible for himself or herself. They have the right and the responsibility to say Yes to what they want, and No to what they do not want, and to communicate their wants, wishes and feelings. They have the right and the responsibility to get what they need in order to grow. Each person is free to make his or her choices in the group and the experience is seen as the result of his or her own choices.

Because encounter sees a person as a unity of mind, body and spirit, it encourages expression of all of these aspects. There has been confusion in the past, and some groups have apparently been interested in emotional and physical expression to the exclusion of mind and spirit. Emotional expression without thought is as useless and dangerous as intellectual expression without emotion is dry and impoverished. The most valuable encounter groups are those which seek to enable people to nourish each aspect of their being and make responsible choices (Schutz, 1973).

Encounter assumes that each of us has a wide range of aspects to our identity and that the more we are aware of these aspects and are able to give them responsible expression, the closer we are to psychological health. In this way encounter is as much about *exploration* as it is about therapy. A person does not have to have a 'problem' to use an encounter group effectively (Elliot, 1976).

Concepts of psychological health and disturbance

One of the major contributions of humanistic psychology in general has been to get away from the idea of 'sick' people and 'healthy' people as a dichotomy. It established that we all have issues to deal with in our lives, and we all have room to grow towards health. It is true that, for some, the issues they deal with are more serious and debilitating in their lives than they are for others. It is also true that it helps to have some idea of what we value as healthy, and consequently what we are working towards in groups. There are a number of factors which are generally regarded as healthy.

First, it is important that we have an adequate sense of self, or identity. This means that we identify ourselves as in charge of our own lives and able to make our own life decisions, rather than being at the mercy of, or in the control of, others whether past or present. It also means being able to set realistic goals for ourselves in our lives, and seeing ourselves as adequate to achieve them.

Second, it is important to have a sense (in thought, feeling and experience) of our own personal rights and boundaries. We should be assertive enough to claim and protect our own rights, whilst respecting those of others. We need to be able to distinguish between self and others in thought, feelings, behaviour and responsibility. This may sound simple, but it is quite common to hear people say things such as 'I felt your pain while you were crying', 'You make me feel guilty', 'I know what you are thinking', 'You feel angry.' Such statements betray a lack of sense of boundaries in distinguishing between self and others.

In making our own life choices, or asserting our sense of boundaries, an ability to say Yes and No is extremely useful. Many people find it difficult to say Yes, or reach out for what they want. As many find it difficult to say No to what they do not want, and feel impelled to say 'I can't' rather than 'I don't want to', with the consequent feelings which go with denial of self.

Third, it is essential to be able to resolve conflicts, both within self and in relationship with others. In some areas of traditional psychology, maturity is seen as the 'achievement of ambivalence' (Winnicott, 1971; Guntrip, 1962), that is, the ability to have both negative and positive feelings about the same person. In any relationship there will be conflicts from time to time. If they cannot be resolved they will result in unequal power relationship, denial of feeling and subsequent impoverishment of the relationship, manipulation, or possibly the break-up of the relationship. Unresolved internal conflicts can lead to splitting, denial of aspects of self, somatic tensions, feelings of powerlessness, depression, diminished relationships with others and so on. For any given person there is likely to be a great deal of correspondence between his or her own inner unresolved conflicts, and the interpersonal conflicts he or she tends to have with others. In order to resolve conflicts we need to be able to confront, negotiate and forgive.

I would include in a list of healthy qualities a willingness to explore and take risks. Without this willingness it is difficult to achieve much personal growth. Particularly in Britain, many of us live under the constraint of thinking that we always have to know what we are doing, which leads to personal conservatism. If we free ourselves from the restriction of never having to make a mistake we are able to act in order to find out, and so by experiment we can find more effective ways of being.

It is important to be able to experience and express ourselves fully and directly, and to be able to communicate our experience (including feelings) to others. This means we are able to talk about, and get help with, any problems that arise in our lives. Finally, I would include the ability to play, whatever age we are.

This is not intended to be a precise definition of health in a human being (if such a thing is possible) but rather a list of indications of health from the point of view of encounter, and qualities a group would tend to work towards. Disturbance, in encounter, would be seen as distortions or interferences in identity, and is therefore indicated by any ways in which we prevent ourselves from being fully alive, and fully being and expressing ourselves (see Schutz, 1967). Although this can take a myriad of forms, there are a number of ways in which this would commonly be seen in groups.

Often people adhere to destructive or limiting life scripts or patterns, which they tend to repeat again and again. For example, some people habitually set up very similar relationships with a series of lovers or bosses or therapists or friends etc. and go through the same repetitive and destructive cycle. The roots of this cycle can usually be found in the person's childhood, and the relationships in which he or she formed his or her identity. It is my belief that this repetition is a series of attempts on the part of the person concerned to meet the same problem again, and this time find a better solution. This belief is also reflected in object relations theory.

Negative attitudes about self are another indication of disturbance: attitudes such as lack of self-confidence or seeing oneself as worthless, bad, sick, a failure or powerless. These aspects have both a behavioural component – how we present ourselves to others – and an internal dialogue component – how we talk to ourselves about ourselves.

Depression can also be taken as a sign of disturbance. When we repress or deny aspects of our *self* we impoverish our personality and our experience of ourself. This leads to loss of life-energy and depression on the one hand, and 'acting out' on the other. This acting out is usually destructive because repression of a part of self is usually accompanied by deep feelings of anger. Since acting out is usually a rebellion against having to interfere with a part of our identity, it is usually done in anger. Destructive acting out is often followed by guilt, and thence depression, and so becomes cyclical.

Acquisition of psychological disturbance

Since there was no central theory-creating figure in the development of encounter groups, and since practitioners of encounter have come from a variety of backgrounds, bringing their former theoretical orientations with them, there has been no central theory of the acquisition of psychological disturbance. Encounter leaders have used, or borrowed from, a number of different theories. Schutz came from an analytical and Reichian background, Egan (1970) from T-groups and social psychology, Rogers was a professor in psychology (though he claimed to have been influenced by many sources), and Synanon created its own theory by trial and error as it went along.

The major theories of psychological disturbance from Freud onwards have all described a process of identity formation. From the point of view of encounter, an essential element in any theory is that of self-responsibility. Within the context in which we grew up – environment, family relations and particular events – we made our own responses and drew our own conclusions about ourselves and our relationship to the world. Identity is the history of our experience in the world *and* our responses to that experience. This is not to say that events in childhood do not have a real impact, but that the child has its own response to the event which determines the nature of the impact. One client says his mother never touched him, except to hit him, for as long as he can remember. Undoubtedly the impact of this deprivation would be painful. His response to this deprivation was to be a 'good' boy. He became very polite and very helpful, and from the age of about four years onwards worked very hard in his mother's shop, all in an attempt to evoke a physical show of affection which never happened. His conclusions were that he could not influence her or others. If someone did show him affection it was a stroke of luck that he had no hand in. No matter how hard he worked he would be taken for granted. He concluded, in a phrase, 'I am powerless to get what I want.' Other children might have responded quite differently – to cry incessantly, to steal, to withdraw into fantasy, would all be understandable responses. The client introjected this situation and drew a conclusion about himself rather than about his mother, that is, 'She's OK, I'm not OK', rather than 'I'm OK, she's not OK.'

As we draw conclusions about ourselves and our environment, and adopt strategies for dealing with others and attempting to fulfil our own needs, all of this is incorporated into our growing identity, and is re-inforced by our environment as it is reflected back to us. Where distortions occur, this is likely to mean that we also limit or repress certain aspects of self. The children who adopt a strategy of being good and polite in order to achieve loving contact are likely to limit, or sacrifice, the more aggressive aspects of their identity such as their ability to demand, compete, or 'go for it'. The children who adopt a strategy of being 'brave' because 'big boys don't cry' may well sacrifice their ability to show hurt or fear, and limit access to their own tender feelings.

The sacrifice of any aspect of self creates negative feelings – pain, anger, and fear. Eric Edwards (1976) says 'The distortion of any individual life produces hate.' Where these feelings are too much to bear, or remain unexpressed, they are likely to be denied. This creates bodily distortions (character structure (see Lowen, 1971)), attitudinal distortions (how we talk to ourselves about ourselves), and behavioural distortions (how we express ourselves in the world).

It should be emphasized that distortions in identity are produced not only in response to individual traumatic events. The steady drip, drip, drip of day-to-day attitudes can be just as potent a force, if more subtle, in the distortion of identity.

Finally, and of crucial importance, this concept of self-responsibility in the formation of identity is not the same as imputing blame. Many clients, in discovering the distortions of self they have made, feel a profound sense of shame. It is not the job of the therapist or group leader to sit in judgement or blame the clients, but rather to accept the choices they have made and help them to make decisions which may be more effective from now onwards.

Perpetuation of psychological disturbance

Psychological disturbance is perpetuated, quite simply, by continuing to think, feel, and behave in the same familiar ways. If we experience and express ourselves in the same way and elicit familiar responses from our environment we create a closed, self-maintaining system. Any divergences from the picture we have created for ourselves can be rationalized, denied, or blamed on other people's pathology. This state of affairs may be re-inforced by others around us, since if one individual in a network of relationships starts to change her way of relating, every other person in that network must change to one extent or another to accommodate her changes (Satir, 1967). It should be understood that any apparently destructive pattern has some pay-off or reward for the person concerned, and behaviour that is not re-inforced in some way by others will be quickly dropped. This reward may be based on avoidance, for example, the person who continually isolates herself does not have to deal with potentially painful conflicts in relationships, and therefore achieves a measure of 'safety'. In order to give up a destructive pattern of thought/emotion/behaviour a person needs to find a different and better way of getting the same pay-off. The person in the example would need to find other ways of making conflicts safer in order to give up her isolation. Fortunately, whilst attitude, emotion and behaviour can be a powerful combination of forces in the maintenance of psychological disturbance, they can be an equally powerful combination of forces for change.

PRACTICE

Goals of therapy

Goals in encounter can be extremely variable. They will vary with leadership style, group format and length, and the particular participant make-up of any group. General aims include:

To increase awareness of self and one's personal style of relating
To facilitate expression of the whole range of emotion
To engender a sense of response-ability, personal power and creativity
To increase skills in personal communication with others

Each group should seek to provide a place where people can go beyond their normal social masks and relate as honestly as possible. As people express themselves in the group their identities emerge, including any problems and limitations. The group can be used to explore such problems, to see how they are related to personal identity, and to experiment with more effective behaviour and expression. In order to create such a place, the group needs to achieve a sense of relatedness between individuals and a balance of honesty, caring, confrontation, challenge and support.

Weekend groups and marathons

On a single group experience it is realistic to expect each person to gain a stimulus to his or her growth. All may well have an important experience that they can take back either into their lives to experiment with, or back into individual therapy or ongoing group to explore further. For instance, someone whose social circle is primarily intellectual may find saying how he or she *feels* very satisfying, or someone who has worked in individual therapy on his or her fear of being assertive may well go back with an experience of having done it with real people. When someone attends a single weekend group, attention should be paid to the integration of each one's experience within the time of the weekend. In the USA it seems that the weekend or week-long residential group has been the common form of encounter, and in groups for the general public the main aim has been to encourage emotional expression and contact. This seems to have been Carl Rogers's main aim in group work. He saw such contact as an antidote to what Maslow (1973) called the psychopathology of the average.

Ongoing groups

Ongoing groups meet for two or three hours each week, usually for a specified number of weeks (commonly between six and ten). Whilst they tend to be less intense than weekend or marathon groups, their week-to-week format is more conducive to the integration of the experience and to the support and re-inforcement of any changes people may make. One theoretical criticism of intensive weekend groups is that even if people make an important discovery for themselves if they go back to the same relationship network the social pressures may well be for them to behave and feel in the same ways they always have done. Ongoing groups can go some way towards ameliorating this effect, and aid the participants in retaining the awareness they gain and the changes they make. Combining weekend group(s) and ongoing groups makes the best of both the intensity and integration aspects.

Over the last few years I have developed what I call the 'rolling ongoing group'. Participants join for a minimum of six weeks, and thereafter drop out any time they wish on two weeks' notice. The group will run for a year or more, and as participants drop out they create a space for someone else to come in. This format allows great flexibility, allows participants to explore a wide range of aspects of self, and allows much more ambitious aims than does a weekend group or short ongoing. In this type of group it is realistic to expect that participants will confront the deeper dynamics of their lives, gain considerable awareness of their own identity, and integrate any necessary changes into their lives. In conjunction with weekend groups it is a powerful and flexible form of group therapy, suitable for a wide variety of people.

Selection

Participants in encounter groups are largely self-selected. However some care is needed with admission to groups. They are not suitable for people who are psychotic, or borderline psychotic, psychopathic, or unduly dependent. If in doubt about a person's ability to handle a group it is probably best to refer him or her to individual therapy until he or she has developed enough strength and contact with reality.

The 'person' of the therapist

The first, and perhaps obvious, thing to say about the people who lead encounter groups is that they should be trained, and have some intellectual framework for the work they do (see Elliot, 1976). Perhaps because encounter sometimes *looks* easy it has had more than a fair share of untrained or 'wild' leaders. However, encounter makes many demands on the person of the therapist.

The most important technique in encounter is ordinary, honest human relating. The leaders should therefore be willing to reveal their own feelings and be warm and supportive on the one hand, and challenging and confrontative on the other. They must be willing and able to deal with the whole range of feelings (including feelings participants have about *them*), and should be aware of a wide range of aspects of their own identity. They should be willing to engage in personal contact with participants in the group. At the same time as being a person in the group, and therefore on a peer level with participants, the leader has also taken an authority position, and must make administrative and therapeutic decisions. This dual role can be the source of much confusion in a group. It must be continually clarified from under which hat the leader is speaking so that personal preferences, feelings and perceptions, etc. are not taken as authority statements and vice versa. There is often ambivalence in the group, with some people wanting the leader to be 'one of us', and at the same time resenting him or her for not being the mythical, perfect authority who knows all the answers and is able to solve all their problems and lead them to Nirvana. There is often ambivalence in the leader about this too. To be able to handle this duality requires an acute sense of personal boundaries, and a great deal of integrity and humility. Without these qualities the leader can easily slip into overinflated omnipotence.

Encounter's emphasis on here-and-now relating does not preclude the possibility of transference. (Here defined as the projection on to the therapist of feelings and perceptions belonging to past significant figures and events.) Encounter leaders should be able to distinguish such elements, and not take them too personally. They should be able to recognize their countertransference responses (a similar distortion on the part of the therapist projected on to the client), and be familiar with their own countertransference issues.

In addition to these elements of responsibility, an ability to play, a sense of humour, a willingness to take personal risks and an openness to joy and spontaneity are all valuable in the encounter leader.

Therapeutic style

Style will naturally vary from group to group depending on the participant make-up of the group, numbers, group format and the personality of the leader. What is appropriate in a long-term group where everybody has had previous group experience and a fair proportion of the group are in individual therapy may not be appropriate in a one-day event where most people are newcomers to the work.

The outstanding thing about encounter as a mode of working is the emphasis on here-and-now interpersonal interactions, and the use of human interactions as a therapeutic tool. The focus of the group will switch between the individual, dyads, subgroups and whole group interactions. Participants will be encouraged to say and express, as directly and honestly as they can, their thoughts, feelings and impulses about self and others. In this way each person gets as honest a picture as possible of his or her impact on other people, both positive and negative. Participants will be encouraged, generally, to be personal rather than 'therapeutic', since it is possible for people to hide themselves behind 'playing therapist' or trying to give help, feedback or insights to another person. However, as the group progresses, and relationships build up, people's genuine personal responses to each other become a real and vital therapeutic resource in the group.

During these interactions the leader will draw people's attention to their ways of making or avoiding contact with others, for example, by eye contact, body language, bodily tensions, breathing patterns and language patterns.

Where behavioural patterns and habitual decisions emerge, people will be encouraged to try out different, perhaps more effective, ways of behaving. This may necessitate the leader working individually with a person. In order to deal differently with the group, the individual may need to do some work with a significant past figure. The leader can use gestalt, role-play, body work, etc. to facilitate this work. It is important to bring the person back to the here-and-now and ask, effectively, 'How does that experience affect your relationships with these people?' so that the person starts to integrate the learning into present-day relationships.

In addition to group and subgroup interactions, and individual work, the group leader will probably use some structured exercises. Simple exercises in communication, movement and interaction can be invaluable in the beginning stages of the group, not only for their intrinsic learning and experience potential but also in that people build up shared experiences and thereby build their relationships with each other. They can be useful as a stimulus to the group, which individuals can then explore further in group time. They are also useful when an issue touches most people in the group. A well-chosen structure gives everyone the opportunity to explore at the same time. However, group structures should be used with care. Overuse of them can limit the spontaneity and creativity of the group and deny people the opportunity to take their own initiatives. If they are chosen inappropriately they can be used as an avoidance by the group and leader of an issue present in the group.

The types of interaction that happen in an encounter group can be extremely varied. Within a short space of time people may converse, play children's games, engage in competitive struggle, reveal aspects of themselves or their history that inspire in others a great sense of privilege at being allowed to see and share, and give very direct, challenging feedback. People may laugh, cry, scream, shout, hug, dance, get bored or frustrated, or very quietly be with each other in a profound sense of shared peace.

The amount and use of group pressure will vary from group to group. The use of excessive group pressure was one of the major criticisms of some encounter groups in the 1960s and early 1970s. However, group pressure exists in any group, whatever the technique, and also in social situations. It takes a variety of forms such as encouragement, persuasion, approval and disapproval, demands, etc. Since it is there it should be acknowledged and can be used therapeutically. It is important that people are aware of their choices in the face of group pressure. If a person is, or feels, coerced into behaving in a certain way, exploring a certain issue, or expressing a particular aspect of his or her self, something is wrong in the process and it will have no therapeutic value.

Whilst people are generally encouraged to express their feelings freely within the group, they will also be expected to make responsible decisions about them. For instance, if one person is in an open and vulnerable state – perhaps experiencing some long-buried pain, or taking a creative step for herself in spite of great fear of doing so – and a second person chooses that moment to confront her with hostile feelings, his feelings may be fine, but his timing shows an irresponsible disregard for the other. He should be stopped by the leader and asked to contain his feelings for a more appropriate time.

Major therapeutic techniques

Having said that honest human relating is the prime therapeutic 'technique' in encounter groups, there are also some specialized techniques in common use which would not normally be seen in other situations. They are all aimed at facilitating understanding, insight, behaviour change, and/or emotional expression.

Direct feedback

Many people come to an encounter group initially because they want to know something of how they seem to other people. Direct feedback is a way of supplying some of that information. One participant receives feedback from one or more other participants, and it should be as direct and accurate as possible. It is helpful if participants call a spade a spade. Since people come to get direct information about themselves, it is counterproductive if others try to protect them from the truth, no matter how painful or pleasurable that is for the recipient.

Direct feedback can be useful in enlightening people about their blind spots. There was a participant in a group who complained that he did not have friends, and that if he did make a friendship it did not last. What the group said to him (which had not been said in social situations) was that he smelled. He did not wash himself or his clothes, and that made him very unpleasant to be close to. Any amount of 'support' would be unlikely to make much difference to the state of his relationships, but that piece of direct feedback was essential – and much less painful than his loneliness in the world.

It is important to distinguish between giving information and *projection*. Description of behaviour and sharing one's own response to that behaviour are the clearest forms of feedback. There is a world of difference between 'I notice that every time you mention your mother you clench your fist' (behaviour description), and 'You are angry with you Mother' (projection).

It is also important to stay aware of the emotional tone of the feedback, particularly where negative feedback is used as a cover for hostility towards the person receiving feedback. This usually makes it much more difficult for a person to take in the information provided in the feedback.

Focus on contact

The leader and group focus on how people make or avoid direct contact with each other. Particular attention is paid to the direction of any interaction. For instance, is what is being said actually being said *to* the person who is primarily meant to hear it, rather than *about* them? Much energy is also devoted to the direct use of language. People are encouraged to make 'I–You' statements rather than talk about 'one', 'they', 'people', etc. and to say what they say as simply as possible, rather than camouflaging a simple statement by hiding it in five paragraphs.

Attention is also paid to the amount and direction of eye contact. In general, people are encouraged to look directly at the person they are talking to. This not only maximizes the impact on the other, but the speaker also gets to see the effect he or she is having.

Checking out

People are asked to check out any projections or assumptions they make about others. For example, if someone working on an issue says 'I don't want to take any more time. People will be bored,' they are asked to check out if that is actually true.

Act as if

People are often asked to try out a new piece of behaviour in order to experience what it is like. For instance, someone who plays doormat may be asked to 'act as if' he has a perfect right to ask for anything he wants. This tool can also be useful if a person *thinks* he has a particular feeling. If he says the words, and adopts the body language and sound of that feeling he is likely to start actually feeling it, if that is what he does feel.

Opposites and exaggeration

Where a person feels stuck, either or both of these techniques can help him to free himself. If someone is frightened and contracts physically, he may be asked to contract even further, and so get a clearer experience of what he does to himself. If he is asked to open himself, he is more likely to experience fully the feeling he is tensing against.

Repetition

If someone makes an important emotional statement and is apparently not connecting with the feelings behind it, she may be asked to repeat the statement two or three times. It often happens that the emotion emerges on the second or third repetition.

Vocalization and movement

Sometimes people get stuck in emotional expression because they cannot think of the appropriate words to go with what they are feeling. Making the sound and movement of the feeling can often free their emotional expression. The words can always be added later.

Confrontation

Confrontation can take a wide variety of forms. It can be positive or negative, intellectual and/or emotional, rational or irrational. Gerard Egan (1970) says:

Generally, confrontation takes place when one person (the confronter), either deliberately or inadvertently, does something that causes or directs another person (the confrontee) to advert to, reflect upon, examine, question, or change some particular aspect of his behaviour. (p. 293)

It should be emphasized here that confrontations are not only about expressing anger (a common myth about encounter). Many confrontations will be dealt with on a level of information, negotiation, behaviour experimentation, or may lead directly to a piece of individual work using gestalt, body work or dramatization. The delivery of confrontation can be factual, kind or humorous as well as angry. However, it sometimes happens that a confrontation becomes intensely emotional on both sides, particularly when there is a lot of projection involved, and the confrontation is carrying a lot of emotional load from the past.

There was a man in one of my groups whose primary defence under stress was to use anger to control other people and the situation. In the same group was a woman who had learned in her family that it was not OK for her to be angry, and had learned to swallow her feelings and cry instead. He made a fairly cutting remark to her about her 'weakness'. She started to cry as usual, but was encouraged by the group (particularly the women) to stand up for herself. She started to fight back fairly tentatively against the man's insults. I asked them to move to the centre of the circle and kneel on the floor, facing each other, with a large cushion in between. The confrontation carried on. After some time of 'trying' (acting as if) she made an emotional connection and her anger really ignited. Her basic emotional statement was 'I will not be humiliated and controlled by you', and the anger she had been swallowing for years started to flood out effortlessly, and very powerfully. He started to look scared, though still trying to use anger to control. I asked them to keep looking at each other and make a sound for how they felt. Her sound was a furious roar, but his became a scream of terror. Soon those feelings subsided and they both started to cry with very deep, painful sobs, and after a while she reached out a hand and made contact with him. This developed into a full frontal hug.

After some time the tears stopped and they hung on to each other with tenderness. I asked them to make eye contact with each other and give some feedback about their experience. She connected with her parental rule about anger and decided it was a rule she did not want to live by any more, and did not have to. She felt very alive, powerful and pleased with herself. He said he had felt as if he was going to die at one point, and then like a hurt little boy. We talked for some time of how he was pushed by his father to achieve and be aggressive, and it was not OK for him to feel fear or show weakness. He still felt somewhat fearful that he had lost the respect of other group members, and was reassured by the feedback that people actually liked him more, and felt warmer towards him than they had done before in the group. He also saw that his original confrontation contained a fair amount of projection. There are a number of points illustrated by this example:

(a) The emphasis on eye contact. The less eye contact people have the more likely they are to treat each other as objects.

(b) The kneeling position is one which facilitates the expression of anger much more than sitting, and seems much safer and more bounded than standing. It is less easy for one person to move away and yet not close enough to touch, and the distance remains stable.

(c) Although the woman received considerable encouragement and support, at no time did she feel coerced into the confrontation, and if she had it is unlikely that she would have reached the depth of feeling that she did. This kind of confrontation cannot be made to happen.

(d) The man's original confrontation was hostile, and at times quite insulting. However, the violation at all times seemed manageable, and provided that she responded from feeling she was unlikely to feel damaged. If she had not responded from feeling or had not found the strength to fight back, the confrontation would have had to be stopped and the issues worked with another way, for example, by gestalt, enactment, or a practice exercise in the expression of anger or assertion.

(e) The expression of feeling in sounds rather than words facilitates regressive feeling, and facilitates the flow from one feeling to another, for example, fear→anger→pain.

(f) When some of the feelings are regressive it is important that the confronters reconnect in the here-and-now and take a new look at each other. Sometimes they will see each other quite differently when some of the emotional energy in the projection is put where it belongs.

(g) Subsequent feedback includes talking about the meaning of the experience and its consequences for present and future decisions. Thus, the experience includes cathartic expression, understanding and insight, and decisions and experimentation with behaviour. In this way it works both on the level of experience of identity and the level of expression of identity.

It should be emphasized that confrontations of this intensity are not the common stuff of encounter and are more likely to happen in marathons and long-term intensive groups than in an ordinary weekend or ongoing group. They are unlikely to happen at all if there is not a fair amount of group cohesiveness already.

The change process in therapy

The change process starts with the clients' increasing awareness of their own mental, behavioural and emotional responses that are uncomfortable or ineffective. This increase in awareness may arise through confrontation or feedback, or simply by experiencing themselves more fully in interaction with others. Where such uncomfortable or ineffective patterns are dis-covered, the client is invited to try alternative forms of behavioural/ emotional expression, and to talk to himself or herself differently. This entails some questioning of the client's own assumptions about, and rules for, himself or herself, that is, questioning distorted aspects of his or her identity. Change in behaviour or thought patterns is often accompanied by emotional catharsis, or the emotional assertion of one's right to be oneself in relation to past significant figures.

Changes in mental, emotional and behavioural responses are incorpo-rated into the person's identity by usage over time, re-inforcement by other group members, and the person's own success experience. This integration takes time, and it is likely that the client will fall into his or her old behaviour patterns a number of times before these changes become permanent. When a person habitually thinks, feels and acts differently, then that person *is* different. The client can aid this process by relating more in his or her life to those who will accept and support the changes he or she makes, and resisting the influence of those who do not like those changes.

Changes in a person's identity are often accompanied by significant life changes, since the person's life is an expression of his or her identity. It is quite common to find that a client changes, or gains more success, in work, relationships and his or her personal creativity.

CASE EXAMPLE

When I first met Marie, she was in crisis. She had recently separated from her husband, was living on her own, and quite seriously talking about suicide. She was desperate in that she did not like the life she had and did not see how to, or believe that she could, change it. In her marriage she had tried very hard to be the person her husband wanted her to be, and thought that to do anything else would be selfish and bad.

Her early life was heavily influenced by her mother, father and grand-mother who lived with them. Her mother was somewhat hypochondriacal. Marie constantly lived with the threat 'If you are bad you will kill your Mother.' She experienced her grandmother as cold, hostile, critical and poisonous, and her father as closed, outwardly unemotional, and ineffectual. There was very little play or affection in the family. Marie concluded that she should try to find out what they wanted and give it to them. She developed a sense of herself as being bad generally, and in addition she could compound her badness by wanting things from her parents, being excited and being emotional. As she grew, she fairly comprehensively annihilated her own personality, adopted an almost permanent smile as a mask, and developed her ability to find out what they wanted of her and give it to them. She became a very 'good' girl and was known as her mother's 'little rock'.

When we started working together she described herself as living inside a tiny box behind her eyes. Her sense of boundaries was extremely weak – to the extent that she did not like inviting anyone into her house because if they did something she did not like she could do nothing about it.

At this point, group work was obviously not appropriate for Marie. We worked together in individual sessions for six months, by which time she had more sense of boundaries and of her right to live her own life. She was more in touch with her body and feelings, and had more ability (and internal permission) to nourish herself. However, despite the progress she had made it seemed that she still was not translating what happened in sessions into relationships in the rest of her life. When she seemed to have developed enough internal strength I suggested she participate in a weekend group. During the course of the group she was faced a number of times with the conflict between what she *thought* in the here-and-now and her old, automatic responses she had learned in her family. She found a considerable gap between what she expected to hear from others and their actual responses to her. Arising out of her assumptions, we did some cushion work around her asserting her rights in relation to her mother. Using the phrase 'I have a right to live my own life', she initially found it too frightening to connect directly to her experience, so we approached it slowly, taking small cautious steps, and deliberately using distancing techniques that people would normally be asked not to use in encounter. For instance, I suggested she say it with an awareness that it was a cushion in a group room in 1985, and see what it was like just to say the words. Then I suggested she say the words as though it was her mother at their present ages, and simply as a statement of fact. She then experimented with adding emotion to the statement. It will be appreciated that to say the statement from her inner child *felt*, to her, life-threatening. Any time it got too scary for her we stopped and talked about the experience. She went some way to making the statement to her mother with feeling. She decided when she had done as much of that as she was ready to. I then asked her to make the statement directly to some of the people in the group. This had the effect of reconnecting her to the group and of bringing her experience into the here-and-now, in relationship to others.

In addition to the direct work we did, several of the exercises in emotional expression and communication were valuable for her. It was also important that she saw and related to others who were working with similar or equivalent issues. On the whole, the experience was positive for her and she joined an ongoing group and did several more weekends.

During this work there were a number of ongoing themes and several 'landmark' experiences. Amongst the general themes were:

(a) Being present in the here-and-now. Since her childhood messages were so powerful, she continually had to work at distinguishing what was happening in the here-and-now and what had happened in her past. When her past fears surfaced, it was particularly important for her to use her eyes to look and check what was happening now.

(b) Being assertive. It was particularly difficult to say what she wanted.

(c) Dealing with her negative feelings. Since she was trained to believe that if she expressed her fears, angers, frustrations and hurts, something awful would happen, to do so in a group was a major adventure, requiring, initially, a great deal of support.

(d) Dealing with boundaries.

(e) Playing. Having been so serious and self-sacrificing throughout most of her life it was both refreshing and useful for her to contact the playful side of herself. To be at all childish was a taboo for her when she came into the group (as it had been during her childhood). As time went on, she initiated such activities as teddy-bear races, play fights, joky bantering and dancing, as well as using a playful element in her therapeutic exploration.

(f) Giving and receiving feedback. She found it very difficult to receive and own any positive feedback. Negative feedback she would tend to blow out of proportion and turn it into a statement 'I am bad.' In time she was able to take in more positivity, and take the information from negative feedback without 'beating herself up'. It also emerged that she was very perceptive about other people if she allowed herself expression, and had a very rich style of imagery.

(g) Use of the body.

In addition to these ongoing themes, which were regularly drawn attention to and explored, there were several important events in her therapy. In one weekend group she challenged one of the men to a wrestling match. During the wrestling, he held her shoulders down. At this point she froze and stopped fighting. The experience of being held down had reactivated memories, and feelings, about a time when she had been abused sexually. She shared with the group some of her memories, which was painful and accompanied by feelings of shame. She had to struggle somewhat with her old script that she was bad if she showed she was unhappy. At what seemed like an appropriate point, I encouraged her to find out what it would be like for her to protest. I asked her to lie on her back with her feet flat on the floor and her knees up, make a thrusting movement with her pelvis, and say the words 'get off me'. Since the pelvic region is a source of great power in the body, freeing it allowed her more power in her vocal protest. She quickly became very angry. As she allowed her energy to flow she started to feel more alive and intact. She came out of her lying down position on to her knees. I gave her a large stick and a pile of cushions. I suggested she bring the stick back over her head, hit the cushions with all of her force, and say the words 'Don't ever do that to me again.' The feeling that emerged was that pure, gut-level, violent anger that is a natural and healthy response to being violated. The latter part of this work was done looking directly at the men in the group.

On another occasion there was a woman in a group with whom she had developed a mutually wary relationship. The other woman was not good at setting boundaries and tended to use hostility as a barrier behind which to hide her vulnerability. Marie found this hostility very reminiscent of her grandmother, and responded herself with fear and hostility. In spite of this hostility there was a mutual attraction between the two women. I suggested they kneel on opposite sides of the circle and experiment with how close or how distant they wanted to be. They moved very slowly towards each other, commenting as they went on how they felt and what they wanted: 'I want you to take a step back.' 'Stay there.' 'I want to take a step forward.' 'I feel warmer.' 'I feel scared,' etc. Each gave the other warning before moving, and as they made their comments more and more in the form of 'I feel . . .' rather than 'You are . . .', each began to feel safer. It was like watching a very slow dance as each explored what it was like to move closer, and established that they could still create distance if they wanted to. They and the group took a great deal of time and patience in this exploration, and after some 30 minutes arrived within touching distance. Both felt very excited as they made physical contact and continued to dance. Someone put on some slow, quiet music, and the group as a whole started to dance with each other.

As time went on Marie became more at home with talking about feelings and allowing herself to show them. She allowed herself to have her own experience without making sure she 'got it right' all the time. She became more adept at asking for what she wanted, and was more willing to show her negative feelings as well as being 'nice'. As she did so, she expanded her creativity and her ability to be truly present in relating to others. She became much more in touch with herself and achieved more satisfaction in several areas of her life, not least of which was a new sexual relationship in which she felt she could be herself.

There remained for her the issue of what would happen if she had an out-and-out row with someone, which was something she was very afraid of. It was one thing to express negative feelings full measure with a cushion, but she feared that if she did it face-to-face with a real person either she would be destroyed or they would. Towards the end of her time in the ongoing group she had angry confrontations with three separate people and, naturally enough, survived all of them, creating closer, more real relationships in the process.

Her struggle with her internal critics (mother, father and grandmother) continues, and events in her life, as well as how she feels, show that she is winning her struggle to be her own, free, self-responsible person.

REFERENCES

Assagioli, R. (1971) *Psychosynthesis*, Viking, New York.

Berne, E. (1968) *Games People Play*, Penguin, Harmondsworth.

Berne, E. (1973) *What Do You Do after You Say Hello?*, Bantam, New York.

Blank, L., Gottsegan, G. and Gottsegan, M. (1971) *Confrontation*, Macmillan, New York.

Boadella, D. (1980) Violence in therapy, *Energy and Character*, Vol. 11 No. 1, January.

Edwards, E. (1976) On the creation of a masochist, in D. Boadella (ed.) *In the wake of Reich*, Coventure, London.

Egan, G. (1970) *Encounter*, Brooks/Cole Publishing Company, Monterey, CA.

Elliot, J. (1976) *The Theory and Practice of Encounter Group Leadership*, Explorations Institute, Berkeley, CA.

Guntrip, H. (1962) *Healing the Sick Mind*, Unwin, London.

Lieberman, M., Yalom, I. and Miles, M. (1973) *Encounter Groups: First Facts*, Basic Books, New York.

Lowen, A. (1971) *The Language of the Body*, Collier, New York.

Maslow, A. (1973) *The Farther Reaches of Human Nature*, Pelican, Harmondsworth.

Perls, F. (1969) *Gestalt Therapy Verbatim*, Real People Press, Lafayette, CA.

Satir, V. (1967) *Conjoint Family Therapy*, Science & Behaviour Books, Palo Alto, CA.

Schutz, W. (1967) *Joy*, Souvenir Press, London.

Schutz, W. (1973) *Elements of Encounter*, Joy Press, Big Sur, CA.

Shaffer, J. and Galinsky, M. (1974) *Models of Group Therapy and Sensitivity Training*, Prentice-Hall, Englewood Cliffs, NJ.

Winnicott, D. (1971) *Playing and Reality*, Penguin, Harmondsworth.

Walder, E. (1971) Synanon and the learning process: a critique of attack therapy, in

R. Siroka, E. Siroka and G. Schloss (eds.) *Sensivity Training and Group Encounter*, Grosset & Dunlap, New York.
Yablonsky, L. (1965) *Synanon: The Tunnel Back*, Macmillan, New York.

Suggested further reading

Berne, E. (1973) *What Do You Do after You Say Hello?*, Bantam, New York.
Egan, G. (1970) *Encounter*, Brooks/Cole Publishing Company, Monterey, CA.
Neill, J. and Kniskern, D. (1982) *From Psyche to System*, Guilford Press, New York.
Perls, F., Hefferline, R. and Goodman, P. (1973) *Gestalt Therapy*, Penguin, Harmondsworth.
Schutz, W. (1973) *Elements of Encounter*, Joy Press, Big Sur, CA.

CHAPTER 5

CO-COUNSELLING

Rose Evison and Richard Horobin

HISTORICAL CONTEXT AND DEVELOPMENTS IN BRITAIN

Historical context

Co-counselling is a therapeutic process which uses catharsis to change rigid, maladaptive modes of feeling, thinking and acting. It is usually learned and practised in pairs, with each participant alternating the roles of counsellor and of client. The techniques of this reciprocal system may also be used effectively in the conventional therapist-client dyad (Pierce, Nichols and Dubrin, 1983). The reciprocal co-counselling relationship forms an excellent training for such expert psychotherapy.

Co-counselling began around 1950 with Harvey Jackins, a man in his early thirties from a poor farming background, having a dramatic personal experience of the healing potential of emotional discharge. Jackins was so impressed that he began to study emotional discharge processes and their beneficial effects. He made no general studies of other therapies although apparently, like Fritz Perls, he was influenced by the ideas and practice of dianetics. By 1952 he had set up a counselling agency in Seattle, Washington, called *Personal Counselors*. This allied a core staff group with part-time student helpers. It was in this setting, often working with highly distressed clients, that many basic techniques of co-counselling were established.

The other characteristic feature of co-counselling – that the counsellor is always a client too – also came from the early days of Personal Counselors. Teaching in ongoing classes started in the 1950s and involved reciprocal counselling – people worked in pairs and each person spent half the time in the role of client and half as counsellor. By the mid 1960s there were several groups of co-counsellors established in the Seattle area.

By the early 1960s a theoretical framework based on their own experiences had been developed by Jackins and Mary McCabe, and was published as *The Human Side of Human Beings* (Jackins, 1965). They clarified the nature of catharsis, as a process which resets mind and body after negative emotional arousal. Such processes included laughing, crying, raging, shaking, yawning. They specified the conditions encouraging catharsis as the emotive re-experiencing of past distresses with a simultaneous awareness that such distresses did not arise from the present-time situation. Mere expression of negative feelings is thus not cathartic.

Co-counselling spread beyond Seattle as teachers of co-counselling migrated around the USA. Jackins subsequently gave many introductory lectures and ran many workshops. By 1970 there was a Re-evaluation Counseling organization (RC). This name arose from the oft-repeated observation that spontaneous re-evaluation by clients followed their emotional discharge. The RC organization expanded until by the 1980s there were organized groups of co-counsellors, known as *communities*, in more than 30 countries of the world.

New theory developed out of the best practice. Issues were addressed by running topic workshops which combined everyone working on their distress with a sharing of the thinking produced. One such issue was liberation.

> The conclusion was that we have to necessarily tackle sexism, racism, adultism towards children and other forms of oppression both inside our community and outside. . . . If we do not, the workshops reasoned, then the daily load of distress visited on our co-counselors by oppression is likely to make them lose their war for re-emergence even if they win battles in their sessions. (Jackins, 1977, p. 11).

This conclusion resulted in new therapeutic techniques within RC, and also in much application of co-counselling strategies to change institutions at grass-roots level. Education, health care, child rearing, challenging sexism, racism and oppression of all kinds are areas in which many co-counsellors have been active throughout the world.

During the growth of RC Jackins remained a powerful central figure, who demanded that RC be characterized by consistency of practice, theory and organization. Any sustained disagreement with Jackins meant people left or were excluded from RC. Some of these people established co-counselling groups outside the RC organization, initially in New England and in Britain. In 1975 a network of these groups called Co-Counselling International

(CCI) was set up by Dency Sargent and John Heron. Co-counselling also goes on outside any organized networks: in communes, women's groups, men's groups, prayer groups, and support groups within the caring professions.

Developments in Britain

In 1970 Tom Scheff, a Californian psychologist, taught the first RC workshops in London. He came again the following summer, following which some of the participants were authorized as RC teachers. John Heron, then director of the Human Potential Research Unit at the University of Surrey, taught the first indigenous class in 1971. He subsequently ran beginners' workshops throughout Britain and Europe: at one of which we, the present authors, were introduced to co-counselling. In 1973 Jackins visited Europe and authorized more teachers.

Early in 1974, after some fundamental disagreements with Jackins, Heron left RC, but continued to teach and develop the methods: as did other early teachers who had also left for a variety of reasons. When CCI was formed there were only a few teachers of co-counselling outside RC, including by then ourselves. Following the first CCI workshop abroad in Connecticut in 1975, a workshop in England established an international committee and guidelines for CCI communities.

Since that time co-counselling in Britain has expanded both within and outside RC. Currently there are over 30 CCI-style teachers actively running beginners' classes. Inside RC there are 26 organized areas, each usually involving several teachers; plus several dozen teachers outside organized areas. RC in Britain takes an active part in the world organization and in applying co-counselling, but has a low profile policy.

Local groups within CCI are self-determined and there is no coherent organization. Nevertheless CCI co-counsellors are influential. Initiated by John Heron, co-counselling continues to be taught by the Human Potential Research Unit and by the British Postgraduate Medical Federation. Cathartic intervention methods in group and individual work have been spread in the caring profession through the Six Category Intervention Analysis and Facilitator Styles courses established by Heron.

We, personally, have been concerned to integrate co-counselling theory and practice with wider psychological and therapeutic principles. We teach classes specifically aimed at members of caring professions. Since 1983 the bookshop sale of our co-counselling manual (Evison and Horobin, 1985) has made the ideas and methods more widely available. Other CCI-style teachers run classes in many environments, including further education.

THEORETICAL ASSUMPTIONS

Image of the person

The theory assumes that everyone is born with tremendous intellectual potential, natural zest, and lovingness, but that these qualities have become blocked and obscured in adults as the result of accumulated distress experiences (fear, hurt, loss, pain, anger, embarrassment, etc.) which began early in our lives.

Any young person would recover from such distress spontaneously by the use of the natural process of emotional discharge (crying, trembling, raging, laughing, etc.). However this natural process is usually interfered with by well-meaning people ('Don't cry', 'Be a big boy', etc.) who erroneously equate the emotional discharge with the hurt itself.

When adequate emotional discharge can take place, the person is freed from the rigid pattern of behaviour and feeling left by the hurt. The basic, loving, cooperative, intelligent, and zestful nature is then free to operate.

(cover of any issue of RC magazine *Present Time*; see References)

This statement, originating with Jackins and his collaborators, would also be subscribed to by co-counsellors within the CCI tradition. There are however differences in the way different writers express the image of the person, and the intellectual framework used.

In John Heron's theoretical statements existential tensions in the human condition are considered to cause primary distress; the accumulation of which leads to interpersonal tensions and hurt which he calls secondary distress (Heron, 1979).

We have a biological/psychological framework, and relate the image of the person to evolutionary and learning theory perspectives. Firstly, human beings have a highly developed capacity for learning, which is enhanced by the ability to use symbolic representation of the world in language. Secondly, as their basic motivation system, humans have built-in emotional reactions to significant aspects of the world. Positive feelings form the natural ongoing state, intensified when people succeed in satisfying their bodily needs or in mastering problems. Negative feelings are intermittent states occurring in response to threats to survival and well-being; they focus people's minds on the threat and mobilize their bodies for action aimed at changing the situation. Thirdly, humans have a capacity for caring and co-operation with others; they are highly successful social animals.

These three capacities are interrelated. Thus our emotions are not unfortunate vestiges of our primitive animal nature; humans are excellent at learning and problem-solving because they are highly emotional, not despite it. Moreover some of our basic emotions are social, for example love, embarrassment and shame. For a discussion of emotions as motivators see Tomkins (1963).

Significantly, just as recognition of threat acts to switch on negative feelings, the perception that the threat has ceased activates innate off-switches. The processes triggered by the off-switch are those of emotional discharge, and their result is reduction of bodily arousal and release of attention compulsorily focused on the threat. The reality of the physiological reset following catharsis has been demonstrated in several studies (e.g. Karle, Corriere and Hart, 1973).

Concepts of psychological health and disturbance

Psychologically healthy people proceed from birth to death as active learners enjoying the challenge of solving problems; they enjoy working with others; they develop their all-round potential through each stage of life; they react with appropriate negative feelings to immediate threat, physical or psychological. If they succeed in mastering a threatening situation the knowledge is added to their experience and skills. After failure, recognizing when the threat is past, they spontaneously discharge their inappropriate emotional arousal. After discharge ends they have a body/mind state of alert flexibility, with maximum choice over the next task.

Psychological disturbance is considered to consist of rigid, compulsive responses – feelings, thoughts and behaviours. Such responses are termed *patterns*. Unlike habits, patterns are not under direct voluntary influence and do not change when circumstances alter. Indeed patterns are highly resistant to change: even when the individual, perceiving himself or herself as destructive to themselves or others, tries to change. It is considered normal for everyone to have some patterns. The extent of psychological disturbance will depend upon how many patterns a person has, how intense are the negative feelings involved, and how much the patterned behaviours clash with social norms.

The psychologically healthy person will have very few patterns. Such people will be expressive of positive and negative emotions with their bodies and creative in terms of problem-solving and the expressive arts. They will not be subject to feeling depressed, powerless or alienated. They will have a strong sense of self-worth, while being caring and co-operative with others. They will be assertive and negotiate with others when needs clash.

Acquisition of psychological disturbance

Psychological disturbance results when a distressing experience with no positive outcome is followed by failure to discharge the negative feelings aroused. The whole sequence is recorded in the person's memory. Subsequent reminders of the original threatening situation, arising when elements of it re-occur, result in a perception of current threat and production of the relevant distressing feelings. These feelings then drive the negative thoughts and futile actions with which the person previously responded as no other responses are available. The whole set of responses is labelled a *pattern*. Patterns equate with neurotic responses: 'The normal person learns from their experience, the neurotic is condemned to repeat it.'

Patterns are not limited to neurotics; in normal development there will be many distressing experiences in which the child fails to obtain a positive outcome. Such experiences may be traumatic, like sexual assault, or they may be minor but occur frequently, as in the basic socialization processes of weaning and toilet training.

Although the most influential patterns are usually established during infancy, they can develop at any age; battle neuroses are examples of patterns from traumatic situations to which all normals are susceptible (Swank, 1949), and John Holt's (1964) book *How Children Fail* provides vivid documentation of patterns produced in school situations.

A mechanism for the acquisition of self-punishing patterns is shown in experiments by Stone and Hokanson reported by Martin (1972). In these experiments participants learned that a self-inflicted electric shock prevented a worse shock being inflicted by another person. Once learned, this self-punishing behaviour continued after the other-administered punishment had ceased, because there was no way for the person to learn that the situation had changed.

Patterns which are destructive of others arise from situations in which the child has been a victim of adult aggression. Undiscriminating input of information by the distressed child means that the words and actions of the person causing the distress are also memorized in a patterned fashion. These behaviours are then available to the 'victim' when in later life he or she finds himself or herself in the power role. Thus those people who have been victims of oppression become oppressors themselves when circumstances give them the chance. Wyre, in his work with sexual offenders, notes both the difficulties of changing their ingrained violence and that many of them had been victims of sexual assault themselves (Swift, 1986). Frude (1982) in his research into child batterers notes correspondences between the nature of their physical assaults and the punishments they experienced as children.

Further models of pattern acquisition are provided by Seligman's ideas on acquisition of anxiety and his concept of learned helplessness (Seligman, 1975).

As there is no way to prevent distressing failure experiences, the key factor producing psychological disturbance is the inhibition of the emotional discharge processes. Anything which prevents emotional discharge taking place will increase the chances of pattern formation and hence increase psychological disturbance.

Perpetuation of psychological disturbance

After a pattern has been established, the unevaluated data present in memory from the original situation can be triggered by a fragmentary reminder of the original situation. Thus smelling hospital disinfectant can evoke the anxiety which was part of a distressing illness; a mocking laugh can bring back the helplessness experienced when being bullied by an older child. The more distressing the experience, the more generalization of threatening stimuli is likely. This production of negative feelings through situational reminders is termed *restimulation*. This is a general phenomenon, as is shown by asking people to talk through recent upsetting events in their lives, when many report re-experiencing the feelings, not merely recalling them.

Restimulation is demonstrated in Interpersonal Process Recall, a therapist training system developed by Kagan (1980), in which viewing of interview videos triggers memories of influential thoughts and feelings the person did not verbalize at the time. Some research made continuous physiological measurements during the initial interview and during its review. These measurements showed parallel emotional arousal between an episode in the original interview and during recall of that interview (Kagan, 1986).

Each time a pattern is restimulated it is strengthened. So if the person does not find an opportunity to discharge the distress which holds the pattern in place, the disturbance worsens throughout the lifespan.

Another way patterns are perpetuated arises from the socialization of the emotions. Discharge is reduced or eliminated, using comforting, distraction or punishment: 'There, there dear, there's no need to cry!' 'Oh, look at that funny doggy!' 'If you don't stop I'll give you something to cry for!' The patterns acquired through this socialization are key ones which shape the person's personality. Tomkins (1963) discusses this, linking various adult psychological disturbances to family styles of socializing emotional expression. An example is the parents' use of shame to control a child's emotional expression, which in the extreme results in the syndrome of emotions, thoughts and actions observed in paranoia.

The patterns directly set up when discharge is inhibited are known as *control patterns*. These constitute intrinsic psychological disturbance and because they inhibit discharge processes, they act to perpetuate existing patterns and increase the chances of future pattern formation.

A lack of trust in others is a further factor in pattern perpetuation. The patterning process is like conditioning. Modern views of human conditioning emphasize the importance of cognitive influences. When experimental subjects were told conditions had changed and punishment would no longer follow a signal, conditioned fear responses previously produced to the signal were immediately eliminated for many of them. A recent re-analysis showed that this only occurred for people who trusted the experimenter. People who distrusted the experimenter only ceased to react when they experienced the truth for themselves (Dawson and Schell, 1987). In everyday life, opportunities to check that conditions have changed are often minimal; particularly in cases where a patterned response originally pre-empted a worse punishment. Since patterns are typically installed by those persons who give the child care and affection, so the child learns that positive figures in his or her life cannot necessarily be trusted. This lack of trust acts to perpetuate patterns.

A further force acting to perpetuate psychological disturbance arises when patterns are tied into the person's self-concept. These patterns arise when children are prevented from exhibiting spontaneous human behaviours, for example emotional discharge and sexual behaviour. Such inhibition can only be achieved by some form of punishment, applied on numerous occasions. The implicit message to the child is that some important parts of him or her are not valued or acceptable. This will frequently be re-inforced by explicit value judgements of goodness and badness applied to the whole person. Because such patterns are attached to the person rather than to specifics of the person's behaviour, they are in continuous restimulation and hence thought of as part of the personality and not susceptible to removal. Such patterns are termed *chronic*.

Finally, many patterns are perpetuated by being re-inforced by the social and political institutions of our culture. This arises when poor self-concept patterns key into a person's membership of a particular population group, for example, 'You're emotional and weak because you're a woman!' Although the social basis of such oppression is economic, the psychological basis is the installation of patterns in individuals. Thus individual psychological disturbance is perpetuated by society's norms and institutions: black children in our society who have had inferiority patterns installed will experience corroborating evidence in the unemployment and discrimination to which they are subject. Once such patterns are set up socialization processes will ensure that they are perpetuated across the generations not just within an individual's life.

PRACTICE

Goals of therapy

Co-counselling concerns people learning how to help themselves and others change in order to lead more satisfying lives. The goal of therapy is for the person to spend more time operating in the flexible, caring, problem-solving mode and less in a patterned mode – with fewer negative feelings which are inappropriate in kind, intensity or duration; with fewer rigidly compulsive thoughts and behaviours. This means disrupting patterns not just escaping them temporarily. To achieve this in counselling sessions the tactical aim is for the client to discharge as much as possible.

People may be motivated to use co-counselling in different ways: for emotional first aid in a crisis; for problem-solving in difficult areas of their lives; to change their personalities; to be empowered to change the world.

However restricted the therapeutic goals of an individual are, it would always be a goal to transmit the basic theory concerning distress, patterns and discharge to that person, so that they could apply it to their life, not just in counselling sessions. Similarly the skills used in therapeutic sessions not only form a vehicle to reach the person's immediate change goals, but learning the skills is seen as a goal in itself since they are potentially tools for use in the world. Using these tools, individuals can:

(a) Become more aware of their strengths and abilities, which are consequently more readily available when needed, and so can be built on and developed further
(b) Learn to focus their attention where they choose, without being unwillingly or unwittingly distracted by distress
(c) Experience less distress from the negative events in their lives, both today's and those from yesterday which still take up time and attention
(d) Break up the destructive patterns which inhibit their flexible intelligence and hinder new learning and creative action.

The 'person' of the therapist

In the co-counselling reciprocal relationship, partners experience each other as client and as counsellor. The experience of the therapist-as-client adds extra dimensions to the person of the therapist. Partners-as-clients are vulnerable, struggling, human beings in need of assistance in getting rid of distresses, however successful their lives appear. In addition, clients will celebrate self and others, discharge a variety of emotions, demonstrate emotional healing, and show changes in their lives. The impact of this on the therapeutic relationship is threefold: the therapist is known as a complete human being, successfully changing; mutual modelling of the client role will enhance the learning of appropriate client behaviours relative to therapy where no such modelling occurs; mutual trust will be built up because of the reciprocal self-disclosure involved (Jourard, 1968, p. 26), and this facilitates therapeutic change.

Two related issues are the specific contract covering the counsellor role and the skills and qualities found in an experienced co-counsellor. There is a minimum contract in which the counsellor aims to offer unconditional acceptance, by communicating a high level of supportive attention to the client and by refraining from giving negative judgements of the client; interpretations of client's material; advice on the client's problems. The counsellor also has responsibility for time-keeping, and for assisting the client to return to a distress-free state at the end of their counselling session. An individual who cannot keep the contract is regarded as unsuitable for reciprocal pairs work, and screening with this in mind is recommended in introductory classes.

Within CCI clients decide on the intervention contract they want. The first possibility is the *minimum* contract described earlier where no counsellor interventions are made. This is likely to be used when the client is an experienced co-counsellor, working with a less experienced partner. In this case clients will act on technique suggestions they make to themselves. The second possibility is a *normal* contract. Here the counsellor makes interventions when the client is having difficulties doing so. In the third possibility, an *intensive* contract, the counsellor picks up every distress or discharge cue, and intervenes to facilitate more discharge. An intensive contract is used when the client is working on chronic patterns; that is, those patterns which are continuously activated, examples being negative self-concepts such as 'I'm not worth loving' and 'I don't deserve to have what I want.' Such a contract assumes the counsellor is highly skilled in offering interventions.

Typical changes occur as people progress as co-counsellors. Working with a variety of partners results in exposure to a wide range of human distresses, and the experiential learning that intensive emotional expression does not equate with being bad, mad or out of control; contrary to the cultural stereotype. Analogously, seeing women expressing anger and men crying serves to disrupt deep-rooted assumptions concerning gender differences. Thus the experienced co-counsellor is accepting of a wide range of client behaviour, and trusts the potential for emotional healing in human beings. In line with this Jackins (1983, p. 31) lists the following counsellor attitudes as facilitative of clients working successfully: approval, delight, respect, confidence, relaxed high expectations, love.

The person of the therapist as represented by an experienced co-counsellor can be summarized using the criteria considered desirable in a teacher of co-counselling. He or she is emotionally expressive, discharges readily in all modes, is aware of and working on own chronic patterns. He or she can offer full attention, communicate unconditional acceptance to others, is continually looking for and appreciating the person behind the patterns. He or she is sensitive to the differences between distressed emotionality and discharge; can act to facilitate discharge, and interrupt destructive behavioural patterns in others. He or she has a strong sense of own self-worth and can act powerfully in the world. See John Heron's description (1978, p. 1).

Therapeutic style

The co-counselling therapeutic style has a number of important strands.

A focus on catharsis

Co-counselling assumes that all types of clients will benefit from discharging distress and breaking patterns, and these assumptions apply to all personalities and types of problems.

Reciprocal therapeutic relationship

Co-counsellors typically work as reciprocal pairs with a clear contract on permitted behaviours. When people have one-way therapy because they are too distressed to fulfil the counsellor role, there is encouragement for them to move to pairs work as soon as possible; firstly in addition to one-way therapy, and after suitable progress to exclusively reciprocal pairs.

What are known as transference phenomena in other therapies are the subject of special co-counselling routines. In these a client explores who his or her counsellor reminds him or her of; what about the person triggers the reminders; and then separates the person of the counsellor from the positive or negative reminders.

Explicit teaching of theory and practice

Co-counselling validates clients' ability to think for themselves, using an explicit contract and the teaching of theory and techniques, to maximize client co-operation. People usually start co-counselling by attending classes in theory and practice; and there is encouragement to engage in ongoing study. In the case of one-way use of co-counselling techniques the teaching will be interwoven into sessions rather than given in separate classes.

No interpretation or advice

Co-counselling assumes that clients are the experts on their own lives; they will generate their own meaningful interpretations and make their own best decisions, after freeing their flexible intelligence to operate in those areas of experience previously locked up by distress. Therefore counsellors do not offer interpretations or advice.

Working from strengths

Working from strengths is crucial to the relationship style.

The counsellor communicates maximum acceptance and support for the client, being available for eye contact and offering supportive touch.
The client is encouraged to appreciate himself or herself in terms of positive qualities, skills, and successes in life.
At the end of the session it is the counsellor's responsibility to help the client to maximize his or her positive feelings and sense of self-worth, rather than leaving the client experiencing his or her own distresses.

Deliberate use of balance of attention

The major interventions by the counsellor aim to set up the conditions for discharge, namely a *balance of attention*. The client relives the negative feelings from previous upsetting events while part of his or her awareness is focused outside the distress with knowledge of present safety. A balance of attention is a basic condition of change in all therapies. Though explicit statements of it are rare, Holden discusses the idea as a necessary condition for primalling (Holden, 1977, ch. 6), and at the other end of the treatment spectrum, Paul Dewald, a psychoanalytically orientated therapist, also describes the same conditions as necessary for client change (Goldfield, 1980, p. 274).

Explicit behavioural and emotional goals

Clients are encouraged to set goals for change in their lives. Work done against patterns in sessions is used to provide the clients with tools to combat the patterns in their lives between counselling sessions.

Major therapeutic techniques

The major techniques can be grouped into four strategies: emotional discharge, attention-switching, celebrating, and target practice. To break

Figure 5.1   Graphical representation of aspects of emotionality pertinent to cathartic therapy. Various 'simple' emotions are plotted on to a space, the dimensions of which are bodily arousal (high-low) and hedonic tone (positive-negative).

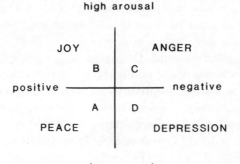

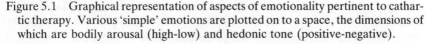

Figure 5.2   Heavy arrows indicate changes occurring during discharge, and the preconditions for the process to commence (i.e. arousal, plus a balance of attention between distress and present safety) are noted.

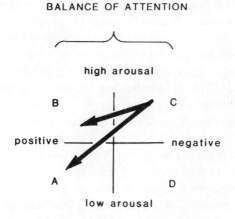

patterns these strategies are usually woven together, though each is a therapeutic strategy in its own right. Emotional discharge is emphasized in this section as it is the major strategy used in co-counselling.

Aids to discharge

Using the discharge strategy means achieving a balance of attention in relation to the distresses that are being dealt with. The techniques used will depend upon clients' co-counselling skills, the material they are trying to deal with, and the state they are in when an intervention is made. Typical techniques appropriate for different client states are given in Table 5.1 and these will be referred to by the letters of the sections they appear in.

Underlying the choice of technique is a two dimensional model of emotions. One dimension is the hedonic tone of the the emotion – positive or negative. The other dimension is the level of physiological arousal the person has. On this model we can plot typical emotions as shown in Figure 5.1.

Emotions which can be directly discharged are those experienced in quadrant C – the more highly aroused negative feelings like anger, fear, grief, disgust, embarrassment. Discharge occurs when the person experiences such an emotion whilst also being aware that the bodily arousal and focused attention is not appropriate to the present-time situation he or she is in. In this case attention is divided between the states in the right hand and left hand of Figure 5.1. Discharge can be visualized as a movement across the figure from quadrant C to A or B, as indicated by the arrows in Figure 5.2. Techniques for achieving a balance of attention, with the client starting in different quadrants, are described as follows:

(a) *Increasing client's awareness of safety.* If the client is experiencing an aroused negative feeling without discharging, his or her attention is all in quadrant C. The counsellor will then seek to increase the client's awareness of present safety, to direct some of the client's attention outside the distress, focusing it in quadrant B to obtain the needed balance of attention. Relevant techniques are given in Table 5.1, section A.

(b) *Increasing client's awareness of a distressing memory.* If the client mostly has attention in A,B quadrants, then interventions use restimulation to enable the client to re-experience the distressing feelings, thus creating a balance of attention. Typical techniques are given in Table 5.1, sections B, C, D.

(c) *Increasing the client's arousal.* This is used when clients are in low arousal states, experiencing feelings typical of quadrant D. Increasing arousal transmutes quadrant D feelings into C feelings, for example depression transmutes into anger, anxiety into fear, alienation into grief. Direct movement from quadrant D to quadrant A is very difficult. Techniques in Table 5.1, sections D and E, increase arousal directly or indirectly. If the client does not appear to be progressing with the chosen distress, whatever is obstructing him or her is worked on as this is the distress on top – see section G.

The techniques used in the preceding (a), (b) or (c) assume that the client is talking through recent upsetting events, which is how beginning co-counsellors start. Such events involve underlying patterns, which clients typically become aware of when working through a series of related incidents. Clients will spontaneously think of earlier incidents, but these can

Table 5.1: Appropriate techniques for observable client behaviours

Client behaviour	Appropriate counsellor suggestions
A. Shut down or lost in distress. Insufficient attention in present time for balance of attention. Needs pulling out of hurts.	*Attention-switching* Focus attention outside distress: with simple descriptive tasks; actions needing attention; requests for positive memories.
B. Unfocused talking. Talks *about* distress. Asks 'Why?' Rationalizes. Seeks interpretations.	*Focusing on specific events* 'Tell me about a recent event that's an example.' Suggest that client: talks in present tense and uses literal description; role-plays self in past incident.
C. Whilst trying to focus on an event client: a. Moves into past tense. b. Is vague, lacks detail. c. Uses indirect speech.	*Focusing on specific events* 'Say that in the present tense.' 'Describe the room.' 'What was he wearing?' 'Talk directly to the person as if they're present now.'
D. Gives cues for distress and negative feelings: e.g. Stresses or stumbles over words. Pauses. Changes facial expression or gestures – eyes water, fists clench. Very tense in part or whole of body. Scratches. Makes aggressive or negative judgements, putdowns of self or others. Uses 'oughts' or 'shoulds'.	*Intensify distress cues* Suggest client repeats distress cues; talks loudly; involves body; uses counsellor to role-play words and actions which cause distress. *Intensify by going against distress cues* Suggest client says and does the opposite of the distress words, postures, gestures. If sagging suggest bodily arousal; if very tense suggest relaxation. Suggest using a parody or comic relief if distress feels heavy.
E. When client is using basic intensifying techniques, but not discharging as a result.	Demand loudness, and involvement of body. Try 'going against' distress; if already doing this, add a 'Yippee!' to end.
F. Counsellor uncertain about what's going on for client. Ambiguous cues. Change of expression without comment.	*General enquiry* 'What's the thought?' 'What's the image?' 'Where are you now?' 'Tell me what's on top – any order.'
G. Client not progressing with chosen distress area: – saying 'I'm stuck!' 'I can't!' 'That's silly.'	Treat client's words as cues for negative feelings – even when said as 'asides' or 'earnestly' – use intensifying as in E above.

– In grip of pattern which inhibits discharge. (Control pattern)

As above, but suggest 'going against' immediately; propose actions which interrupt patterns – tearing up cardboard, or acting actions which go with discharge.

– Client in conflict about what he or she wants or having competing distresses.

Suggest two cushions, one for each side of the conflict – client works first on one then the other, allowing each side of conflict a full say and aiming to discharge on both cushions.

H. Giving cues for patterns:
  a. Client verbalizes an association. 'I'm reminded of a person/place/event.'

Following pattern connections
Encourage focusing on that association. Get client to tell story, or talk directly to key person thought of, as appropriate.

  b. Client working on recent incidents in which people involved are authority figures, or suggestive of archetypes.

Useful interventions: 'Who does this remind you of?' 'Who are you really saying that to?' 'Try saying that to your father/mother.'

  c. Client's recent distress appears out of all proportion to its cause.

Check for earlier causes of restimulation: 'What's your earliest memory of a situation like this?' 'How about scanning through times when things like this happened?'

I. Client discharging.

Encourage the discharge: 'Let it go!' 'You'll feel better if you let it out.' When discharge slows down, get client to repeat the initial 'trigger'.

J. Client has identified major pattern, particularly chronic patterns.

Suggest direction-holding: the sustained, energetic, repetition of a direction, with appropriate posture, gestures, etc.

K. Client emerging from discharge and having lots of attention free to choose what to do. (In present time.)

Encourage taking time for re-evaluation. 'Take some time to think out loud on that situation.' 'How will you be different in the future?'

Client spontaneously brings up new memories, new ideas, new insights, new solutions.

Encourage client to follow up on these.

Client has plenty of free attention, and there is time in the session.

Encourage: Thinking out loud on broadening topics, e.g. 'My goals for the next 5 years.' Specific action planning. Self-expression, e.g. dancing, singing, painting.

L. Client approaching end of a session while still caught up in distress, or with discharge still occurring.

First, use attention-switching techniques so client finishes session with maximum attention out of distress. Then suggest using target practice – select as appropriate to time available and the work the client has done.

Stage reached by the client:
– Unfinished business.

Ask for 'What's left unsaid?' i.e. uncensored thoughts put into words. Then consider separately rehearsing for next time, e.g. 'What could you say for real, next time?'

– Present distress shown to originate in past – particularly when in early childhood.

Ask for separations of present person from past distress. E.g. 'I'm no longer the child who had to earn love – I'm now a smart, strong, skilled adult.'

– Client ready to consider and maximize changes in their life in the light of identified patterns.

Directions the client has used for discharge in sessions noted for use in life situations when patterns likely to be evoked.

M. End of session very close.

Encourage client to celebrate self, energetically, with words appropriate to work done.

also be evoked by the counsellor asking appropriate questions, as in Table 5.1, section H. Once patterns have been identified they can be worked with directly, without the need for talking through events where the patterns are restimulated. The technique used is called *direction holding*, a direction being a slogan which precisely and powerfully contradicts a client's pattern, provoking discharge. See Table 5.1, section J.

Attention-switching

Attention-switching moves mind and body from negative feelings into positive ones; from quadrants C,D to quadrants A,B in Figure 5.1. Such movements rely on our feelings adjusting to match the focus of our attention. This is part of everyday experience; research evidence is reviewed by Kovacs and Beck (Izard, 1979, p. 427). This strategy is used within sessions to achieve a balance of attention and also at the end of sessions so that clients do not leave overwhelmed by distresses. See Table 5.1, sections A and L.

Celebration

Celebration involves clients attending to, and actively voicing, appreciations of their positive qualities, skills, and successes – anything mastered or learned; so enhancing self-esteem. Celebration results in the client's positive resources being more readily remembered, so attention is less likely to be overwhelmed by distress in threatening situations. Also, although celebration is engaged in when the client is mainly in quadrants A or B, it goes against chronic self-put-down patterns, and hence the client will often discharge. RC has recently emphasized celebratory techniques using the label 'counselling with attention away from distress'.

Target practice

The target practice strategy involves clients practising breaking patterns, and substituting the new actions and thoughts which they wish to apply in their lives. Patterned responses are labelled as relevant only to past events; directions on which the client has discharged in the session are identified for use when the pattern is activated in the client's everyday life; future role-play is used to restimulate a pattern and practise interrupting it; the clear, distress-free thinking that occurs after discharge is applied.

All the four main strategies are operated flexibly; the counsellor trying one technique after another until discharge starts. The counsellor observes the client carefully, and encourages repetition of whatever triggers client discharge. Typically clients will discharge briefly and then cut it off. Tactically, repeated discharge on a situation or a pattern is encouraged until no more occurs. This may take many sessions, with more than one form of discharge occurring sequentially with the same material. Spontaneous ending of a discharge process is observable with noticeable relaxing of facial and bodily tension; clarity of thinking; access to new information about the distress, spontaneous interpretations, or ideas for action.

The change process in therapy

The possible changes experienced by clients during therapy can be viewed in terms of a spectrum:

(I) Emotional first aid → (II) Problem-solving → (III) Personality change → (IV) Transpersonal development

Movement from (I) to (IV) corresponds to gaining free attention and an increasing ability to think and act outside patterns. Major change occurs at each stage though the stages overlap and as different areas of distress are opened up there is recycling from later stages back to earlier ones. Clients with distresses and problems dominating their lives start work at stages I and

II. However even when motivation to co-counsel arises from a stage III or IV issue, clients need experience of stages I and II to learn the techniques, and to identify their chronic patterns, both necessary for work in stages III and IV.

Emotional first aid

The major work at this stage involves recovering the ability to discharge, When a client arrives at a session distressed, awareness of the safety contract and the counsellor's attention may be sufficient for the client to discharge. After discharge the client experiences relief from the negative feelings, often involving dramatic shifts to relaxed positive feelings and appearance. Re-evaluation phenomena commonly occur – recovering of occluded memories, re-interpretation of problems, new ideas for actions – such re-evaluations facilitate pattern-breaking in everyday life.

Thus the first important learning is that discharge is a route out of distress, with the post-discharge state being enjoyable and conducive to clear thinking. This learning goes along with an enhanced judgement of when oneself or others are in distress; with acceptance of a wide range of emotional expression as being desirable; with experience of warm supportive human relationships as being normal; and the experience of hope and empowerment.

Problem-solving

The problem-solving stage evolves naturally from emotional first aid as spontaneous re-evaluation occurs. Problem-solving can also be deliberately engaged in after the client gains facility in discharge. The focus is likely to be on being competent in particular situations, for example whether or not to get a new job, or the process of obtaining a divorce. After discharging clients will start to use target-practice techniques to enhance disruption of patterns in their lives. A useful technique is role-playing a difficult future situation including restimulating patterns and then practising interrupting them.

Skills learned in the counsellor role become available for use in the client role. Practice in deliberate switching between positive and negative feelings states, along with the client making suggestions to him or herself, results in part of the person's awareness becoming organized as a 'director'. This director will monitor feelings and behaviour, and initiate attention-switching or discharge as appropriate. This is like having an 'inner counsellor', who remains detached from the turmoil of the person's feelings and can intervene to change what is happening. This inner counsellor transfers to life outside sessions, with individuals increasingly able to retain some free attention when highly distressed, and able to choose not to go along with patterns.

Negative feelings are experienced as more sharply focused, more intense, but lasting for shorter periods. For example tendencies to depressive feelings may be replaced by anger focused on particular events. Scheff (1983) demonstrates these differences before and after discharge in therapy sessions. Clients move from particular problems to tackling their distresses in areas of life such as sexuality. As skills develop and change occurs in relation to particular distresses, underlying patterns become clearer and accessible for work, including eventually chronic patterns.

Personality change

Personality change requires the breaking of chronic patterns, that is, those in continuous restimulation, which appear to the client as 'my personality' or 'how the world is'. Working on chronic patterns can feel like trying to cut off an arm or leg, and many people stop co-counselling at this point. Such chronic patterns are tackled by a combination of intensive contracts and major use of direction-holding in sessions, with aware use of directions when restimulated in life at large.

The need for an intensive contract puts a premium on counsellor skills and RC has devoted much attention to improving counsellor skills, developing methods of coaching counsellors. Specific personality changes will depend upon the patterns worked on. General changes are that people experience an enhanced sense of self-worth, and increased ability to take charge of their own life. Assertive behaviour increases and apologetic or aggressive responses to others decrease. Inner counsellors gain in strength and expertise.

Transpersonal development

Transpersonal development covers social liberation and spiritual openness: they are both ways in which a client interacts with issues transcending individuality. For instance, having gained a measure of freedom from his or her own chronic patterns, the client can grasp the interactions of individual patterns and social oppressions. Although patterns are owned by individuals they also express an unaware collective consciousness. Work on collective patterns is done in groups who share the same experiences in society. Such work needs members of other groups to act as allies, able to stand outside and provide a collective balance of attention.

Breaking chronic patterns becomes focused on acting in the world as in the use of commitment techniques. Within sessions, directions which are commitments to act outside sessions are used. Outside sessions the person acts in ways that simultaneously go against his or her own patterns and those of oppressive others. Thus action in the world becomes a crucial therapeutic technique without which complete re-emergence of the person from his or her patterns cannot occur. Many co-counsellors are active in this type of action in local government and commercial organizations and the political sphere; there are case histories in RC literature (e.g. *Present Time*, January 1986, p. 5).

Alternatively stage IV can involve clients in spiritual growth. Experiences of altered states of consciousness encourage clients to work in transpersonal areas (e.g. *Present Time*, January 1986, p. 54). John Heron includes a transpersonal self as part of his model of being human and his 1974 co-counselling manual included transpersonal direction-holding as a further-on technique. He continues to be active in developing exercises on transpersonal themes suitable for co-counselling work (Heron, 1984).

CASE EXAMPLE

A client's relationship with her mother over several years is described. During this period the client was regularly engaged in reciprocal counselling with a variety of partners. The relationship was repeatedly addressed, though other issues were also tackled. Progress was from stage I to stage IV.

At the time of starting to co-counsel the client J. was in her early thirties, married, with a child aged four; and worked full time as a teacher in Higher Education. Her marriage relationship was stable and her husband also took up co-counselling. At work J. was enthusiastic and sought to improve her skills. However, she found dealing with people stressful; under a confident exterior she was self-conscious and unsure of her abilities to make relationships. She was overconscientious and typically ended term in a state of nervous exhaustion. Over the years she had been teaching, several depressive episodes had resulted in time off work and medication.

J. experienced her relationship with her mother as difficult. She felt disapproved of for being an inadequate housekeeper, for not producing a grandchild and, when she did, for returning to work when the child was still young. She had been frequently told by her mother that she was forgetful, thoughtless, careless and unloving.

J.'s parents lived some distance away and rarely visited. When they did her mother frequently became upset, and was loudly abusive about J.'s inadequacies and past failures. J. was unable to defend herself, choked over words, and was liable to cry. Both J. and her father would become targets for her mother's blaming. After shouting, her mother usually sulked, sometimes for a day or more, until sufficiently placated by her husband. During this time J. found herself helpless and depressed, and unable to get on with her own life until her mother had returned to some semblance of normality.

Another problem which emerged, connected with the maternal relationship, was that when under attack from superiors J. could not defend herself, even when she perceived the accusations as unwarranted. J. behaved as with her mother, choking and crying. This had happened with her previous employer; following which she had been very angry and found another job.

Just before starting co-counselling, J. had suffered several weeks of depression after a typical episode with mother. During the training J. worked with the teacher. Faced with the teacher role-playing mother, J. experienced herself as giving up and being unable to hang on to her sense of self-worth. After the training weekend J. began working in a pair. She worked on her mother following upsetting episodes with her. She was angry at her mother's current behaviour, and at what she thought her mother had done to her as a child. After discharge J. felt strengthened and knew more clearly that she was not responsible for her mother's distresses. J. became more able to be with mother without anger spilling out inappropriately. This was mainly emotional first aid, moving into problem-solving.

Next, anger started to give way to grief, J. felt unloved by her mother. Love had been conditional upon her mother's approval, and she had never been able to win that approval. Directions such as 'I want your love, mummy!' and 'I'm fine as I am mummy!' triggered prolonged crying. Resolution came with the re-evaluation 'Of course my mother loved me – whatever I felt, she did the best she could.' J. could still experience the need for approval from others as important but viewed this as distress arising from the past, and not currently relevant. J. was starting to work with her chronic patterns.

Then a key event occurred. Mother wished to be given a room in J.'s house to store surplus property. J. agreed to provide storage, but not the use of a whole room. When J.'s parents arrived with a van load of belongings, a long row resulted. During this row J. broke various patterns. Firstly, she was able to talk and respond without choking. Secondly, she refused to discuss past failures, and focused the conversation on the present situation. J. insisted that she would store the property, but in the manner of her own choice.

At one point mother became hysterical and threatened to attack J., who promptly slapped her face – something she would never have dreamt of previously. Mother was horrified, became more abusive, and eventually rushed off. J. was now crying and feeling helpless. She was aware of the pattern-breaking she had done, but it was not enough. She then departed for a friend's. On arrival she was still crying and her friends reacted with advice not to see parents at all if this resulted. J. had a clear thought 'I know what happens, my mother makes me feel and behave like a helpless little girl. The reality is I'm a mature women with many skills, and my mother is old and ill and insecure – and, if she was not my mother, I have counselling skills I could use with her.' This thought produced a sense of release and calmness, and was followed by 'I can go back home tomorrow and behave differently – use my counselling skills.' This was what she did.

J. regarded this episode as spectacular pattern-breaking; she knew she need not be caught again behaving and feeling as a small child. She was fully aware of the operations of her 'inner counsellor' during it. She now had a capacity to remain detached and patient with mother.

In counselling J. used directions such as: 'You no longer have power over me!' and 'I'm no longer the little girl who couldn't earn her mother's love.' These progressed to 'I'm still the same even if you disapprove of me.' A further step was applying this direction to distress with others and using 'I have a place in this universe no one can take away' to discharge the grief.

Progress was indicated by an incident in which J. talked to mother over the telephone. After coping well with being attacked, J. became very distressed. Putting down the telephone she looked for a counsellor. However alongside the upset was the knowledge of what it was all about – she had been caught again in the 'little girl' distress and her 'inner counsellor' gave her instructions to discharge in order to return to her normal self. This took about ten minutes of intensive discharge and celebration of herself. A few years earlier, recovery could have taken ten days.

Further progress occurred after J. spontaneously introduced her own daughter to a group of people by saying 'This is my delightful daughter!' In her next co-counselling session J. used the direction 'I am a delightful daughter.' Copious crying discharge resulted. Over time this direction became believable and celebratory. This transition corresponded to acting powerfully and looking after both parents during her father's terminal illness, confronting her mother's disapproval whenever necessary. J. coped with many hysterical outbursts from her mother, who would say she never wanted to see J. again.

The current relationship with her mother is more amicable than it has ever been. Mother's behaviour has changed very little, but J. is rarely caught by her mother's distress, and has the option of taking the counsellor role. J. notices when she is angry, avoids directing it at her mother, and discharges it later. Corresponding changes have occurred with regard to other authority figures. Recently J. confronted an awkward and manipulative administrator, who was putting her down, and denying her version of what took place. J. planned the crucial meeting, remained calm despite his bullying, demonstrated objectively that he was in error, and secured his agreement to putting things right.

In general J. is less self-conscious, and less in need of others' approval. She is perceived as warm and caring and readily makes satisfying relationships. Her confidence in her job skills has vastly increased, and she is no longer drained by demanding work. She is still working on some aspects of her chronic patterns. In particular, on being non-judgemental of others whilst being willing to interrupt their destructive patterns. She is moving into stage IV – acting effectively in promoting social change.

FOOTNOTE ON NOMENCLATURE

The processes and ideas described here are widely known as co-counselling. Re-evaluation Counseling and Co-Counselling International are the names of international networks of co-counsellors. Within the USA the terms *Re-evaluation Counseling* and *Co-counseling* were registered as service marks by Personal Counselors Inc., marking the fact that RC considers its fusion of process, theory and organization as unique.

REFERENCES

Dawson, M. E. and Schell, A. M. (1987) Human autonomic and skeletal classical conditioning; the role of conscious cognitive factors, in G. Davey (ed.) *Human Conditioning*, Wiley, Chichester.

Evison, R. and Horobin, R. W. (1985) *How To Change Yourself and Your World* (2nd revised edn), Co-Counselling Phoenix, Sheffield.

Frude, N. (1982) Child abuse as aggression, in N. Frude (ed.) *Psychological Approaches to Child Abuse*, Batsford, London.

Goldfield, M. R. (1980) Effective principles of pyschotherapy, *Cognitive Therapy and Research*, Vol. 4, pp. 272–89.

Heron, J. (1978) *Co-counselling Teachers Manual*, British Postgraduate Medical Federation, London.

Heron, J. (1979) *Co-Counselling* (revised edn), Human Potential Research Project, University of Surrey, Guildford.

Heron, J. (1984) Brief note on transpersonal co-counselling, *Firelighter*, Vol. 2, pp. 1–3.

Holden, M. (1977) The sensory window and access to primal pain, in A. Janov and M. Holden, (eds.) *Primal Man*, Sphere, London.

Holt, J. (1964) *How Children Fail*, Pitman, London.

Izard, C. E. (ed.) (1979) *Emotions in Personality and Psychopathology*, Plenum, New York and London.

Jackins, H. (1965) *The Human Side of Human Beings*, Rational Island Publishers, Seattle.

Jackins, H. (1973) *The Human Situation*, Rational Island Publishers, Seattle.

Jackins, H. (1977) *The Upward Trend*, Rational Island Publishers, Seattle.

Jackins, H. (1983) *The Reclaiming of Power*, Rational Island Publishers, Seattle.

Jourard, S. M. (1968) *Disclosing Man to Himself*, Van Nostrand Reinhold, New York.

Kagan, N. (1980) Influencing human interaction – eighteen years with IPR, in A. K. Hess, (ed.) *Psychotherapy Supervision: Theory, Research and Practice*, Wiley, New York.

Kagan, N. (1986) Personal communication.

Karle, W., Corriere, R. and Hart, J. (1973) Psychophysiological changes in abreactive therapy – Study 1: Primal therapy, *Psychotherapy: Theory Research & Practice*, Vol. 10, pp. 117–22.

Martin, D. G. (1972) *Learning-Based Client-Centered Therapy*, Brooks/Cole Publishing Company, Monterey, CA.

Pierce, R. A., Nichols, M. P and Dubrin, J. R. (1983) *Emotional Expression in Psychotherapy*, Gardner Press, New York.

Present Time, A quarterly Re-evaluation Counseling magazine, Rational Island Press, Seattle.

Scheff, T. J. (1983) Toward integration in the social psychology of emotions, *Annual Review of Sociology*, Vol. 9, pp. 333–54.

Seligman, M. E. P. (1975) *Helplessness*, W. H. Freeman, San Francisco.

Swank, R. L. (1949) Combat exhaustion, *Journal of Nervous and Mental Disease*, Vol. 209, pp. 475–91.

Swift, A. (1986) Article discussing Ray Wyre's work, in *The Guardian*, 9 March, p. 13.

Tomkins, S. S. (1963) *The Negative Affects*, Springer, New York/Tavistock, London.

Suggested further reading

Jackins, H. (1980) *Fundamentals of Co-counseling*, (1981) *The Benign Reality*; (1985) *The Rest of Our Lives*, Rational Island Publishers, Seattle.

R C Magazines. For Instance: *Caring Parent*; *Classroom*; *Men*; *Recovery and Reemergence*; *Sisters*; *Well Being*; *Wide World Changing*; *Working for a Living*; *Young and Powerful*, Rational Island Publishers, Seattle.

Scheff, T. J. (1979) *Catharsis in Healing, Ritual, and Drama*, University of California Press, Berkeley, CA.

CHAPTER 6

PSYCHODRAMA

Ari (Joel) Badaines

HISTORICAL CONTEXT AND DEVELOPMENTS IN BRITAIN

Historical context

The history of psychodrama, an action technique of group psychotherapy, is essentially a history of Dr J. L. Moreno, a Viennese psychiatrist. He is the founder of psychodrama, creator of its theory and techniques, and considered by many to be the father of group psychotherapy. Eric Berne (1970), the founder of Transactional Analysis (TA), writes:

> In his selection of specific techniques, Dr Perls shares with other 'active' psychotherapists the 'Moreno problem': the fact that nearly all known 'active' techniques were first tried out by Dr Moreno in psychodrama, so that it is difficult to come up with an original idea in this regard. (pp. 163–4)

Moreno was born in Rumania in 1889 or 1892, but his family shortly thereafter moved to Vienna. He attended the University of Vienna, and then joined its philosophy department. Moreno received his medical degree in 1917 and began the study of psychiatry. He met Freud, and related this anecdote. Freud asked him of his plans, and during their discussion, Moreno (1946) said. 'You see patients in the unnatural surroundings of your consulting room. I meet them in the streets . . . in their natural environment. You analyse their dreams. I shall give them courage for new dreams' (p. 6).

The birth of psychodrama is said to have occurred in 1921 at Moreno's

Theatre of Spontaneity where he applied his improvisory techniques to problems of relationships, individuals and small groups.

Experiencing post-war Europe as rather sterile, Moreno emigrated to the United States in 1925 and continued to develop his method, wrote prolifically, and at the 1932 American Psychiatric Meeting he used the term *group psychotherapy* – apparently for the first time. In 1936, he established the Moreno Sanitarium which for many years was the centre of psychodrama training and treatment. It served as a residential treatment centre, often treating very disturbed patients in the psychodramatic method. From this period until his death in 1974, Moreno (and his wife, Zerka) continued to expand and refine the psychodramatic approach into areas of education, military selection and management, prisons, industry and personality theory. Similarly, he has influenced the fields of anthropology, sociology and of course psychiatry. Today, Moreno's influence can be seen in role-playing, sociodrama, family therapy, other 'body-mind therapies', and in many of the newer approaches to therapy such as encounter groups and sensory-awareness sessions.

Psyche refers to the mind, the mental life of an individual comprising the intellectual, emotional and impulsive activities and predispositions. *Drama* comes from the Greek word which means action, or a thing done. Psychodrama, then, can be seen as a method which uses action and drama to explore the psyche and whose aim is to enable individuals to resolve conflicts in a micro-society (the group) on the psychodramatic stage. This stage attempts to emulate life, but free from its usual constraints and restrictions, it permits enacting and re-creating problem areas. It is not just the participant's realistic life problems which are portrayed, but also the psychological dimensions: the unfulfilled wishes, unspoken fears and feelings – thus combining the physical and psychological realities to give a basic truth, which led Moreno to call psychodrama the 'theatre of truth'.

Moreno states that psychodrama did not come from the theatre; in fact, it told him what not to do. Moreno (1969) sought an encounter between one's real self – his or her *I* or *Thou* (not his or her shadow nor role as an actor), and another's real self. Thus, encounter was seen as a meeting between two people, on a most intense level of communication, which was unplanned and spontaneous.

Action methods in approaching and dealing with the world of the participant encourage the experiencing and expressing of any emotions aroused by actions taken in that world. Old feelings may be stirred up at the same time, and these too may be expressed with the same intensity as that with which they were first laid down. This process of abreacting stored feelings, leading to new perceptions and understandings, is called *catharsis*. Aristotle introduced this concept, but Moreno noted that in Greek drama the catharsis occurred in the audience, the spectators; in psychodrama it occurs not just in the spectators but primarily in the actors who produce the drama. These actors simultaneously liberate themselves from the drama, their problem situation in everyday life.

Developments in Britain

Psychodrama continued to expand geographically in the United States as those who trained with Moreno brought it to new areas of the country, but the tremendous upsurge in interest in all of the 'new therapies' through the human potential movement led to its introduction into Britain. In the late 1960s and early 1970s various psychodramatists came to Britain to run workshops, usually through one of the growth centres. Howard Blatner, Joel Badaines and Marcia Karp were among the first to reside in Britain.

This meant that people could experience psychodrama on a consistent basis, but there were, at that time, no opportunities for training in Britain. In the early to mid 1970s this was rectified by the establishment of two training opportunities, one through Joel Badaines and the other through Marcia Karp at the Holwell Centre for Psychodrama. A diploma course was established through her centre in 1980 which essentially had the same standards as the American certification process to be a psychodrama director (practitioner). The diploma requires a minimum of 780 hours of psychodrama training and experience, as well as a short thesis in publishable form. While having no legal status, this is an important step in giving the public some indication that those so certified have shown a certain standard of competency and training. Several have completed the course and are running psychodrama groups in various sections of England, and in York there is a training programme as well.

Zerka Moreno has, since 1981, made an annual trip to England to lead a variety of workshops which have been well attended, and have given an opportunity to work with a highly skilled pioneer in the field. An annual conference was first held in 1983, and at the second conference in 1984 the British Psychodrama Association was formed. There were three categories of membership which helped to set some national standards:

1. Full membership, for those who have completed the Holwell Centre diploma or other equivalent training
2. Training membership, for those currently involved in training at Holwell Centre

3. Associate membership, which is open to those who have an interest in psychodrama but do not fit into the first two categories.

As individuals from the various professions attended these psychodrama workshops, they attempted to introduce the method into their own fields; psychiatric hospitals, day centres, marriage guidance, university courses, etc. Various national conferences also included psychodrama experiences and/or trainings in their programme.

Today in Britain psychodrama has gained greater acceptance in the more established fields of education and mental health. While, so far as I am aware, there are no specific positions for psychodramatists within the National Health Service, there is an increasing use of psychodrama by trained personnel which is accepted and even embraced by the institution concerned. From personal experience, I am aware that many organizations have sought consultation on introducing psychodrama into their treatment mode, or supervision for their staff who are already utilizing psychodrama as a treatment modality.

THEORETICAL ASSUMPTIONS

Image of the person

Foremost in Moreno's image of the person was the belief that he or she is a spontaneous individual, interacting with others in a continuously creative process.

These two terms *spontaneity* and *creativity* are the cornerstone of Morenean theory. Spontaneity is not a wild, uncontrolled response. Instead it is a readiness and an ability to meet new situations adequately, and familar ones with direct vitality rather than a rigid, fixed approach. The spontaneous person will move into a situation with ease. Spontaneity is present at birth, and develops unevenly during one's lifetime, peaking in childhood. Similarly there are individual differences in the amount of spontaneity a person is able to use at any given time.

Spontaneity is the catalyst for creativity. Moreno found it difficult to describe, but its chief characteristic is that the results are new to the individual, but not necessarily to the rest of the world. The major outcome is a new relationship that has been created which in the experience of the creator did not exist before. To be creative for Moreno meant not just being adaptable, but actually responding constructively to new situations.

Finally, Moreno perceived the person as a co-creator, co-responsible with the rest of humankind; and thus an individual's life and welfare is linked to all of mankind, the two being seen as currents flowing together, mixing and influencing and co-acting one upon the other.

Concepts of psychological health and disturbance

For many role theorists, a role is what a person plays at any given moment, but for Moreno the person is the cluster of roles that he or she develops. A role essentially was a unit of behaviour which an individual portrays at a given moment, in a specific situation, and is related to the persons and/or objects involved in the situation. Some roles are adequate and useful while others are not. Roles also may be under- or over-developed or not developed at all. Thus, the healthy person will seek and adequately take a variety of roles which lead to fulfilling, adaptable lifestyles. Moreno stated that the past structures a person's roles, the present governs the action of these roles, and the future sets the goals. The healthy person will by utilizing his or her spontaneity and resultant creativity, integrate the past, present and future into each role.

Thus for Moreno the ideal person would be one who is fully using his or her potential. As each person meets external challenges, those who are most healthy are those who draw on their own potential for freedom to solve their problems.

Moreno differentiated three kinds of spontaneity. The first is marked by the novelty of the response, but it is inadequate for the specific situation. Children and psychotics often display this type of spontaneity: in reply to 'What day is this?' a psychotic stated 'Mr Gooday'.

The second kind of spontaneity has adequacy, but lacks novelty. Trite, repetitious responses, which may sometimes be seen as smart repartee, are good examples of this second form. These first two were thought to be false forms of spontaneity.

The third, true spontaneity contains an adequate response which is both novel and adequate, and hence has every chance of being truly creative (Bischof, 1964).

It can be seen that Moreno viewed the role-player who was successful in developing new relationships and successful roles as likely to be healthy, while those who suffered from deficiencies in the above would be seen as disturbed.

There are two further concepts which need to be clarified in terms of psychological health and disturbance. The 'social atom' is the smallest living unit which cannot be further subdivided and in which there exists a reciprocity in the relationship. Thus a family, a friendship (both characterized by a long history and intense feelings), or a brief interaction (e.g. between waiter and customer) all represent social atoms. It merely describes the state of the particular relationship in that it is a value-free concept.

The relative freedom from psychological disturbance for Moreno also depended on an individual adequately taking roles and developing new ones in society, aided by his or her spontaneity and creativity. As one does not act in isolation, but co-acts and co-creates with others, a balanced, open social structure is also required.

Acquisition of psychological disturbance

In our increasingly mobile and complex world, change is likely to occur in a person's life situation at almost any time. Significant people in a social atom may leave, work may terminate, economic and/or environmental changes may arise, and the individual may wish to develop new roles which initially could create stress. Cultural roles may also shift, adding new pressures. As long as the person has sufficient freedom to meet these changes, the person's own equilibrium in relation to his or her social and cultural atoms will be maintained. If, however, people are unable to be sufficiently creative to meet these changes, a disequilibrium (often experienced as symptoms and feelings of distress) will become manifest, and according to Moreno (1940) will be reflected in the disturbance of interpersonal and interrole relationships. Lack of spontaneity is also a basis for anxiety in that the person may feel inadequate in new situations. If the person is unable to muster sufficient resources, there will also be a ripple effect, creating disequilibria in the life of those close to the individual. If these disruptive influences persist, it is likely that a state of psychological disturbance will develop not only for the individual but, to a greater or lesser extent, for those others as well.

Moreno believed that individuals co-act, and the co-action between individuals he called *tele*. Tele is a two-way process of reciprocation, and is responsible for the two-way multitude of feelings among people in relation to one another. Tele can be positive, negative or ambivalent, and may be for objects and/or symbols as well as for people. Those friendships which just flow are those with a mutual positive tele.

This phenomenon has important implications for the mental health of the individual. Starting in childhood, if for example a young girl is forced to spend a significant time with people with whom she feels little positive connection, and this is mutual, she will begin to feel different, unaccepted and even rejected. Again, if she is lacking in sufficient resources to resolve the problem, she may withdraw and become isolated or become overly aggressive, etc. Furthermore, such an individual is deprived of practising in childhood a variety of social roles. It is obvious that if this pattern were to continue into adolescence and adulthood, more persistent forms of psychological disturbance would become manifest.

In the normal course of development, as the individual grows, her telic relationships proceed from other persons then to include objects (toys, bicycles, antiques) and finally to symbolic tele (spoken and written words, the national flag, etc.). Through the years of development, the individual may have greater success with one of these forms of tele, preferring it to the exclusion of the others. According to Bischof (1964) those individuals or societies which favoured tele for persons are characterized by a high degree of emotionality in their relationships. Those who have a high tele for objects tend to be more technically oriented, and if it is overemphasized there may be little caring for persons or ideas. Ascetically oriented societies serve as illustrations of symbolic tele organizations. Thus, if an individual is living in a society or subculture which emphasizes one form of tele, while the individual requires a different emphasis or overall balance, and this situation persists, it is likely that he or she will demonstrate considerable signs of psychological disturbance.

Moreno does not offer a clear statement regarding the causative factors which limit people having or utilizing their spontaneity. He does say (Moreno, 1974) that humankind has done everything to discourage its development; instead people stay with the safe, the known, and become rigid, fixed and in a sense non-risk-taking. Moreno adds that spontaneity may be so poorly developed because people fear their own spontaneity, or because they simply do not know how to use it. Until this changes, Moreno says, humankind will suffer from psychopathy and sociopathy because we cannot mobilize our creativity.

The outcome of this process is called the *cultural conserve*, and this can be anything which preserves the values of a particular culture. Thus a book, film, rituals, ceremonies, social customs and events are all examples of cultural conserves. They do benefit both the culture and the individual in that one does not have to keep on creating the same patterns for everyday situations – they are just there. Furthermore, the cultural conserve provides a sense of continuity for a culture, and a sense of security. It also provides a set of roles for the individual to use.

There are four broad categories of roles. The first to appear are the *psychosomatic* roles. These emerge through interaction with the primary caretaker (often the mother) and can best be described as a pattern of roles involving bodily processes: the eater, eliminator, sleeper, etc. From further interactions with this primary caretaker and others, *social* roles develop; these are the roles an individual takes in relation to other people: husband, father, boss, tennis-player, etc. are typical social roles. Each culture stamps roles, especially the social roles, with its own particular mark. Thus an assistant in a large London department store might behave differently from his or her counterpart in a small Greek village shop, reflecting particular cultural values and styles. Such roles are called *cultural* roles. And finally, those roles which are perceived as outside everyday interactions with other people – God, witches, the devil, animals – are known as *fantasy* roles. These roles are linked with the ability to separate reality and fantasy, and with the use of imagination.

Role-playing is the 'royal road' to the creation of a truly spontaneous person, but it can become a source of psychological disturbance. If, for example, a person holds too tightly to a role, it too becomes conserved. For example, if a husband feels that his role includes only the traditional aspects of the masculine husband, but his wife insists that he expand his role to include helping around the house, there will be psychological stress.

Bischof (1964) suggests that if roles are frozen in the past, regressive and infantile behaviour may be seen: for example, a 30-year-old man may be described as 'just a little boy'. Roles which focus only on the present often are without goals, and fluctuate in accordance with the stimuli at hand. And roles which are solely future-oriented do not deal with the issues in the present, and often exist at a fantasy level: for example, 'Next year when my book is published all my problems will be over.'

Further sources of psychological disturbance lie in role confusion. All of us are aware of certain roles which are important for us if we are to have some degree of satisfaction in life, or even to avoid undue stress. This occurs at work, at home, in social relationships and so on. Sometimes, however, just what roles are expected may not be so clear. This is most likely to be the case during adolescence when at times there is an expectation that the person behaves like an adult, while at other times it is child behaviour that is expected. Such role confusion can cause considerable stress, and expresses itself often in the exclamation 'I just don't know what they want from me!'

A closely related factor is the concept of being role-locked. Here one attempts to minimize one predominant role and to develop a more creative one, but those in the social structure fail to note and respond to the newer role. The former delinquent who is still blamed by the police for local vandalizations, and the adolescent who becomes more responsible but is still treated as if he or she were irresponsible are examples of being role-locked. Role-locking manifests itself in intimate and family relationships, in work and most other environments as well as many different kinds of groups. If the individual cannot escape from an undesirable role in which he or she is locked, it may lead to signs of psychological disorder, and the person may be forced, if it persists, to leave the situation permanently.

Perpetuation of psychological disturbance

Any of the preceding situations, if prolonged, can lead to the perpetuation of psychological disturbance. Additionally, behaviour that becomes stereotypical, compulsive and habitual is devoid of spontaneity, and according to Blatner (1985) comprises much of what is called *psychopathology*.

At a cultural level there may appear a social pathology, in the form of rigid bureaucracies, prejudice, and tradition for tradition's sake when those traditions no longer serve a beneficial function. Moreno foresaw a situation where a 'robot-like person' would evolve who survived in a conserved and conserving environment, devoid of any creativity, freedom or responsibility; in such an environment psychopathology would flourish.

Starr (1977, p. 270) suggest that the origins of psychosis lie in the child's early experiences with fantasy and reality. In infancy fantasy and reality may intermingle, but gradually become separated out. But an incomplete separation can leave the person prone to a confusion between reality and fantasy, and such a confusion would be self-perpetuating. Telic attractions towards imaginary people or for objects or symbols over positive social relations would also pave the way for the perpetuation of psychological disturbance.

Starr also points out that while telic strength is considered by Moreno to be genetically determined, Moreno's overall theory of severe psychological disturbance does not necessarily assume a genetic or constitutional basis. His theory emphasizes individual responsibility and choice in that the person selects special roles (which the mental health professionals would describe as reflecting moderate to severe psychological disturbance) which will enable her or him to create an environment and produce a drama which will bring greater fulfilment than any other roles would. The psychotic state, for example, often reflects the taking of fantasy roles (Jesus Christ, the devil, etc.) to the almost complete exclusion of social roles, and even psychosomatic roles – manifested in their reluctance to eat or in catatonia, to move.

Role confusion is also a contributory factor in the more extreme forms of psychological disturbance. The psychotic may sometimes be Jesus Christ and sometimes not. Role confusion may also be a source of disturbance for the neurotic to the extent of being too confused to assimilate enough of a socially required role to take it in any adequate way. Thus a phobic person remains at home because he or she cannot adequately perform the required tasks associated with the various roles required outside the home. A similar explanation may be seen in the process of institutionalization.

Faulty social atoms and poor social structures can perpetuate psychological disturbance. If social atoms are faulty, the person will have major difficulties in building satisfactory interpersonal relationships, enhancing mutual telic attractions and experiencing gratifying membership in groups. The culture or mini-society in which our experiences are embedded may be either supportive of or hostile to spontaneity and creativity, and if hostile may well make it more difficult to deal with or lose psychological disturbances.

PRACTICE

Goals of therapy

The following are the goals of psychodrama.

1. To increase the spontaneity-creativity level of an individual, so that the person plays existing roles more effectively and can develop new and more satisfying roles.
2. To assess and utilize untapped creative potential in the participants through support and challenge.
3. To provide a safe environment for a cathartic and insightful experience in such a way that it leads to further integration.
4. To enable individuals to discover how they form, maintain and change their social atoms.
5. To free a person from stereotyped (conserved) behaviour and to help him or her to develop new and more appropriate (spontaneous and creative) approaches to current experiences, life situations and roles. This is perhaps the ultimate aim of a psychodrama session.

Psychodrama aims to facilitate the deeper understanding of the many dimensions of emotional conflicts by enacting them rather than just talking about them. With the development of additional roles the sense of self can be strengthened. Through enactment the person is able to learn more of the relative effectiveness of body language, and to differentiate between thoughts, feelings and actions. Using models (other group members) the protagonist (focal person in a psychodrama) can see in action more appropriate behaviour and can then try it out as a form of rehearsal for life itself. Finally, as psychodrama is essentially a form of group psychotherapy, the goals of group psychotherapy would also apply here: such things as acceptance, encouragement of openness and self-disclosure, development of a non-judgemental attitude toward the problems of others, increased empathetic understanding, group support for change, risk-taking, etc.

The 'person' of the therapist

Psychodramatists must be aware of the seriousness of the work which they undertake. Out of that awareness comes the desire to be adequately trained and to be made aware of their own personal dynamics which might influence the direction of their work with others. A good background in group dynamics and group process as well as an awareness of non-verbal communication are also essential. Naturally, psychodramatists are spontaneous and creative in their use of methods, and in their own lives. They are open with participants, share from their own life experiences when relevant, and through engagements which treat clients as real and worthwhile persons, help clients to experience the richness of human interaction. They have ethical principles which forbid them to exploit the resulting relationships.

Psychodrama directors will also be comfortable with highly emotional, sometimes volatile scenes, and be able to keep their attention focused on the work occurring; at the same time they are aware of the mood of the group and the emotions generated by the work of the protagonist. It is equally important that they are confident enough not to need dramatic explosions to occur, and that their own needs are not met exclusively through groups; that is, their own lives are in order.

Therapeutic style

Moreno had faith in the wisdom of his patients, and a firm belief that through the psychodramatic process each person would make the necessary connections and gain insight and change through new perceptions. Reflected in these beliefs is the generally non-directive style of most psychodramatists. This means that it is the client who chooses the content, but the director will be active in selecting the methods and techniques to enable the client to adequately explore and experience the issues at hand.

The director will be real with the client, but that will not be an excuse for the expression of all the negative feelings toward the client. Such an expression is not considered therapeutic under the guise of 'modelling anger', 'letting it all hang out', 'being real', etc., and neither is it considered an example of healthy spontaneity. Because of the belief in each person's own wisdom, most directors convey to the group that each and all will be responsible for their own pace and direction, respecting their right to grow and change following their own path in their own time. Still, it is hard for some novice psychodramatists to stay patiently with a protagonist who works slowly and cautiously with little spontaneity, especially if the director wants to impress his or her audience (no longer a group!) with the ability to produce dramatic results through explosive styles. It often leads to pushing the client, and the client resisting with equal strength. The experienced psychodramatist may suffer from similar needs, but will be aware of them, and not transfer those needs on to the protagonist. Similarly, while striving for effective psychodramatic productions which enable the protagonist to experience deeply, the director is not thrown when things do not go smoothly all the time, and can adapt the method and technique in accordance with the needs of the moment.

The psychodramatist adapts his or her style to the particular group and its purpose. Thus in a new group of inexperienced participants, the director will be perhaps softer, more gentle, engendering a trusting and supportive atmosphere, proceeding at a pace which is tolerable to the group. In accordance with the situation, directors may be firm and confronting, but will not attack the integrity of the person. Frequently they are open, warm and supportive, and also humorous – Moreno emphasized the therapeutic aspects of humour. In a word, they are spontaneous.

Major therapeutic techniques

The psychodrama session is as lifelike as possible, but unhindered by the frozen patterns of daily life. In the psychodrama theatre, as opposed to the traditional theatre, the ideal is to be free from scripts. It is not a place where the patient comes to show his or her wounds, and have them healed by a skilled professional; instead all the initiative, all the decisions arise from within the protagonist. The psychodramatic stage provides the protagonist with a space which is flexible and multidimensional, where the individual who has lost his or her equilibrium (Moreno, 1946) can find it again.

In the application of psychodramatic techniques, the director follows a set of guidelines which are briefly summarized here. (I am appreciative of Zerka Moreno's unpublished paper on rules and techniques upon which this and the following section are based.) The protagonist enacts her or his conflicts, rather than talking about them, all in the here and now, regardless of when the actual event occurred. Speaking in the past tense removes the protagonist from the immediacy of the present, and he or she becomes more of a storyteller. The protagonist is directed to respond 'as if it is happening to you in this moment, for the first time', and this brings about deep involvement.

By encouraging the maximum expression of thoughts and feelings, the protagonist is free to include delusional and hallucinatory material as well as fantasy and projections; this is particularly beneficial for the repressed or inhibited individual. In contrast, some have difficulty in restraining the expression of thoughts and feelings, being impulsive or psychopathic perhaps; psychodrama is also a technique of restraint, either through role reversal or through the taking of roles in the drama which require patience and restraint.

Role reversal means taking the role of significant others in one's own drama, as when a female protagonist takes the role of her husband, perceiving the world through his eyes, heart, body and soul. Through projection, identification and other psychological mechanisms, the protagonist has taken into herself with varying degrees of accuracy those persons, situations, experiences and perceptions from which she is now hurting. To overcome the distorted perceptions and other manifestations of imbalance, role reversal can free the protagonist to grow beyond those negative experiences and to recover her spontaneity.

Psychodrama begins with a warm-up which may be verbal, fantasied or physical. Eventually the group attention becomes focused on one person, and this will be the protagonist. A beginning point is conjointly decided – a scene or situation from that person's life. The others in that scene are represented by 'auxiliary egos', usually selected from the group by the protagonist. The scene is begun, and sooner or later role reversal will take place, the director suggesting that the protagonist and one of the auxiliary egos change places. Not only does the protagonist gain a deeper understanding of that person, but also experiences her environment, herself and significant others from such a different viewpoint that a change in perception often occurs through role reversal itself.

Another technique is *doubling*. (Another person is sometimes chosen by the director, sometimes group members volunteer who feel strongly identified with the situation and feelings portrayed by the protagonist, but usually the protagonist selects her own double. This double stands next to the protagonist and imitates her physical movements.) Its major purpose is to facilitate the protagonist's awareness of internalized thoughts and feelings by the double's clear but brief expression of these thoughts and emotions. In other words, the double speaks on the protagonist's behalf. If working with very withdrawn patients the double may do much of the expression, but if the protagonist is very active and expressive, then the double's role is reduced. Different directors may emphasize different aspects, or the same director could encourage the double sometimes to focus on feelings, other times on interpretation and integration of thoughts and/or feelings, and other times (all in the same piece of psychodramatic work) on being supportive. Multiple doubles (more than one person doubling the protagonist) are successful in portraying conflicted parts of the protagonist or the various roles that the protagonist plays in life. Multiple doubles can be powerful in ameliorating the crippling effects of self-rejection and criticism.

People often get stuck in the present out of fear of the future. By using a technique called *future projection*, the protagonist can experience the future in the present. A specific time and situation is portrayed as realistically as possible. Thus a woman who feared leaving her husband out of a fear of loneliness portrays her life six months hence as if she had left her husband. It is Saturday night in her new flat, and she is aware that she has many friends around her, and the possibility of a new romance. Two weeks later she moved out of the marital home.

It is possible to suffer from 'act hungers' – that is, wishes for events which never happened, or which are unlikely to happen. Such events can be set up and played out as what is called *surplus reality*. This enables the protagonist to let go of the pain of the hunger and to come back much refreshed.

Learning new approaches can be enhanced through the use of *models*. Another person in the group can demonstrate emotional expressions, communication skills and so on that the protagonist lacks. As in all the other techniques, the goal is to help the protagonist to discover his or her own approach to the problem, with models giving some ideas which the protagonist may or may not wish to incorporate into his or her solution. Related to this is the use of *rehearsal* for practising how a person will actually behave in a concrete situation in the near future. Psychodramatic methods create a safe environment for individuals to first experiment with a variety of approaches, and then select those most useful for his or her particular situation.

The use of modelling and rehearsal can be expanded to include role training by practising new behaviour. This training occurs in small steps until the behaviour becomes sufficiently integrated into the person's role repertoire. Through the technique of doubling, individuals also expand their role repertoire by being involved in unfamiliar roles; taking auxiliary ego roles has a similar effect. The director may utilize this effect by asking participants to take roles which would expand their repertoire. A person who has difficulty restraining his or her anger may be invited to portray a husband who is described as emotionally overcontrolled and restricted. When selecting an auxiliary on this basis, it is called *therapeutic role assignment*.

In a long-term group, especially when the group looks at who the participants are who are most and least chosen, based on a specific criterion, individuals become clearer about the reasons for their choices, and gain valuable feedback about themselves. Such a long-term group also provides opportunities for the client to learn more about his or her social atom and how to maintain, and when necessary, change it. Through honest, supportive disclosures, transference-based distorted relationships can be transformed into mutually positive tele-based connections. The psycho-dramatic method itself can be applied to examine sources of conflict and anxiety as well as support and strengths within the progaonist's social atom.

Through cathartic experiences, through taking a variety of roles, the use of imagination and play, and the opportunity to experiment through drama, the level of spontaneity and creativity is enhanced in the individual partici-pating in a psychodramatic session.

After a protagonist has completed his or her work, the group joins together in a circle where sharing occurs. Participants share their emotional identifications with the protagonist in a non-judgemental manner. This is of value not only to the protagonist, helping her to feel that she is not alone in her problem, but sharing can be of therapeutic benefit also to those who identify with the problem. Sharing may even become the warm-up to the next action session.

Briefly, psychodramatic techniques lend themselves to dreamwork, to family and couple therapy, and they are equally adaptable in a wide range of settings and with various populations: children, the severely disturbed, adolescents, prison populations, etc.

Historically psychodrama is primarily a method of group psychotherapy, but it is also a powerful adjunct technique in individual psychotherapy. Most frequently, the therapist will use psychodramatic techniques whenever they will enhance the therapeutic process, or facilitate the client reaching any of the goals discussed earlier. There are, however, additional role demands placed upon the therapist. She or he must be able to take a variety of necessary roles for the client's therapy, often in quick succession, and simultaneously maintain control over and focus on the overall direction of the session. Additionally, the therapist must portray those roles in a sufficiently convincing manner so that the client is emotionally engaged and benefits from the psychodramatic action (Stein and Callahan, 1982). Skilled therapists also pay careful attention to the effects of the therapist taking specific roles (role of client's mother or father, for example – often a critical and punitive role) on the overall therapeutic relationship (transference issues). Essentially, as Stein and Callahan report (1982, p. 128),

> Therapy is intensified through engaging the individual in action on many levels, in an atmosphere of heightened realism and immediacy. In a sense, the client's world is not merely talked about but is brought into the room, where it can be directly examined and gradually transformed.

The change process in therapy

Moreno was convinced that people could best develop their spontaneity on the psychodramatic stage where natural barriers such as time, space and everyday resistances are obliterated. Moreno uses the term *catharsis* as an emotional purging, but adds that the common principle producing a catharsis is spontaneous dramatic action (Moreno, 1945). Insight is a by-product of catharsis and may occur simultaneously with it, or following the cathartic experience. He suggested that through the psychodramatic process, with its sensory stimulations in combination with the emotional catharsis, a restructuring of perceptions occurs.

The ultimate, private, yet almost universal nature of most people's work encourages both those who are participating actively and those who are in the 'audience' (group members but not taking an active role) to become increasingly involved to the extent that the emotional release of the protagonist almost becomes theirs as well, as if they are silent partners in the psychodrama. Therefore it is not only the protagonist who is able to change, but also the other members, perhaps as they see themselves reflected in the enactment.

Many forms of therapy would agree that the expression of suppressed feelings is a basis for change. As an example, suppressed individuals tend to be constricted in roles requiring the expression of feelings. Psychodrama encourages the ventilation of such emotions by bringing them on to the stage and into the appropriate scenes. Examining attitudes that one holds towards others and towards oneself is facilitated by doubles and auxiliaries; this again can lead to important changes in feelings about oneself and one's social atom and its associated structures.

Similarly, through such measures as role reversal, the protagonist gains a deeper understanding of past emotional events which have influenced basic attitudes toward themselves. As an example, Sue felt inadequate and rejected by her father because of his high expectations of her. Through portraying him (role reversal) in her psychodramatic session, she came to realize that they were ones she could not possibly live up to, and that those unrealistic expectations were partly based on his insecurity and his subsequent need for her to succeed for his benefit.

Once the point of 'act completions' (or 'act fulfilments') or emotional peak has been reached, some integration of the work is sought. In this phase of the enactment, the protagonist's equilibrium is restored through group support and by using what was learned from the enactment to develop a sense of mastery over the problem. In this second phase of the enactment, the protagonist will often utilize new perceptions and his or her available creativity to formulate more effective role behaviour for solving the problem. If necessary, such techniques as modelling and role-training can aid in this process. Opportunities for practising are provided. At the end of this phase, the protagonist is likely to feel more competent in his or her ability to cope with the situation, regard himself or herself more positively, and frequently be able to gain a strong sense of group support and care. This, in turn, should support his or her motivation and determination for change.

Fine (1978) indicates that there are three aspects to change through psychotherapy: cognitive (thoughts and perceptions), affective (emotions and feelings) and behavioural (motivations and actions). The first stresses changes occurring through modification of the protagonist's beliefs about himself or herself and others, and enables more rational decisions to be made. The affective dimension focuses on the emotional release of blocked feelings (catharsis), while the third suggests that more effective behaviour is required (developing effective roles). As can be readily seen, with the psychodramatic method, all three are included. Psychodrama's potency is further enhanced in that it takes place in a group setting, thereby making the transition to everyday life easier than would be the case in individual therapy.

Blatner (1985) indicates that an important component of change through psychodrama lies in the fact that 'in the production of psychodramatic enactment, they are in fact practising the process of co-directing, of being in a sense the playwright of their own experience' (p. 56).

CASE EXAMPLE

Jo was a 40-year-old woman, married for 20 years with four children. I first met her in the outpatient unit of a psychiatric hospital in London. She had been advised to come following her second brief hospitalization for depression, suicidal thoughts and feelings of guilt and low self-esteem. Her family were interested in her welfare and her husband was supportive and involved.

In attempting to understand Jo, my goal was to gain a picture of her social atom, her effective and ineffective roles, and the range of roles available to her, as well as the earlier and current events which helped to form her basic attitudes to herself and others.

Jo was the eldest of three siblings, the others being younger brothers. Her father abandoned the family at an early age. Her mother was sickly and frequently bedridden. She demanded of Jo obedience and conformity, and controlled her through guilt, withdrawal of approval, and her infirmities. Jo, from nearly her earliest memories, recalled that she always was in the caretaker role. Saddled with initially having to help mother consistently around the house, and then by age ten, essentially taking over the role of mother, she strongly developed the roles of babysitter, cook, dishwasher and decision-maker. She learned these roles well, but at the expense of play and imagination; all of which gave her little opportunity for spontaneous interactions, or the development of her own spontaneity. At school she was lethargic and tired. Because she always had to go straight home after school, she had little peer contact. This situation was furthered by rejections from peers and ridicule by the teachers. Thus she suffered from restricted and unsatisfying social atoms both at home and at school. Coming from a different socioeconomic background than most of her peers led her to feel even more inadequate and different.

During childhood and adolescence she concentrated on roles which would win her mother's approval and acceptance. In early adolescence her social atom shifted dramatically and suddenly with the unpredicted death of her mother. Unfortunately this event occurred during one of the few times that Jo was developing a new role of rebellious teenager. She had refused to remain home one Saturday night to babysit her younger brothers and mother. At a school dance she was notified by the police, and racing home, discovered her mother had just died, leaving the following message: 'My death rests on your shoulders.' From there she went to a children's home while her brothers were fostered, increasing her sense of worthlessness. Here Jo become very withdrawn, but was obedient, tried hard to please, and was very helpful. In her roles she was very constricted and apparently insecure. The home was marked by frequent changes of staff and children. She remained there until she was 18 and then lived by herself, and worked as a waitress where she met her husband.

He was described as a kindly man but as one who believed in the traditional stay-at-home role for his wife. They have four children. When she became a mother, she functioned much as she had in her first family.

When she felt very depressed and consumed with guilt she entered the local psychiatric hospital. This gave her temporary relief, perhaps because for the moment she was able to take more of a care-receiver role. Essentially, however, her condition did not continue to improve, and the manifestations of psychological disturbance were maintained.

With consultation, Jo formulated the following goals:

1. Provide for a corrective emotional experience which could release her from her guilt and suppressed anger, and meet the act-hungers for love and approval.
2. Modify her critical attitude towards herself.
3. Get free from her role-locked position by developing more appropriate roles (expand her role repertoire), especially in the area of care-receiver,

and those which would bring her satisfactions.
4. Develop and maintain a more open social structure which would support change and bring more satisfaction in interpersonal relationships.

Jo joined an ongoing open-ended psychodrama group for outpatients. It met weekly for three hours, and consisted of about 15 members. Initially she was quiet and rarely expressed herself. However, with the support of the group, their general interest, and accepting, non-critical attitude, she began to relate events in her life. Her first experience on the psychodramatic stage occurred when she was chosen (not surprisingly) for the role of caring mother. Lest she become role-locked, I began to make therapeutic role assignments, frequently selecting her whenever the role requirements allowed Jo to be nurtured, assertive or demanding so that she could safely experience these new roles.

Eventually, Jo asked for time in the group to talk about her mother's death. Greatly encouraged by the group's interest and suggestion that she do an enactment, she proceeded. She began the action by creating the kitchen on the psychodramatic stage and enacting a scene where she was trying to serve dinner, discipline the boys and meet her mother's demands. Jo became restricted, compliant and tearful. She resisted any expression of anger, but continued to try to please.

In the second scene, she informed her mother that she was going to the dance, and in spite of her mother's attempts to keep her at home, Jo went. Several other group members spontaneously enjoy the dance scene, enhancing their own and Jo's spontaneity. This scene is now interrupted by the arrival of the police, who inform her of her mother's imminent death. Using surplus reality, mother this time has not died, and accuses Jo of causing her approaching death. Jo breaks into tears, throwing herself upon mother's bed, begging for forgiveness, exclaiming that she had never meant for mother to die. Jo promises to be good always if only mother will live (and the astute double re-emphasized – 'Always'). I ask Jo to reverse roles with her dying mother who is seeing her daughter for the last time. The auxiliary (now as Jo) asks 'her mother' (now Jo) for her forgiveness, and if she really blamed her? Softening, suddenly, and in a very sincere, moving voice, 'mother' (Jo) forgave her daughter, and indicated that she never really held her responsible. 'I only said that because I wanted you to feel guilty for leaving the boys and me alone. It was not your fault.' And spontaneously, without prompting, Jo (still as mother) told 'her daughter' how much she did appreciate all that she had done. Reversing back to herself, Jo then allowed herself to receive her mother's forgiveness.

Suspecting that underlying her grief was anger, I invited Jo's double to portray (as a mirror) Jo as that obedient, helpful little girl seen in the first scene. Watching this portrayal, Jo was very moved, and when she was invited to say what she wished, she began to express her anger for the way her mother had treated her. Voice raised, fist shaking (with the physical and verbal support of her double), Jo ventilated some of her anger. When she finished, she smiled broadly and said: 'That felt really good; I should have done that a long time ago.'

In that session two other scenes took place. In the first, Jo 'met' her mother again – this time Jo was herself, at her then current age. Summarizing the scene that occurred. Jo enacted elements of forgivenness, presented herself as a competent and worthwhile person, and shared her accomplishments with her mother (whom she did love); Jo also checked again that her mother really did not hold her responsible for her mother's death. This provided additional confirmation and relief, and strengthened the changes which were beginning to occur.

People often ask 'How can Jo be sure of her mother's forgiveness?' The answer lies in that Jo's 'mother' who will or will not grant the forgiveness is the mother that Jo has internalized – the mother that Jo carries within herself. In a sense, it is for Jo to decide whether she can forgive herself. In the psychodramatic context, conditions are such that the protagonist is able to reach a higher level of spontaneity and can evolve a more creative response as we have just noted.

For repair work, and to satisfy additional act hungers for approval and love, a final scene placed Jo in a new family which desired and loved her. Equally important for the development of a new role and in the formation of this psychodramatic family, Jo was able to make decisive choices as to whom she wanted to play the various roles. She successfully chose individuals who would be able to give her warmth, support, love and praise, and not those (as I initially feared) who required what she was seeking, thus casting her back into familiar roles. A typical day in a five-year-old's life was presented, full of joy, adventure and spontaneous play. The 'parents' were particularly effective in conveying a real sense of pride and pleasure in their daughter; she was encouraged to try new things as well. The scene ended with the parents tucking her up in bed, with warm hugs and loving, nurturing exchanges. That it was potent for her and many others in the group was revealed through the many misty eyes.

Jo returned to the circle, and initially there was a warm silence, everyone sitting with their arms around their neighbour, but Jo's double holding her with both arms. Slowly participants shared their identifications, and praised Jo's courage and perseverance.

In the sessions that followed, Jo rehearsed confronting her husband with her wish for greater freedom, and slowly she began to develop new roles. She joined a local choir and occasionally went to films with new-found friends, many from the group. In another session, she indicated that she had become friendly with a man, and wanted to pursue a friendship with him, but did not know how to go about it. Using models, mirroring and role reversals, plus a conversation with the part of herself (played by an auxiliary) that was fearful and discouraging, claiming she was spending too much time away from the home (not at all realistic), she gained sufficient confidence and permission to follow through with her wish.

In one of her final sessions, she confronted herself (using multiple doubles and role reversals) around the issues of her high demands and critical attitude when she failed to meet those self-imposed standards.

Over the eight months in the group, she maintained a much improved and expanded social structure, and continued to receive warm support from the group members. Each year I have received a brief note from Jo, and she has had no further deep depressions nor has she required hospitalization. She sometimes still gives herself a hard time, but is able to manage that, often by reminding herself of the work she did on this, and the group's very reassuring and positive feedback to her which followed. She had continued, with her family growing up and her husband more accepting of her outside life, to maintain and expand her social structures, and is involved with many outside activities which she enjoys.

REFERENCES

Berne, E. (1970) Book review, *American Journal of Psychiatry*, Vol. 126.

Bischof, L. (1964) *Interpreting Personality Theories*, Harper & Row, New York.

Blatner, H. (1973) *Acting-in: Practical Applications of Psychodramatic Methods* Springer, New York.

Blatner, H. (1985) *Foundations of Psychodrama: History, Theory, Practice and Resources*, Blatner, PO Box 768, San Marcos, TX 78667–0768.

Fine, L, (1978) Psychodrama, in R. Corsini (ed.) *Current Psychotherapies* (2nd edn), F. E. Peacock, Itasca, Illinois.

Mendelson, P. (1976) Sociometry as a life philosophy. Paper presented at the 34th Annual Meeting of the American Society of Group Psychotherapy and Psychodrama, New York.

Moreno, J. L. (1940) Mental catharsis and the psychodrama, *Sociometry*, Vol. 3, pp. 209–44.

Moreno, J. L. (ed.) (1945) *Group Psychotherapy: A Symposium*, Beacon House, Beacon, NY.

Moreno, J. L. (1946) *Psychodrama*, Vol. 1, Beacon House, Beacon, NY.

Moreno, J. L. (1969) *Psychodrama*, Vol. 3, Beacon House, Beacon, NY.

Moreno, J. L. (1974) The creativity theory of personality: spontaneity, creativity and human potentialities, in I. Greenberg (ed.) *Psychodrama: Theory and Therapy*, Souvenir Press, London.

Moreno, Z. (undated) *Rules and techniques*, Unpublished paper.

Starr, A. (1977) *Rehearsal for Living: Psychodrama*, Nelson Hall, Chicago.

Stein, M. and Callahan, M. (1982) The use of psychodrama in individual psychotherapy, *Journal of Group Psychotherapy, Psychodrama and Sociometry*, Vol. 35, No. 3, pp. 118–29.

Suggested further reading

Blatner, H. (1973) *Acting-in: Practical Applications of Psychodramatic Methods*, Springer, New York.

Blatner, H. (1985) *Foundations of Psychodrama: History, Theory, Practice and Resources*, Blatner, PO Box 768, San Marcos, TX 78667–0768.

Greenberg, I. (ed.) (1974) *Psychodrama: Theory and Therapy* , Souvenir Press, London.

Moreno, J. L. 1946) *Psychodrama*, Vol. 1, Beacon House, Beacon, NY.

Moreno, J. L. (1969) *Psychodrama*, Vol. 3, Beacon House, Beacon NY.

CHAPTER 7

BIOENERGETICS

Geoffrey Whitfield

HISTORICAL CONTEXT AND DEVELOPMENTS IN BRITAIN

Historical context

Alexander Lowen opened his workshop in London in 1975 by saying 'Bioenergetics is a psychotherapy which seeks to harmonize the body and the mind.'

Bioenergetic therapy was evolved by Dr Alexander Lowen who was himself a client and pupil of Wilhelm Reich, who was a colleague of Sigmund Freud. Bioenergetic analysis owes its roots to Freud for his understanding of analytical material, to Reich for his understanding of character armour and structure (i.e. chronic muscular tensions and the shape of the body), and to Lowen for bringing together the work of these two men plus his own integration of the grounding and breathing principles that combine to make the basis of bioenergetic therapy.

In 1958 Lowen set up the Institute of Bioenergetic Analysis and since then the movement has attracted a following throughout the world. It has developed in the United States of America from New York and the Eastern Seaboard through a number of states to the West Coast where there are strong state organizations in California and elsewhere.

It has many affiliate organizations in Canada and there is growing interest in South America. In Europe too there have been training programmes resulting in the formation of viable societies in France, West Germany, Holland and Belgium. Thus, while there may have been critics, it has attracted a significant following in the professional therapeutic world.

A journal was commenced in 1985, under the editorship of Philip Helfaer of Connecticut, to gather together material of particular interest to those acquainted with bioenergetics. The Institute offers a biannual international conference for members to meet where presentations are given and exchange of ideas is encouraged. These are held in different countries and alternate between the European and North American continents. The major concern of the Institute is the training of existing professionals and the maintenance of adequate standards. While this is an appropriate concern, there is much work still to be done to ensure that those standards apply to everyone within the organization. It will take time to develop and organize this and other issues critical to standards of professional training.

It will be interesting to see if the Institute is able to avoid many of the hazards that befall young organizations. Certainly, there are differences of opinion within the membership of the Institute and, while there is much tolerance, the Institute sometimes functions in an authoritative manner with a high degree of centralized control in the hands of a few.

Bioenergetic analysis is the term used by those who are affiliated to the International Institute of New York. Naturally there are many people who are involved with bioenergetic therapy who are outside that particular framework. Not everyone who practises bioenergetic therapy in England has necessarily had anything to do with the organization in New York, nor indeed do many of those who practise bioenergetics in fact have recognition by that Institute, nor even do they seek it. Doubtless, in the future, bioenergetics will find its own way of growing and developing, but few would doubt the immense debt that is owed to Reich and Lowen for their massive contribution to the understanding of body–mind therapy.

Developments in Britain

Prior to any formal training programme being established, David Boadella, a contributor to this book and then an educationalist in Dorset, created and edited a journal for bioenergetic research entitled *Energy and Character*. This has proved a lively and informative publication which is widely appreciated by many in the therapeutic world. Dr Frank Lake in 1969 referred to the work of Alexander Lowen in his pamphlet on the schizoid personality. The Boyesen Centre in Acton, London, had its own therapeutic and educational emphasis on body energy and doubtless this will be referred to elsewhere in this book.

Eventually, in 1978, a formal structured training programme became available to professional therapists in Britain. Until 1976 the normal pattern organized by the International Institute was for professionals to attend a number of weekend workshops, usually on a monthly basis, for four years, which were normally centred in New York (although various state organizations sometimes set up their own training programmes elsewhere). Clearly it was not viable for British professionals to travel regularly to New York for their training.

In 1976 I attended the Biannual Convention in New Hampshire, USA, and discussed with Alexander Lowen and others the possibility of bringing a trainer from the United States to Britain for three separate weeks each year. This took two years to establish but, in September 1978, the first training workshop was held at the University of Sussex. The trainer was Dr Myron Koltuv, who later, with Dr Scott Baum and Dr Harry Brown, became the training team and I was the British training co-ordinator and took part in the training programme as a trainee.

From the outset it was very difficult to attract sufficient interest in England from professionals who wished to be trained in bioenergetic analysis. The costs were very high by British standards and the criterion demanded for would-be trainees was also very exacting, that is, they had to be willing to undertake the training workshops together with personal therapy and, later, personal supervision. It was expected that they would be academically and/or professionally qualified prior to undertaking what amounted to postgraduate specialist training. Fortunately there was sufficient attendance from the European professionals, principally from Belgium, to enable the programme to develop. Although it always struggled to be viable, the training programme was eventually completed. Training progammes are still available in Europe, that is, Belgium, France and Germany, and others may be in the process of being developed.

The nature of the four-year minimum training means that many find the course too demanding and not every programme is completed. There are also difficulties with organization, leadership and accreditation which sometimes create conflict. There have been accusations of high-handedness and insensitivity and as yet there is no platform for grievances to be discussed in a supportive and clarifying environment. Criticism is not always readily heard nor willingly scrutinized but, hopefully, a readiness to listen and respond, rather than react, will become part of the growth of this virile and creative organization.

THEORETICAL ASSUMPTIONS

Image of the person

Bioenergetics is a development of the Freudian theories of psychodynamics taken to a somatic and expressive level. It sees human problems having their origins in the afflictions of early life; anxieties and stresses are the conse-quences of, and defences against, the eruption into the present of those intolerable events which, stored in memory, are reactivated by a present experience. The combination of conflict in the present making connections with the past induces a loss of well-being and the onset of the threat of non-existence which is manifested in a variety of psychological and physical disturbances.

The analytical work of Freud is inadequate in bioenergetic terms. The psychological trauma is profoundly expressed in physical terms which Reich called *character armour*. While the basic Freudian psychosexual develop-ment is seen as fundamental to the understanding of the person, bioener-getics sees physical manifestations of character tension and armouring which also must be attended to if there is to be therapeutic effectiveness. For example, there are limitations for a person with a masochistic character structure, in bioenergetic terms, understanding his burden-bearing nature but who concludes therapy still with bowed shoulders and a stoop. His body must be in harmony with his mind so that the energy of the body is available to him.

Bioenergetic therapy believes in the growth of the person rather than cure. Alexander Lowen said in 1976 at the biannual conference in New Hampshire: 'We do not believe in cure.' Nothing can stop the past being reactivated. We need to find ways of letting people live with their problems in a profoundly different way so they are unfettered by the past and go on to enjoy life. Thus, there is a deeply humanistic element, stemming from a Freudian base. This optimism is due to a profound belief in the value of the person and his or her capacity to overcome the distress of the past and move on to a richer dimension of life.

Concepts of psychological health and disturbance

Psychological health is to be found in the harmony of the body and mind. Energy produced by the body should not be used to maintain tensions and defences but to create a consciousness of authority and aliveness resulting in the feeling of well-being and pleasure. This emphasis on the body as well as the mind is fundamental at a time when society has psychosomatic illness and distress at such unprecedented levels.

Lack of psychological health is revealed by a loss of energy and adequate breathing, absence of spontaneity and graceful movement and in the inhibition of self-expression. When the body is tense it cannot be freed simply by exertion or relaxation, for tension is only a symptom of the difficulty. It is, however, not only a symptom but a signpost to the origins of the presenting need. It thus provides the direction for inquiry so that therapeutic intervention can be effective in the diagnosis and treatment of psychological disturbances.

> This emphasis on the body includes sexuality . . . but it also includes the even more basic functions of moving, breathing, feeling and self expression. A person who doesn't breathe deeply reduces the life in his body. If he doesn't move freely he restricts the life of the body. If he doesn't feel fully he narrows the life of his body. And if his self expression is restricted he limits the life of his body.
>
> (Lowen, 1975).

When acquired in early life psychological disturbance results in unnecessary body shapes and tensions which are perpetuated throughout the years. Bioenergetic therapy indicates where the trauma is located in the body and provides an opportunity for reliving those traumas and expressing the hitherto repressed material, thereby producing a body with a new shape and a new flow of energy which is available to develop a new way of life for the person concerned.

The concept of psychological health seeks a free flow of energy coursing through the body of the individual giving vitality, energy and pleasure. Clues to the original disturbance lie where the energy is visibly restricted, and where there are tensions is further evidence of unresolved traumatic experiences. Where there is no pleasure in life and instead there is anxiety, depression, neurosis and even detachment from the person and those around him or her, this psychological disturbance will be revealed in a multitude of presenting somatic patterns. This is the area of bioenergetic therapy.

Acquisition of psychological disturbance

Until recently the acquisition of psychological disturbance has always been centred in the life of the child from birth until the end of the Oedipal phase. However, it is seen by some who practise bioenergetics and who have been influenced by the work of the late Dr Frank Lake (1981) that one has to consider prebirth issues. It is considered possible that significant tensions are formed within the body of the unborn child as a result of the traumas it has received while still in the womb because of the mother's own tensions and difficulties. It would not be fair to say that this point of view has been given a great deal of space in bioenergetic literature to date. These are early days and much more research and observation needs to be done before anything other than cautious propositions can be considered. When the infant experiences psychological pain it will use its body to cut off from the pain by tensing of the muscles. In addition, if there is no adequate outlet for the release of the feelings that go with the suffering, it will further tense the body to contain those feelings. The result is a body that is shaped by the misuse of the muscles to absorb hurt and control the responses which would be unacceptable if expressed. This results in the bioenergetic concept of character armour and leads us to the five basic structures of character analysis (Reich, 1961).

It needs to be stressed that rarely are there pure types of character structure. Most of us have a mixture of more than one and these need to be dealt with in the complicated intertwining of different issues. For the sake of simplicity, let me deal with, in turn, the way the physical disturbance of the early years is acquired in the body by identifying each separate character structure.

The schizoid character

The *schizoid* character is by definition split off from himself or herself and from others. It is diagnosed by Alexander Lowen (1969) as having been established at birth or soon after because of the hostility of the mother towards the child. This is particularly communicated through the hostile gaze of and physical handling by the mother of the newborn infant which causes the child to be terrified. In order to separate from its own terror and to detach itself from the antagonism of the mother, it cuts off from its body awareness and identifies with the mother in negative feelings against itself.

The oral character

The *oral* character is one who has experienced being abandoned in the first nine months of life by a mother who may have loved it at one time, indeed probably did, but unfortunately failed to offer the consistency of love that the child needed at this time of dependency. This has been made clear since the post-war period and particularly in 1975 by the work of Mahler. The child having experienced abandonment is constantly searching for the warmth and love which has been removed at a catastrophic level. Therefore it is always in a state of vulnerability and near to collapse; it is always seeking, yearning, longing for the restoration of the blissful nature of that bonded, symbiotic relationship with the mother.

The psychopathic character

In Britain the term *psychopathic* character has criminological connotations but that is not what is meant here. The psychopathic character is someone who has been controlled and overpowered, normally by the father. As a youngster of two or more it decides that having been overpowered there is only one way to survive in life and that is to overpower everybody else. So they become either aggressive or passive psychopathic characters.

The masochistic character

The *masochistic* character has been swamped and smothered by the mother. By two or three years of age an infant has experienced having its rights taken away and not allowed to have any needs of its own; its major task is to carry the burdens of those around it. Saint Christopher might well be his or her patron saint.

The rigid character

The *rigid* character is someone who metaphorically has a steel chest. He or she gives the impression of being able to relate well and this is because normally he or she has had a fairly untraumatic life experience thus far. However, at the age of three or four he or she experiences the tragedy of having his or her heart broken by some outside event. It is my personal belief that the rigid character is an early manifestation of Oedipal material when the child's early sexuality is rebuffed by a fearful parent.

Perpetuation of psychological disturbance

Each individual will perpetuate his or her own body shape/structure with little conscious awareness that he or she is so doing. For example, if a male learns to be a burden bearer in early life, his shoulders will retain the distinctive bearing shape of the masochistic character. While his behaviour will normally also reflect this, there equally may be reaction patterns of behaviour to disguise the early hurts or to compensate for them and their consequences. This principle would be so for all character structures in each individual.

The schizoid character is someone who lives very much with his or her cognitive awareness rather than the emotional side of his or her life. The person becomes out of touch with his or her process and feelings and this is reflected somatically in the lack of vitality in the body and in the eyes. The eyes are not completely detached as with the schizophrenic, but they do not connect easily with people. The body is nearly always one that is lean, has no nourishment and has little sense of being other than a burden that has to be carried around for the rest of life. Often, with a rueful smile, he or she will admit to having no awareness of his or her body whatsoever. Unconsciously, there is normally a profound sense of antipathy and hostility towards the self believing that 'In me dwelleth no good thing.' This negative view of the self becomes very destructive and makes therapeutic work difficult.

The oral character constantly seeks for intimacy. Sadly, because of its own sense of having been abandoned it will always act this out and expect to be abandoned later. Therefore his or her relationships are often temporary and very volatile. The body shape is frequently round and soft and has a quality of longing and the need for support because it has collapsed. The significant part of the oral character structure is seen particularly at the sternum where there is nearly always a depression. One might say in metaphorical language that they have a hole in the heart. And certainly that, emotionally, is what the infant experiences.

The psychopathic character is always needing to control a relationship and have the people to whom they are relating in bondage either by their passivity or by their aggressiveness. If they cannot control a relationship, their own lives or what they are involved in, they are in danger of collapse. Actually, the psychopath is trying to compensate for his or her own internal collapse, which is close to the oral position where the love was never given and sustained. The body shape shows the chest being held up as though needing to be standing over someone rather than being stood over. In contrast, the legs are usually very underdeveloped and relatively weak.

The masochistic character has classic burden-bearing shoulders which contain the rage and resentment at his or her own loss of freedom. The buttocks are tensed, with considerable restriction in the pelvis, which inhibits freedom of sexual movement and expression. The chest is also restricted by the holding in against humiliation and there is powerful loathing turned in against the self.

The rigid character has resolved never to allow his or her heart to move out again in an intimate relationship and to risk emotional injury once more. Therefore he or she may be able to relate extremely successfully in all sorts of ways – socially, personally and so on. However, at the deepest level, they are never able to combine the surrender of their hearts with intimate relationships, particularly at the level of sexuality. On the one hand, their sexuality always gives rise to acute anxiety and, on the other hand, relationships will be devoid of rich sexual satisfaction when intimacy is part of the relationship.

These are the five basic patterns of psychological disturbance which are perpetuated in life.

PRACTICE

Goals of therapy

There will be four major factors when working with a client in bioenergetic therapy; they are: character analysis, grounding, breathing and energy. Whatever the presenting problem may be, the critical issue of character structure is central to the therapeutic process. If a client presents himself or herself with depression, that will only be explored in the context of his or her character structure, that is, the permanent issues which are visible in the body, of which the presenting problem is only perhaps an indication. For the purpose of diagnosis, which is critical to therapeutic effectiveness, the knowledge and use of character analysis is fundamental. One of the goals in therapy is to alter that character structure so that the tensions and armouring are eliminated, and where necessary, physical posture is altered. Then the body may take a more harmonious and free expression of movement, unhindered by the earlier character structure.

The second factor is that of grounding. In his earlier work with John Pierrakos, Alexander Lowen found that instead of working in the horizontal position of vulnerability, it was more beneficial to work standing in an upright position (Lowen, 1975). By doing this clients not only physically contact the ground with their feet, they also discover their body and their authority to stand for themselves in life instead of leaning on other supports like a spouse or a job, illness, fame or wealth, etc. Fear of falling is a basic human fear. Persons who experience such fear are rarely in full contact with the ground, although they touch the ground when they stand or walk. The therapist will always have grounding as one of the ongoing focal points for this client.

The third factor is breathing. While everyone breathes, those who are anxious or under stress will usually breathe less. Reich found that the holding of one's breath reduced the person's contact with pain, both physical and emotional. We all know this by experience. Part of the wince response to pain which enables us to control the feeling is to hold the breath and tighten the muscles. Thus contact with the pain is diminished. This may be effective, but eventually it becomes a learned, unconscious process to cut off feelingful contact with the distress in our bodies caused by emotional and physical needs. To increase the breathing increases the contact with the feeling which may be temporarily distressing, but if the breathing is developed, it is possible for the feelings to be released. This discharge of feelings may be dramatic but it means that the body is released from tension and the breathing is available to energize and nourish the body.

The fourth factor is the principle of energy. Energy is visible in the body by the colour of the skin, the temperature of the body and the movement of the muscles. Where a person is free from stress there will be bodily harmony which includes the free flowing energy within the person. The bodies of most clients who present themselves with a problem will indicate a lack of energy. This is often due to a holding back of the energy because it is connected to a withheld expressive force. Where there is a breathing, grounded, tension-free person, the energy produces a sense of being alive. Where the energy is locked up, there is a lack of vitality. Thus therapeutic effectiveness will include dealing with the resistance to the spontaneous energetic flow so that energy is available to the body for its vital and harmonious functioning.

The goals of therapy naturally depend on what is actually wrong with the person. The following is a brief synopsis of therapeutic goals for each of the five character structures. These brief statements do not deal with the difficulties and time factors which are involved and the reader is referred to specialized references at the end.

The schizoid character

The persons who have a major schizoid issue are those who have generally had a terrifying experience at birth or soon after, which has taught them to split from their bodily awareness for that is the place where they meet their suffering. It is not enough only to talk to these clients in analytical terms. The client needs to begin to discover that he or she is out of feelingful contact with his or her body. I remember a client who said to me that he did not realize he was crying until he felt the wet running down his cheeks. If in fact he can be facilitated to go through this process of impasse he can begin to realize that he does not have to live outside his body and he can go on to find ways of exploring meaningful relationships.

The oral character

For the oral characters therapy is of course quite different. These persons need no introduction to their body: they are consumed with messages coming from a variety of sources from within themselves. However, the psychological experience is of deep, desperate pain and anguish, with the sense of being in daily threat to their life. The goal for this person is to meet the experience of early childhood abandonment and to express that violence and rage at the beloved object, who not only removed the infant from the sense of being loved, but removed themselves as well. Because the body of the oral is very ungrounded and unsupported it is crucial to work with the legs in order to enable the client to find the authority within his or her own body. Then the client can support himself or herself, and find that he or she does not need to collapse when feeling the old fears threatening his or her very existence.

The masochistic character

The goal for masochists is to learn to have needs of their own and to meet those needs and not see their life as being constantly in the service of others. Repeatedly, masochists will slip back into those well-tried areas of needing to take care of everybody and needing to be very understanding of those who afflicted, smothered and seduced them. For the masochist to release pent-up rage against the smothering by mother is pivotal. The release of the energy in the shoulders not only expresses the buried resentment but begins the move towards freedom from the burden of guilt which so successfully kept him or her in bondage through the years. The release of pelvic tensions provides a gateway for the discovery of the full range of sexual potency.

The psychopathic character

The goal working with psychopathic characters is to enable the clients to let themselves experience their concealed vulnerability instead of using their energy for control and power as their defence. When a person's life has been centred on power and control, to ask him or her to relinquish them and become vulnerable and open is a massive task. One has to meet the ultimate sense of shame and impotence which was such a dread-filled experience when the parent was overpowering the child at a tender age. This means developing the energy in the legs to provide a real sense of authority and integrity in the body, together with melting the upheld chest, with its pride and fear, into surrender and vulnerability.

The rigid character

The goal for rigid characters is to open their heart to its tenderness and its softness so that they can release the feelings held within the steel-like ribcage which has protected them from further heartbreak which they originally experienced in excruciating reality in the formative years. The rigid character finds it difficult to reach out and be open to his or her own need. The rejection of those original yearnings meant not only pain but shame for having such feelings.

In addition there is great anxiety about sexual feelings because of the way they were responded to in the early years and through the Oedipal phase. This created great confusion about feelings of love in the heart and sexual expression of the body. Therefore the two issues are necessarily kept separate from each other. For the sexual erotic feelings to combine with the open heart of tender love is a therapeutic objective with considerable obstacles to overcome.

The 'person' of the therapist

I have already described the training requirements for the therapist. Just as important as the training, however, is the nature of the therapist. It is important that bioenergetic therapists convey within themselves some of the elements of integrity, authority, groundedness and resolved conflicts. It would be hoped that they would represent, not an élite corps of super therapists, but humble students of therapy themselves, always seeking for their own ongoing therapy and supervision. It would be unlikely for a therapist with adequate training to see clients as character structures; rather he or she would see them as persons, in a full Rogerian sense, despite the emphasis in this chapter on much technical detail. Their empathetic resonance would convey their own sensitivity to the pain, defences and resistances of the client. Defences are seen as survival mechanisms, to be respected rather than scorned.

In common with Freudian analysts bioenergeticists work closely with the positive and negative transference. Because of the work that takes place with the body of the client the transferential material becomes clear in the very early stages of the therapy and continues throughout. They would be sufficiently sophisticated to work continuously with these factors and seek supervision for themselves to deal with their own countertransference which will also be a strong element in the therapeutic process. When the therapists are without supervision, they have succumbed to hubris or the pride of believing that they can see all the issues in their client and be untouched within themselves.

Because they are unlikely to believe in cure, but rather the growth and development of the person at emotional and somatic levels, they will see themselves as fellow travellers with their client, and both on the same road. At the same time, they are the ones who have learned about their own defences, character structure, and energy flow and so are able to offer insights and support so that the client can respond to his or her own rising levels of awareness.

The diagnostic element which plays a large part in bioenergetic therapy is seen, not as labelling a person with an irremovable blemish but as friendly information for the client to use to enter more deeply into the significance of the uncovering of his or her own issues. The basic disciplines of empathy and respect, when combined with the therapist's awareness of his or her own pathology, produce a support system for the client which results in the creation of a team of two therapists, one of whom is the client. This humble awareness is powerfully creative in the therapeutic process. Therapists offer themselves with the authenticity of those who, knowing of their own pain and suffering, seek to facilitate others in their quest for release from the fixations of the past and to live creatively in the present.

Therapeutic style

This is a highly individual matter because each therapist will have his or her own style. However, there may be a number of common factors.

Because therapists are working largely with the unconscious they will make a great number of interpretations. This is not always well received and the therapists will need to beware of opening themselves to the charge of arrogance. Thus while some practitioners have given the impression of bioenergetic therapy being a noisy event with heavy interventions to produce maximum effect, my experience is that the more sophisticated are likely to be fairly relaxed about their interventions and the way they are offered.

Considerable attention will be focused on the environment of the practice. For example, I have armchairs where the client can sit comfortably and talk at an intellectual and emotional level. However, there is also a changing room where the client can change into appropriate clothing, normally shorts for men and shorts and a top for women. They are encouraged to bring their own clothing if they so desire. There are a variety of mirrors so that the client can see his or her body full length and at different angles so that from the outset he or she can observe both posture and character structure. The room will contain a number of features. It is well-bounded with sound-reducing components, for example, double-glazing, heavy curtains, padded walls. The colours are soft and harmonious and the room temperature comfortable. I have a variety of accessories: a mattress for working in positions of vulnerability, a heavy punchbag for clients to strike and kick, cushions of various sizes for holding and hitting. The indispensable tool is the breathing stool which is used for clients to develop their breathing and which will be referred to later in greater detail.

The style of each therapist will be an individual matter but attention will be focused on the harmony of the body and mind, or lack of it. Bioenergetics has sometimes been accused of overemphasis on the body to the exclusion of the mind and certainly I have experienced practitioners who have made this explicit. However, this would be more a comment on themselves than the therapy model. Thorough bioenergetic work involves the interaction of the body and the mind. It follows from this that there will be a great deal of interpretation by the therapist, especially in the early stages of therapy.

Major therapeutic techniques

There is a variety of techniques available to the bioenergetic practitioner and I will confine myself to those of breathing, grounding and discharge. In practice they are interwoven but for the sake of clarity I will endeavour to refer to them as separate techniques.

Breathing

Reich emphasized breathing as the root of energy. This is the critical factor for the flow of energy, because breathing enables the person's body to become oxygenated and alive. When one breathes deeply, the muscle blocks and tensions are revealed because it is possible to see where the flow of energy is limited or halted. So breathing is of critical importance, both diagnostically and therapeutically. The energy flow of the person can be seen first through the movement of the body, second in the temperature of the body, and third in the colour of the skin. It is possible to see where the energy flows and does not flow. Thus, somebody who may have blue or white hands indicates not only lack of energy but where in fact there is a psychotherapeutic issue. The task of the therapist is to ask what those hands really want to do. Do they want to reach out to love or to destroy or something else?

One matter which is still in fact a mystery is the connection between breathing and memory. It does seem clear that when someone's body becomes energized through deep breathing, a memory system is opened up to those deeply buried recesses of the mind and it is then possible to have greater access to the hidden material of the unconscious. The circulation and respiratory systems work harmoniously to provide not only energy but evidently access to the past also. Deep breathing also assists the release of muscular tensions. Exercises which produce deep breathing are plentiful, for example jumping, hopping, striking, etc.

The bioenergetic breathing stool, over which the client leans backwards, produces immense stress on the held chest and enables the client to release the holding and to breathe deeply. This release can also open the hidden psychological traumas which were concealed by the musculature armouring.

The stool itself is about 21 inches (55 cm) high with a padded top over which a client can place himself or herself in a variety of positions, depending on the place of tension and the appropriate need at the time. It is a conventional technique, commonly used in bioenergetic therapy for it is effective in enabling clients to contact their body, their breathing and their feelings.

Lastly, breathing is used as one of the techniques to enable a person to support himself or herself. Breathing produces the energy for a collapsed body to support itself. To fail to breathe sufficiently is to have an unenergized body which will not function with effectiveness and will need alternative support systems. Thus breathing techniques are critical not only for diagnosis, memory and release, but also for energizing and the creation of a somatic life-support system.

Grounding

Grounding has not always been well explained but it is simply and profoundly the principle of persons using their legs to contact the ground and thus be in touch with the authority in their own bodies. They are able to find that they can stand in the world instead of being metaphorically swept off their feet by the pressures and demands of the past or present.

Having stated it fairly simply, I must also say that this is very difficult for people to achieve, particularly if they have spent their lives operating 'in their heads' or those who are always in threat of collapse like the oral or psychopathic clients. The techniques or exercises to achieve grounding sound simple but take time and patience before the feelings of authority become available to the client.

The first grounding technique or exercise can be called a bioenergetic stance, which is to stand upright, with feet shoulder-distance apart, toes slightly turned in, the weight on the balls of the feet, the knees, pelvis and neck soft, the head upright and the jaw relaxed, the breath drawn into the chest through an open mouth and exhaled richly so that the stomach moves. This enables the person to breathe fully and to have the benefit of an energized body. This is diagnostically creative, for the lack of energy due to holding will reveal therapeutic issues.

Another grounding technique is the arch or bow. Lowen (1975) shows that this has its roots in Taoist philosophy 'aimed at attaining harmony with the universe through a combination of body movement and breathing technique' (p. 74). The body is put into the shape of a bow by having the feet placed apart, with the shoulders above the feet, but the pelvis drawn forward so that there is a curved line or arch between the pelvis and the feet and the shoulders. The arms are drawn behind and fists placed on top of the buttocks. By breathing fully, the body will be energized and balanced, in harmony with itself.

A very simple technique which I use regularly is to take up the posture of the bioenergetic stance referred to above and then to lower the pelvis so that the client moves into his or her haunches until the heels are about to come off the ground. In this position which is close to the sitting position, stress is put on the legs and contact with the ground via the legs is quickly established.

Discharge

As the techniques of grounding and breathing produce energy or charge, so there are techniques which provide for the discharge of feelings. Most of us have unconscious aggressive and tender feelings that are repressed. So that clients can meet and own their concealed material they will need to be facilitated to express themselves verbally and physically. By its nature the character armour will defend the clients from those expressions because they will reveal the secret, frozen needs which have caused such affliction. There is a variety of striking techniques involving fists, sticks or arms in the prostrate, kneeling and upright positions. These will release the hidden aggression in the hands, arms, shoulders and back. Similarly, kicking the feet and legs will open up the locked aggression in the pelvis and legs.

Singing and shouting techniques will open the hurt and anger held in the throat, neck and chest. Vocal and verbal expression will normally accompany the striking and kicking activities also.

Of equal importance is to harness techniques which release the soft and tender feelings which are also held in the body. To ask for help, to express one's need, to admit one's vulnerability is difficult for many people and almost impossible for some. It would be usual to have the client lie down on a mattress on his or her back so that the client is in a vulnerable position, with feet flat on the mattress and knees raised so that contact with the ground is present. Many techniques can be implemented, for example reaching out with the arms, calling for the desired person, reaching out with the lips in a feeding, sucking movement, making verbal requests, such as, 'I need you', 'Please help me', etc. Such contrived behaviour can quickly lead to contact with reality and the discovery of deep loss, sadness and need. Equally it can lead to the discovery of rage at having been neglected, deprived or rejected. Therefore therapists must have a wide repertoire of skills so that they may accompany the client where the discoveries take them, that is, the ambivalent feelings of love and hate, reaching out and withdrawing. Being on a mattress, it is easy to move between the ambivalence of softness and anger, weeping and striking, demanding and surrendering, loving and hating.

To open the body to its sexuality can be effected in both the upright and prostrate positions. By breathing and grounding in the standing position a number of pelvic movements can be innovated, especially the gyration 'hula-hoop' movement. This is too clumsy in the prostrate position but apart from bouncing the pelvis (with care) and jerking the pelvis upwards in an assertive or aggressive movement, it is more limited.

The art of the therapist is to know when exercises are appropriate and how intense should be the nature of the application of the technique. One must bear in mind one of the principles of Dr Murrary Cox (1978) who speaks of the timing and depth of an intervention being two of the vital considerations for an effective therapeutic process.

The change process in therapy

When clients come to therapy there are numerous unspoken attitudes which need to be addressed. The clients will normally have a presenting problem which they will expect the therapist to resolve for them. Thus they probably see themselves in a lesser position as the patient or supplicant, while they see the therapist as superior or the expert. By attitude and expression, the therapist will seek to alter this distortion so that they may consciously work at the transferential issues together. Hopefully the clients will gradually move from their attitude at the commencement of therapy to the point where they become their own facilitator and therapist. The paradox is that without the therapist they would not make this transition. Nonetheless, the therapist will continually be nudging the client to become responsible for his or her own growth and development. This will mean that therapists have to create a safe environment for the client to work in. They will have offered the client an authentic relationship out of personal integrity. They will also have worked so that the two persons form a therapeutic alliance where defences are respected and understood as critical survival kits from the past which are now obsolete.

Bioenergetic therapists will take note of all the material that is presented and give it attention because it is that which distresses the client and exhibits his or her need. However, they will also address themselves to the next layer of represented need which is the character structure of the body of the client. This 'body reading' not only will give information which goes beyond verbal expression but will indicate where deeper issues are awaiting therapeutic intervention.

This third layer is where the repressed and therefore unconscious material is stored. All the responses to the original violation need to be released. This means returning to that fourth layer of the vulnerable, needy infant who experienced the affliction. It is that vulnerable final injured core state which received almost the final *coup de grâce* by the client himself or herself, that is, the abhorrence toward his or her own vulnerability which will ally with the unconscious determination never again to be in that parlous state or even to acknowledge its existence.

While there may be much alternation in the ebb and flow of therapy nonetheless gradually through the therapeutic work these four layers, two external and two internal, will be revealed and clarified in detail. Ultimately two things are crucial for a satisfactory therapeutic resolution. One is to work so that the basic being of the person is respected as deserving of worth and value rather than disdain and abhorrence. The other is to expect a physical change in the body in terms of appearance and energy. It is expected in bioenergetic therapy that there will be significant physical alteration in the bodies of clients because of the recognition of and work on the musculature and posture of the clients. The outcome of these two factors would be expected to produce a change in the way clients relate to their intimates and their world.

CASE EXAMPLE

This case example will necessarily be abbreviated. It concerns a lady whom I shall call Ellen. She came to me in her sixties saying she was to retire in a few years' time and wanted to equip herself so that she could enjoy her retirement without the burdens which had been besetting her through all her years. She had been brought up on another continent, in a community of English expatriates and therefore had the typical English stiff upper-lip attitude, but more than that, her deep schizoid issues were seen in her body – clipped voice, narrow minimal breathing, and tensions throughout her body, through her neck, chest, stomach, pelvis, knees and ankles. Her body was split into two sections, the upper and lower halves not appearing to belong to each other; the top being underdeveloped and the bottom overdeveloped from the pelvis down. She had large legs which were to compensate for the fact that she had no confidence in them or her capacity to stand with a belief in her own authority. Certainly she had no energy in her body, but she had a good mind, being intelligent, educated and alert. Within her professional field she was highly skilled, well-considered by her peers, and constantly seeking to be creative within her work and with those for whom she was responsible.

The first issue became clear when she stood in the classic bioenergetic position because when she relaxed her mouth she began to weep and to weep copiously. She was immediately in touch with her deep sense of loss and gradually over a period of time she came to discover that her body was held in its position to protect her from the feelings of loss and sadness that she had experienced as a tiny infant and thereafter. She had experienced great deprivation in her infancy. Her mother was very young and anxious and found it difficult to cope in a foreign environment. The client felt alienated from her mother and within herself. She was hyperactive as a child, was deeply hurt by the behaviour of those who were supposed to make her feel loved and secure, and she felt devoid of any sense of personal worth and value. She became sick and had to return to England for medical treatment while still a child. In yet another foreign setting she was away from her familiar if unnurturing environment. Her medical situation deteriorated and she became permanently affected physically despite long periods of hospital care.

Her place in the family became one of being usurped by another sibling who was with the family when she finally returned to them after more than three years' separation. Because of her infirmity she felt awkward personally and socially. This compounded her earlier sense of anxiety and fear and she felt out of touch with herself, lacking in spontaneity and vitality. In therapy her sense of loss of any real awareness of well-being was expressed in great bouts of weeping. Later this gave way to the understanding that there was a reverse side to this sadness which was some fearful anger and rage because of the affliction she had experienced as the result of being treated with coldness, without feeling and with typical distancing which abounded in that culture at that time.

She spent some months working through the details of those two sides of the same coin; her loss and sadness on the one hand, and her anger and rage on the other, as this affected her contemporary life. She came to see that much of her contemporary relationships and present life was contaminated by the psychopathological issues which repeatedly presented themselves and clouded every relationship in which she was involved, both personally and professionally. She saw that her whole life was taken up with these contaminations from the past and, because she was keen and task-centred, she was able to greet each piece of information about her current situation as a discovery which would enable her to live differently.

Over the months her body softened and she began to have an awareness that within her plaster-cast of a body there was in fact a warm live person. With sensitivity and no little difficulty she gradually entered into an awareness of her sexuality and the prohibitions that were there. She had lived out of feelingful contact with her body all her life and the idea of its being the basis of pleasure and of surrendering to its natural, creative, sensual process evoked strong conflict. However, she knew of the possibility of release and its freedom which awaited her if she could overcome the daunting nature of the obstacles that were in front of her, that is, of meeting the vitality and sensuality lying beneath the tensions in her body.

Gradually she found her way through to allowing her legs to give her authority to stand in the world, so that she really felt them and experienced the energy and the confidence they could give her. Previously she had relied on those very large legs to support her, not because they had any energy or strength, but because she needed legs that size to hold her up. Otherwise she had nothing to support her. She became open to the energy that came to her through her breathing which then circulated in a body that was alive. Previously she had existed within a downward spiral of fear, which produced tension, followed by lack of breathing, resulting in the deadening of the body. Slowly she created an upward spiral by breathing, contacting her body, allowing the body to leave the tensions behind and receive the energy from the breathing. She not only became more open to herself, her own processes and her own awareness; she ventilated her anger and sadness repeatedly over a long period of time with the whole range of discharge techniques of striking, hitting and shouting. Gradually she found herself less poisoned by the early traumatic events and found that the cathartic experiences were indeed cleansing the bitterness that had contaminated her life over the years.

Her encounter with her vulnerability which she had protected through her life by cutting off from it, brought great fear. However, now supported by her body she could remain vulnerable and explore new ways of relating to people. This affected the way in which she saw herself and those around her. Her speech became different as well as her manner of addressing people. She became less critical and less negative. She also became more open to her husband and her family. She learned to reach out and to ask for help from those around her. She was able to rejoice in not only reparenting herself and making up to herself for what her parents had failed to give her, she also became able to heal the wounds they had created for her. So she moved beyond the constant battle with her parents to the point where she was able to make peace with them by seeing the restraints under which they had lived, and which they had passed on to her. She entered into the deep delights of becoming a grandmother, welcoming her own softness and vulnerability, able to live with a deep sense of peace and hope for the future.

She finished the therapy at the end of three years with strength for today and bright hope for tomorrow, conscious that she had begun on the pathway where she was able to leave the hobgoblins and foul fiends of the past. She found an openness towards herself and others even before her retirement years came to pass.

She has not been 'cured' for there is no such thing in bioenergetic therapy. She had found for herself a way out of her sharpness with people and herself, and this opened a way to be different with others. She found that her body could be a reservoir of support and good feelings for herself. She did not have to be tense and ill with psychosomatic ailments. She found a suppleness as she discovered the energy and vitality in her body. That discovery of the harmony was the beginning of a new appreciation of herself which could be rediscovered each day as she left behind the past struggles within her body. She was able to own her anger and need because she saw that there were good reasons for their existence, that is, the natural response to physical and mental suffering while unprotected as an infant and child.

She found a new appreciation of her parents within herself, though they had been long dead. She valued herself as a person, not because she had overcome her sins and failures but because she found she had a value in herself, as she existed in the present. This self-acceptance gave her a tranquillity, which was in marked contrast to the harsh self-critical attitude she had possessed earlier.

Just as important was her awareness that she was still on a journey. There had been no conclusion to her working on herself. Her past would still present itself and she could easily return to the old survival kits. However, with her psychological awareness combining with her body as a continuous, ongoing self-therapeutic activity she felt ready to conclude her formal therapy to her own satisfaction.

REFERENCES

Boadella, D., *Energy and Character*, Journal published by Abbotsbury Publications, Weymouth.

Cox, M. (1978) *Structuring the Therapeutic Process*, Pergamon, Oxford.

Lake, F. (1970) *Clinical Pastoral Care and Schizoid Personality Reactions*, p. 49, Clinical Theology Association, Oxford.

Lake, F. (1981) *Tight Corners in Pastoral Counselling*, Darton Longman and Todd, London.

Lewis, R. (1976) Premature ego development. Paper given to Biannual Convention of International Institute of Bioenergetic Analysis, New Hampshire.

Lowen, A. (1969) *The Betrayal of the Body*, Collier Macmillan, London.

Lowen, A. (1975) *Bioenergetics*, Penguin, Harmondsworth.
Lowen, A. and Lowen, L. (1977) *The Way to Vibrant Health*, Harper & Row, New York.
Mahler, M. (1975) *Psychological Birth of the Human Infant*, Basic Books, New York.

Suggested further reading

Lake, F. (1981) *Studies in Constricted Confusion*, Clinical Theology Association, Oxford.
Lowen, A. (1971) *Language of the Body*, Collier Macmillan, London.
Reich, W. (1961) *Character Analysis*, Simon & Schuster, New York.
Verny, T. (1982) *Secret Life of the Unborn Child*, Sphere, London.
Whitfield, G. (1982; 1984; 1986) Prebirth issues. Papers presented to Biannual Convention of International Institute of Bioenergetic Analysis, USA, Mexico and Belgium.

CHAPTER 8

BIOSYNTHESIS

David Boadella

HISTORICAL CONTEXT AND DEVELOPMENTS IN BRITAIN

Historical context

Biosynthesis is a somatic psychotherapy which I developed in the early 1970s. My approach grew out of many years' experience with Reichian therapy, so it is necessary first to give a brief background to Wilhelm Reich.

Reich was a psychoanalyst working with Freud in Vienna in the 1920s. He kept alive the early work of Freud and Breuer which focused on the energy-economy of the neurosis, and the expressive release of emotion. Reich developed his method of character-analysis in Vienna and Berlin, which saw the character as a defensive protection against threats to primary needs. Some years later, in Copenhagen and Oslo, Reich developed a method called *vegeto-therapy* which worked directly with the somatic roots of character resistance, in the form of a system of muscular tensions which Reich called *armouring*. The neurosis was physiologically anchored in these tensions and in associated disturbances in the rhythm of breathing. Reich saw the stasis of libido expressed as a stasis of sexual energy which resulted in reduced capacity for deep contact and gratification in orgasm. Vegeto-therapy used touch and expressive movement to elicit repressed impulses that were locked up in the muscular armour. The client was helped to recover the function of pulsation in the tissues and expressions, and this emerged spontaneously as the muscular armour was dissolved.

I received my personal therapy from Paul Ritter in Nottingham between 1952 and 1957, and subsequently took a further training in vegeto-therapy from Ola Raknes, Reich's principal therapist in Norway.

In the late 1960s two separate developments emerged out of the Reichian tradition and took root in London. The first of these was biodynamic psychology, a method developed by Gerda Boyesen in Oslo, which worked with a variety of forms of massage to free blocked energy. When she moved from Oslo to London in 1969 I set up her first professional seminars, published her theoretical papers, and led several dozen groups for therapists-in-training at the Boyesen Institute of Biodynamic Psychology. The second development was bioenergetic analysis, which was created by Alexander Lowen and John Pierrakos in New York. In 1968 I helped to arrange Lowen's first European workshop. Two years later I founded the *Journal of Bio-energetic Research*, and was invited by Lowen to be the guest at his first International Conference, in Mexico, in 1971. My journal published articles by all the leading therapists who wrote about bioenergetics. I subsequently worked as a guest trainer for a dozen or so bioenergetic training programmes.

My approach to therapy was powerfully influenced not only by Reich and his successors, but by a number of workers who emphasized the deep importance for the understanding of both health and sickness, of insights gained from embryology, and the study of life in the womb.

Foremost of these was Stanley Keleman, the director of the Centre for Energetic Studies, in Berkeley. Keleman has a broad and rich background not only at the Institute for Bio-energetic Analysis, where he is a senior trainer, but at the Centre for Religious Studies, led by Karlfried Durkheim in Germany; and with Nina Bull, director of Research for Motor Attitudes at the College of Physicians and Surgeons, Columbia University, New York. Keleman taught me how to read the expressive qualities of a person, the central importance of the *formative process*, and how to begin to understand the emotional anatomy of the body.

Developments in Britain

The term *biosynthesis* was first used by Francis Mott, an English analyst working with a configurational psychology rooted in depth studies of womb-life. Mott was a patient of Sandor Fodor, who had been a patient of Otto Rank. Mott was in discussion with Roberto Assagioli, the founder of psychosynthesis, one day. Mott said that his work was a biosynthesis because it dealt with the organic roots of the life-process in embryonic existence. In spite of this Mott however worked only psychologically: his principal tool was dream interpretation.

Mott's work was greatly expanded and developed by Frank Lake's research in England into prenatal psychology and primal integration. Frank Lake practised a deep form of regressive therapy that he developed in England during the 1950s, at first using LSD, and later, more effectively, by stimulating changes of consciousness due to deepened breathing. Lake was a therapist in the tradition of the British Object Relations approach, led by J. D. Fairbairn and Harry Guntrip. I introduced Frank Lake's dynamic approach to London, and began to see that my approach to therapy involved a bringing together of three different traditions that had developed from Freud: *one* traced through Reich, Lowen and Gerda Boyesen, focused on libidinal energy flow; *one* originating with Rank, and coming down to Francis Mott, focused on prenatal experience; and *one* coming through Melanie Klein, the object relations therapists, and Frank Lake, focused on the mother–infant relationship.

The integration of these approaches was first presented in a lecture I gave called 'Stress and Character' at the Tavistock Institute for Human Relations, London, in January 1974.

After Mott's death I adapted the word biosynthesis to cover my particular therapy and to distinguish it both from bioenergetics and biodynamics. The word means 'integration of life'. It was chosen to describe the fusion of three streams of libido which differentiate in the early weeks of embryonic life, which are regularly split up in neurotic states, and the integral functioning of which can be shown to be essential to somatic and psychic health. These concepts are fully described below.

In 1976 I was asked to become a director of the newly formed Institute for the Development of Human Potential in London, which had been set up by David Blagden Marks, the director of the first European Growth Centre. Here I taught the principles of therapeutic integration for six years. In 1982 I formed the Centre for Biosynthesis to co-ordinate a network of training groups which, originating in Britain, had now spread to 30 other countries in Europe, North and South America, Japan and Australasia. The Centre has no building and will resist becoming overattached to structures or organizational hierarchies. Biosynthesis is an open and not a closed system. Thus it is not a final or fixed set of theories or methods, but a continuously evolving network of concepts and practices drawn from many sources and integrated into a higher level of order. Like an ecological system it thrives on diversity, yet is unified by the coherence and co-operative interplay between its component skills and principles.

THEORETICAL ASSUMPTIONS

The image of the person

The word *person* comes from the Latin 'persona'. The persona was a mask that hid the face of the individual behind it. He could not be seen, but his voice could be heard. He was recognized through sound, *per sona*.

Biosynthesis inherits from Reich the view that a person can be understood at three levels of existential depth. At the surface we see the mask: a protective armouring of character attitudes formed as a defence to threats to the integrity of the individual in childhood or earlier. The nature of these threats will be considered presently. The character defences present a false self which hides the true self which was threatened in infancy. When the character defences begin to loosen, a secondary layer of painful feelings, including rage, anxiety and despair, appears. Beneath this is a third primary layer of core feelings of well-being, love and basic self-confidence. The frustration of this layer creates the secondary distressed layer; and the repression of the distress and protest in turn creates the mask.

The character defences allow people to be typed, according to the pattern of the defences. In biosynthesis we are more interested in the defence system as a form of *survival strategy*. The resistance needs respecting for its life-protective function, and the unique qualities of the individual that are contained and represented in the character patterns, need to be recognized, elicited and valued.

A person's uniqueness is grounded in the physical body, and embodied in the tissues. So the qualities of personal life are reflected in qualities of muscle tone, facial expression, breathing rhythms and the organization of excitement. The therapist sees people whose bodies have been conditioned by the restrictive images they took on from their internalization of environmental demands. To see a person clearly is to see through these restrictive images encapsulated in the character, and beyond the constricted conditions imposed by the muscular armour.

Biosynthesis does not see that a person can be reduced to the ground of the physical body. Recent research has confirmed the ancient teaching that we have an energy-body that extends beyond the physical body, and encompasses it. This energy-body is called *bioplasma* in the Soviet Union, and *perispirit* in the work of the Brazilian biophysicist, Hernani Andrade (1968). In mystical tradition it corresponds to the *aura*.

Biosynthesis recognizes these two modes of existence, somatic, and transsomatic, and seeks to relate them so that a person feels at home in both worlds. The emphasis is on organic form and somatic liveliness as expressions of a person's uniqueness, and is complemented by the recognition that these are incarnations of qualities of an essence that may transcend both birth and death, in biosynthesis we refer to this transparental dimension as the *inner ground* of a person. Much of the therapeutic work consists of helping persons to embody this inner ground in their outer life; and to discover by deepening their contact with the rich life of the body, a true form for their inner field.

Concepts of psychological health and disturbance

Since in biosynthesis we work with the unity of body, mind and spirit (or essence), it is not possible to see psychological health apart from bodily and spiritual health.

Health is founded in a rhythmic wave-function, a pulsation of joyful and pleasurable life-activity. This pulsation is seen in the bioplasma:

> In a person who is alive and streaming, the energy centres are glowing and pulsating; they emit light, and are indispensable for the amount of energy that is metabolised into the organism. . . . This is a pulsating energy configuration that has many colours and variations of hues and appears as if it is shimmering and oscillating and pulsating with life.

(Pierrakos, 1987).

The expansion and contraction of the energy field corresponds to the processes of swelling and shrinking in the tissues of the body. The pulsations of the cerebrospinal fluid (10¾ 14 times a minute), the rhythms of the brain, the beating of the heart, the wave-like processes of breathing, and the stretching and relaxing of muscle, all express this fundamental oscillation of the undisturbed life-process. The following aspects are developed from Ola Raknes (1971).

Somatic aspects of health.

1. Breathing is regular and rhythmic, with free and easy movements of the chest. The peristalsis in the abdomen is neither spastic nor flaccid, but functions with a sense of inner well-being.
2. The organism is in a state of good tonus (eutony). The muscles are able to move easily between states of tension and relaxation without being chronically rigid or collapsed. Blood pressure is normal and the vein pump in the legs is functioning well.
3. The skin is warm with a good blood supply. The face is lively and mobile. The voice is expressive and not mechanical. The eyes are contactful and luminous.
4. Orgasm is also a rhythmic involuntary pulsation, with gratification, and a

feeling of love for the partner. Sexual feelings and heart feelings can be felt for the same person.

Psychic aspects of health:

1. The ability to relate outer expressions to inner need, and to be able to function from primary life-needs and to distinguish these from secondary addictions.
2. The ability to make contact with another person without idealization or projection, or other distorting defences. The ability to distinguish genuine contact from substitute contact, and to value and cultivate the former.
3. The ability both to contain feelings and to express them, and to make decisions over when it is appropriate to do which.
4. Freedom from anxiety when there is no danger.
5. The courage to act in defence of what one believes to be right, even when there is danger.

Spiritual aspects of health:

1. Contact with deep personal sources of value that communicate a sense of ongoingness and meaning.
2. The existential strength to deal with life-crises without getting trapped in despair.
3. The sense that life is a process of ever-deepening respect for one's own heart and the hearts of others.
4. Freedom from neurotic guilt and the willingness to face real responsibility.

If these are the qualities of health, disturbance is the loss of these qualities. In the aura it will show as a dulling of lumination, and a sluggishness or frenetic overactivity in the vibratory quality of the field. In biosynthesis we recognize three different forms of armouring:

1. Visceral armouring. This is a breakdown or dysfunction in the peristalsis or the breathing. There will be a tendency to chronic hyperventilation (overbreathing) or hypoventilation (underbreathing), and to a closed system in the abdomen (irritable gut syndrome). In extreme forms these dysfunctions may get expressed as disposition to asthma, or colitis.
2. Muscular armouring, and tissue armouring. The muscle tone can be disturbed in two directions: hypotonus (weakness, lack of energetic charge), or hypertonus (tightness, overcharge). Tissue armour is related to the disposition of tissue fluids and the effectiveness of the vein pump, which when it gets sluggish can produce a variety of fluid-distribution disturbances that have been described in detail in the work of John Olesen (1974). In extreme forms we see tendencies to rheumatic pains or to

cardiovascular disease (hypertension, heart stress).
3. Cerebral armouring. This can show as disturbed cerebrospinal rhythms; or as disturbances to the bioelectric charge processes in the brain (the transcephalic current); or to the flow of the brain hormones. It can show as disturbances to vision and to eye-contact. The tendency to obsessional thinking or the schizophrenic thought disorder would be more severe expressions of cerebral armouring.

There is a danger of dividing people into sheep and goats, the healthy who do not need therapy and the sick who do. It is more realistic to see health as a spectrum and to recognize the capacity for neurotic responses in so-called well people, and the capacity for health in even quite disturbed individuals. Indeed, all progress in therapy depends on the therapist tapping the hidden reserves of health in his or her client.

Acquisition of psychological disturbance

Whether with Freud we see the origin of neurosis in the Oedipal period, or with Melanie Klein we seek it in the first year of life, or with Lake and Mott we carry it back to the prenatal period, the effect of the clash between human needs and the 'civilizing' process is to break up the unity of the organism. This loss of unity effects the functional integration of three germinal layers of the body. In the fetus these develop during the first week of life, as inside (endoderm), outside (ectoderm), and middle (mesoderm) of the developing cell mass. In the body of the child or the adult we see loss of connectedness between the main organ-groups that correspond to these three germ layers:

Endoderm: digestive organs and lungs
Mesoderm: bones, muscles and blood
Ectoderm: skin, sense organs, brain and nerves

The effect of this splitting is to cut action from thinking and feeling; emotion from movement and perception; understanding from movement and feeling.

There are locations in the body where these disjunctions are most focally placed: between the head and the spine, at the nape of the neck; between the head and the trunk, in the throat; and between the spine and the internal organs of the trunk, at the diaphragm.

It happens that these three locations correspond to three major phases in the maturation cycle of infant development.

Birth pressure is experienced strongly at *the back of the neck* and across to the brows. It can split the connection of head to body. Oral and weaning problems stress *the throat* and confuse breathing with sucking. Anal and genital repression both function through tightening *the diaphragm*, the natural bridge between breathing and movement.

Three streams of affect can be identified in fetal life (Mott, 1956). They exist in pulsating waves of sensation moving through different parts of the body. The first of these is a flow of umbilical affect from the placenta through the umbilical cord to the centre of the body. If the mother is enjoying her pregnancy and is emotionally happy her sense of well-being is communicated to the child. But before birth the fetus is also affected through the umbilical cord with strongly negative emotional states from the mother. Negative maternal affect can be communicated through the blood hormones. In the period after birth the early handling of the infant's skin, eyes and ears can create basic patterns of under- or over-sensitivity, in addition to the fetal affect the infant brings with him or her from the womb. Handling of posture and movement can create disturbances of the kinesthetic sense, and create numerous startle response patterns.

Character defence patterns are learned ways of trying to cope with these early stresses. The various character types described in psychoanalytic and bioenergetics can be seen as learned ways of trying to cope with these early stresses. Three functions in particular can be used to differentiate the style of defence that a person uses.

The first is related to the amount of overall energy available for self-protection. We can distinguish a polarity in the quantity and quality of charge present, which will be related to how a person breathes. Overcharge will show as a tendency to fight or react with overexcitement in stress situations, and a tendency either to bottle this charge up or to discharge it explosively. Undercharge will lead a person to react with more passivity and resignation to situations of threat. We are dealing in part with a natural polarity of the nervous system, and in part with response patterns induced by upbringing. Thus we can surround a child with overstimulus to increase the charge-level, or we can bring him or her up in an understimulating environment which gives him or her little challenge. Hans Selye (1964) has shown that some level of stress (challenge) is necessary for health, and overcharge and undercharge are evidence of too much or too little.

The second function is the level of grounding present in a person which is related to the level of tonus. People with strong egos used in defensive ways develop various forms of rigidity in which the body can be looked on as overstrung. Such people tend to be compulsive, and fixated on external reality, especially the drive to work hard at something. If the musculature is undertoned and understrung a person will feel ungrounded. He or she will tend to retreat more into the inner world. Extreme forms of ungroundedness show as tendencies to develop some kind of psychotic behaviour.

The third function is the style of cognition and perception. Linear and logical thinking calls on us to increase our mental focus and to bring it to bear like a searchlight highlighting a particular problem and excluding everything else. In extreme forms this develops into a kind of tunnel vision. The opposite is a more symbolic style of thinking, emphasizing metaphor, free association and the image. This style is more free-floating and defocused.

The interaction of differing polar extremes of emotional charge, muscular tonus and mental focus, involving three different components from the nervous system, produce eight basic personality styles. Frank Lake (1981) shows how a person can be led to flip over from one pole of response to the opposite, as his or her level of 'transmarginal stress' increases. We can see this in the response to cold: at a certain level of cold a person may shiver or run around to get warm, that is, respond by movement. But at deeper levels of cold he or she may conserve heat by huddling under a blanket and reducing movement. This is similar to how a person handles emotional coldness.

Perpetuation of psychological disturbance

The neurotic splitting tends to reproduce itself: character structure writ large becomes social structure (Reich, 1949). The repressed energy of the individual becomes the fuel for political tyranny and counter-terrorism. The beaten child can grow up to become a parent who beats his or her children. When neurotic character tendencies are socially rationalized they create what Reich (1949) called 'emotional plague', a socially well-defended form of dysfunctional behaviour that can express itself in a number of anti-life manifestations, from the nuclear industry, to a repressive school regime, or in the dehumanized technocracy of an overmechanized childbirth, where the needs of the obstetrician may be given precedence over the natural rhythms of both baby and mother.

Neurosis is perpetuated by those forces in society that are collective expressions of loss of contact with healthy life functions.

I have worked therapeutically in some 30 countries and have had a very good opportunity to observe the emphasis created by differing culture patterns. It may be necessary to step outside one's own culture and look at it from the eyes of another, to see its particular form of perpetuation.

In Japan, for example, there is a strong taboo on eye-contact and at the same time a very powerful pressure on the individual to conform to the group norm. The eyes are masked to withhold the individuality. But this is not the personal problem of a particular repressive upbringing, it is the learned ethos of a whole culture pattern, and is re-inforced daily in a thousand ways.

In Latin America fear is much more evident in people's expression and to a higher degree, than most other cultures I work in. This fear can be related to the political situation that many people grow up in. In a professional group I led in Buenos Aires, consisting of humanistic psychologists, approximately one third of the group had been the victim of kidnapping, torture, or severe political repression, or had seen childhood friends killed or caused to disappear.

In California, the home of primal therapy, and a hundred other ways of promoting radical change, at a conference on the politics of the body, people were saying: we know how to fall apart, but not how to come back together. The fragmentation and scatteredness of their multiracial society and their polyglot environment where 'anything goes but nothing comes off' was reflected in their character structure.

Therapeutic systems, designed to ease disturbance and promote better health, can themselves become parts of the perpetuation. For it is easy to turn a therapeutic community into a new form of tyranny, which demands from people the opposite of what their old tyranny demanded. Or to use the delicate transference situation that exists between the helper and helped so as to impose on a person the beliefs and attitudes of another. So in biosynthesis we are also interested in teaching people how to stand up and resist manipulation and group pressure which can sometimes be found even in what are intended to be therapeutic environments.

A further source of perpetuation is in what Freud called the repetition compulsion and is related to resistance. In biosynthesis resistance is related to concepts from biology like homeostasis – the tendency to maintain life as it is, and to the damping of fluctuations, which are qualitative leaps out of the usual states we live in and are conditioned to. But the treatment of resistance leads to a description of the practice of therapy.

PRACTICE

Goals of therapy

The goal of therapy is to restore the person to a state of healthy pulsation in which the basic life-activities are rhythmic, give pleasure, and work for enhanced contact with oneself and others.

There is a problem however in defining this goal. Long ago Mathias Alexander described tensions created by what he called 'end-gaining' and argued that we should pay close attention to the 'means-whereby'.

In biosynthesis the *process* of therapeutic growth is more important than the *product*. If we focus on the product we can easily begin to make demands on the patient that fit our model of health: for example, the demand to be emotionally expressive can follow from the belief that emotional expression is healthy.

In a process-therapy close attention is paid to the direction in which the person who is being helped wishes to move, the problem he or she confronts and the new life steps he or she is seeking to take. If, as can often happen he or she is unclear about these, the therapist works to soften the breathing, and loosen the muscle tensions, to such a point that the client's growth direction and movement-tendency can be directly experienced. There is an *emergent* in the client, a theme, a potentiality, an inner direction, which can be directly experienced by the therapist and helped to unfold. Thus the therapist does not seek to give the client directives, except as a temporary measure, but to uncover the client's inner direction.

What is needed however is for the therapist and client in consultation with each other to determine what is the next step in the client's growth and to help him or her to take that step, rather than to move towards attaining the therapist's goal. The one who needs to develop more surrender and the one who needs to develop more will are both connecting to a process the 'goal' of which may be invisible or visible, and may change as the process emerges.

The 'person' of the therapist

Neurosis is the result of a disturbed primary relationship and therapy, to be deeply effective, in changing this primary disturbance, needs to create a new relationship.

The qualities of the disturbed relationship combine to produce an interference pattern to the rhythm of personal growth. Neurosis is the effect of this interference pattern. The therapeutic relationship needs to interfere with the interference in such a way as to create a resonance with the primary rhythm of growth.

A good therapist with a limited technique will have a good effect on a client in a limited area. Thus a good verbal therapist may help a client to very important insights yet neglect crucial areas of somatic change. On the other hand a bad therapist with a deep-ranging technique can have a bad effect on a client over a wide area of his or her development.

From Paulo Friere biosynthesis takes a basic model of three styles of interaction which define three styles of person for a therapist. The first of these he calls *invasion*, the second *deprivation* and the third *dialogue*.

Invading therapists penetrate the client. They become not a therapist, but

the rapist. They can rape the client with interpretations that shoot
unconscious (in ways that Reich condemned in 1933) or they can be in
by using pressurized body-techniques to force a response and over
client's resistance. (Invasion is a lack of respect for the client's boundaries
and results in a discouragement to the client to trust his or her own
developmental process.)

Deprivation is a state where therapists withhold from the client some of
the basic human nourishments he or she may need for growth. A body-
therapist who refuses words or deprives a client of language experience or a
word-therapist who has no insight into the body may deprive a client of
kinesthetic experience. Fear of 'invading' can lead to 'deprivation'; fear of
'depriving' can lead to 'invasion'. Between these two disturbed modes of
relationship lies 'dialogue'. Dialogue can be both verbal and non-verbal.
Therapists open to dialogue will learn from their client as well as teach him
or her. There will be a more dynamic interaction between them based on
open communication and mutually developed processes. Dialogue is a mode
of contact that creates resonance with the client. This resonance is a
sounding board which can be used to evaluate the appropriation of any
technique being used. The person of the client is of primary importance;
techniques are of secondary importance.

The therapist's person may be too impersonal or too personal. The
impersonal therapist tries to be objective, keep his or her feelings hidden,
remain a blank screen, or practise a specific technique. The overpersonal
therapist is too subjective, makes a symbiotic relationship with the client,
acts out personal needs in the session, and is unable to handle both the
transference and the countertransference. Between these two extremes,
there is room for the sharing of deep human emotions in a warm and human
way. In biosynthesis the body of the therapist is an important tool, the most
basic one. It is the therapist's body which will resonate to many of the subtle
tensions and emotional states in the client. Reich called this process 'vegetative identification'. It means to feel in your own body a sense of the client's
struggle, rhythm, and quality of pulsation.

The body of the therapist is a tool in another sense. Body-to-body
interaction is one of the most powerful ways to learn new developmental
patterns. This includes the use of the hands in touch, but the therapist in
biosynthesis will use at times many other parts of his or her body, the feet,
the back, the head, to help the client to explore new movement pathways.
The therapist becomes at times a 'contact-dancer' who guides the client to a
new experience of the ground of his or her own body. Therapy is then a form
of contact and guidance.

Of course transference and countertransference, with the use of touch, are strong, and the therapist needs to have done plenty of personal work on himself or herself before being ready to participate in this deep form of somatic dialogue in a responsible way that avoids the danger of invasion described above.

The intricacies of transference and countertransference in biosynthesis are described elsewhere (Boadella, 1983).

Therapeutic style

Styles of therapy reflect styles of person. It is important that each therapist adopts a style of being with the client that is congruent and fits his or her individuality. This is different from a style that reflects his or her character, since character is by definition a defensive style of behaviour (Reich, 1949). We are seeking to minimize the effect of character on style, and to maximize the effect of individuality.

There is a second way to look at style, in terms of the degree of activity or receptivity taken by the therapist. In biosynthesis we have a mode of five styles of interaction in terms of the activity/receptivity spectrum.

In *level one*, the therapist is an initiator. He or she suggests, proposes, directs, activates, mobilizes. The client reacts, by seeking to follow the therapist's activity. However the client's reaction is other-directed, not self-directed. The therapist for example might propose a particular exercise to loosen a part of the client's body. And the client might react by doing the exercise rather mechanically at first. Nevertheless level one may prepare the way for *level two* where the therapist is equally active but the client is more *responsive*, answering the therapeutic initiative with more self-motivation, more individuality of response, including modifying the original suggestion. At the other end of the spectrum, *level five* is one where the therapist is largely *receptive* to the client. He or she gives space, allows time, incubates, supports, leaves pregnant pauses, and is more in touch with being than doing. Of course, this may turn into the classic 'waiting game' of a deprivative script, but all waiting is not neurotic. There is a creative waiting that can give the client time to organize his or her experience for himself or herself for the first time. In level five, the therapist permits, allows and encourages the client's natural movements, silences, language flow and emotional expression. In *level four* the client is equally leading the session but the therapist *joins in* and adds something to what the client brings. In movement work the therapist acts physically to support or amplify a movement begun by the client. It is a response similar to that of someone who pushes on a swing that is already oscillating under the action of the rider.

Level three is an intermediate position at the centre of the spectrum.

Therapist and client are both engaged in a process where it may not be clear who is leading and who is following. The process itself is the prime mover, and the two participants are following the inner dynamic of the process. Here the work is at its most dance-like, and here is the most inter-dependence.

At any time in a session any one of these five levels of interaction may be the most helpful. They function as a range of contact and response options, and the more mobility a therapist has in selecting which option is the most appropriate, the better the work will proceed.

If the therapist is too active and intervening when the client is just about to contact a deep inner theme, the client will be led away from his or her true process. If on the other hand the therapist gives permission and space to a client who is in some kind of acting-out pattern of behaviour, then the client will be denied the chance to learn what is hidden behind the acting-out.

So the options in the range of activity and receptivity need to be handled appropriately to be effective therapeutic styles.

Major therapeutic techniques

I prefer to write about therapeutic processes rather than techniques. I do not teach techniques which can be abstracted from context. Context is related to process. Process is the personal dynamic within which a particular structure of experience, or a particular technique, makes or does not make sense.

In biosynthesis there are three primary processes of therapy which are derived from the embryological model. They are called centring, grounding and facing, and are described as follows.

Centring

Centring is a process of helping a person to get in contact with the wave-like rhythm of his or her breath, and with the associated emotional dynamics. Breathing and emotion are profoundly related in that every emotional shift involves some change of breath rhythm. There are specific patterns of breath associated with anxiety, anger, sadness, hope, joy, longing and so forth.

The breathing can be unbalanced by being more in the chest than in the belly or vice versa. And it can be unbalanced in the relative emphasis on in-breath and out-breath. The therapist can help the out-breath in clients who are overcontrolled and overtense by encouraging a free flow of move-ment, for example, in running or other movement work described below. The breath will then tend to follow the movement. For people who tend to minimize their in-breath, and to overemphasize the out-breath, help to stimulate the in-breath is needed. This can be done in a variety of ways: gentle lifting actions of the cervical or lumbar spine at the same time as the in-breath, will support deeper inspiration. A raising and lowering, or opening and closing of the limbs, also in the rhythm of the breath, will also be very helpful. So will a particular form of massage for undercharged hypotonus muscles: I call this massage *womb-touch* as it consists of a gentle squeezing action of soft tissues of the body, particularly the upper arm muscles, in rhythm with the in-breath. The subtleties of these methods are difficult to describe in print. The effect of working with the breath is frequently to promote emotional release (in an overcontained person), or emotional containment in an emotionally volatile person.

In-breath work is helpful in dealing with states of anxiety, helplessness, weakness and sadness. Out-breath work is indicated for conditions of overcontrol, blocked anger, and excessive tension. Many times a person is in a condition where one kind of work needs to be followed by its opposite, as a counterbalance.

Emotional layering

The emotions can be layered, with one emotion that is easy to express being used defensively to conceal a hidden emotion that is difficult to express. The therapeutic principle is to try to elicit the defended-against emotion, and to avoid encouraging the defensive-emotion. Common examples are: anger used to hide sadness and fear; fear used to hide anger or excitement; sadness used to hide anger, or pleasure.

Grounding

Grounding is related to our rhythm of movement and the state of our muscle tone. A person is well-grounded when he or she has the appropriate muscle tone for a particular action or behaviour. Moshe Feldenkrais (1948) speaks of this as the 'potent stance'. The therapist works to release energy from overtense muscles, by transferring the tension into expressive movements and to draw energy into overslack muscles, by increasing the tonus through dynamic resistance against the ground of the earth or the ground of the therapist's body.

Grounding involves vitalizing the flow of energy down the spine and from there into the 'five limbs', both arms, both legs and the head. We work with a wide range of body postures, some of these resembling the asanas of yoga, or the stress positions of bioenergetics.

In biosynthesis however we are primarily interested in posture as an expression of a person's contactfulness. Many of the postures have an evolutionary thrust and are related to developmental stages of life, from the movements of the birth reflex, through creeping and crawling, to standing and walking. These are beautifully illustrated in Stanley Keleman's (1985) book *Emotional Anatomy*. But fishlike and birdlike movements of swimming and flying also often occur as part of the spontaneous regulation of muscle tonus. There is a whole language of shape-flow which has much in common with release dance.

The flow of movement has three major qualitative aspects: a vital, an emotional and a spiritual. The movement expression may be a vitalizing flow of life through the body bringing energy and motility back to previously deadened areas; or it may be an emotional flow, helping a person to translate his or her affective states into meaningful action sequences. For example the client may be helped in a state of fear to strengthen his or her boundary so as to make a more effective protection against threat; or in a state of anger the client may be helped to increase his or her space, so as to feel less compressed and muscle bound; and in a state of sadness the client may be helped to reach out for more contact than he or she usually allows. The movement expression may also bring a flow of spiritual feeling to a person, where the gesture has the quality more of a 'mudra', connecting a person deeply to universal energies much more extensive than himself or herself.

To elicit these shape flows and dynamic postural evolutions, the therapist in biosynthesis learns to recognize the language of movement-attitude which is a bound state of intentionality. If the movement-attitude is loosened an intention-movement may begin. This is like the birth moment of a release-sequence. If the intention movement is supported a movement tendency will reveal itself and will flow in the direction of one of the major pathways described above.

Therapists work with the principles of induction and somatic resonance. They have to be sensitive with their own muscle tone to the muscle tone of the client. The timing of their support will be crucial so as to respect the pacing of the client and also the relationship to the rhythm of the client's breathing will frequently be of crucial importance.

Facing and sounding

Apart from movement expression the principal channels of contact are the eyes and the voice. The therapist works with the qualities of eye-contact as 'mirrors of the soul' and is experienced in how to elicit the different expressions that are withheld from the eyes.

In the eyes-open position there are two main modes of outlook, defensive and contactful. The defensive looking is associated with staring, with watching in a guarded way, or with a dreamy 'far-away' look. Sometimes the gaze can be changed by helping the person voluntarily to increase his or her tendency and then relax it so as to reduce the degree of defensiveness. Sometimes, with the overwatching person, who uses his or her gaze as a form of control, working with the eyes closed will bring more contact with the inner expression. If the eyes are more contactful they will respond to the eye-contact of the therapist and the differing expressions such as longing, anxiety, anger or pleasure can be helped to find expression.

In the eyes-closed position there is also a defensive and a contacful mode. The defensive mode here is associated with withdrawal of contact, and shutting out both intake through the eyes and also the revealing of any feeling. The contactful mode here is associated with paying closer attention to the inner world of experience and is often associated with the emergence of imagery. The skill of the therapist is in distinguishing which way the eyes are being used and in helping the client to face what is being defended against.

In working with the voice there is a recognition that a close energetic relationship exists between tone and muscle tone. We speak of sounding as the development of resonance of the voice so that it can become a powerful expressive instrument. Improvement in voice freedom is associated with improvements in muscle tone. Sounding helps grounding. Clearly voice work is intimately related to breath work.

When we come to the role of language the key factor in biosynthesis is the ability to distinguish between explanatory and exploratory language. Explanation means to flatten: here the client uses words, regardless of content, to give information that carries a sense of feeling or of body behind it. This language is disconnected, and is used defensively. Exploration means to flow out. Exploratory language comes more from the heart and is connected to the person's vitality and motility.

In biosynthesis, we try to ground the language in the body and to develop an easy flow between verbal and non-verbal expression. Often if the body signals become unclear or confused, the therapist will turn to language seeking clarification of the inner feeling. If the language is confused he or she may seek more understanding of what is happening by reading the non-verbal language of the body.

Inner ground

The work with breathing, movement and language forms the outer ground of biosynthesis. Behind this lies the inner ground of a person's essence. This inner ground is associated with presence and being, rather than with activity and doing. The inner ground in breathing may present itself as a meditative state where a person feels the subtler vibration of breath; in postural work it may elicit 'postures of the soul', deep movement forms of spiritual intensity. In language work it may lead to the uncovering of archetypal images of existential scripts, and open up a transpersonal dimension of existence. We seek to connect these two grounds, inner and outer, to each other by constantly helping the client become aware of the bridges between his or her inner life and outer reality.

Contact signals and the elements of touch

In biosynthesis we have found it helpful to consider touch as being related to the four traditional elements of earth, water, fire and air. Each of these is briefly described.

Earth touch. Here the hands are used, with other parts of the body, as support structures. We try to communicate the experience of solidity, that the ground of the earth and of another human being can be reliable.

For people who are overindependent we use the support principle to help them to learn to trust others more and accept more help. For people who are overdependent we use it to help them to take more trust from the ground and from the support structures (back, legs, arms) in their own body. Earth touch is particularly helpful, in this second sense, wherever we are dealing with people with weak boundaries, or who feel ungrounded and over anxious.

Water touch. Here we seek to give the experience of liquidity. The hands become circulators, inducers of currents of energy, increasing the flow of life from the centre of the body to the surface. We can recognize the liquidity of the interior of the body, in the peristalsis of the intestines, described in detail in Gerda Boyesen's (1985) theory of biodynamic psychology. And we can follow the liquid flow of movements in the form of vibrations, streamings, tremblings of the body, as it gives up excess muscle tension and begins to rebalance the muscle tone. Swimming-like movements of arms and legs are also characteristically induced when working with the principle of this element.

Air touch. In air touch the hands are used as gentle pumps to massage the breath rhythm of the person into the body as a whole, and to assist in the filling and emptying rhythm (extension and flexion, abduction and adduction, elongation and shortening) in the overall musculature. Many people disassociate breathing and movement by spasticity and flaccidity in the diaphragm, so this kind of touch can be called diaphragmatic touch since it opens many diaphragms in the body, bringing more pulsation to the crown of the head, and the craniospinal fluid, the pelvic floor, the soles of the feet and the palms of the hands, as well as the diaphragm itself.

Fire touch. In fire touch the principle is warmth and the thermo-regulation of the body. The hands are used as radiators to draw out the inner warmth and bring it to the surface. This can be done directly by warming cold areas of the body, or indirectly by working with the energy field in the space above a constricted area of the body. If both hands are used to create an energy field between the palms enclosing a particular area, the effect is intensified. Hot areas of the body are normally overcharged and need work to dissipate the excess heat by converting it to movement.

The change process in therapy

The process of change is dependent on three factors: the effectiveness of the therapeutic interaction; the depth in the person to which this reaches; and the extent to which changes in the session can be translated into life-events. The first of these has already been discussed in the preceding three sections, so I will confine myself to the other two.

The therapeutic work has been described by Reich (as already shown) as taking part at three levels of depth: a tertiary level of personality, concerned with the character and muscular defences and associated with the social mask. Under this a secondary layer which usually contains a great deal of distress and pain and feelings of loneliness, anger, fear and hurt. Beneath this again and in a primary layer of well-being with feelings of hope and joy, and pleasure in being alive.

Between these three layers there are two transitions. Many therapists are skilled in leading a person from his or her character defences against pain to experiencing pain. In primal therapy there is no concept of a primary sense of well-being, so it is my belief that a client may be left feeling alive but in distress for long periods of time, because of the conviction that the pain is primary.

Due to the widespread existence of pleasure-anxiety, many clients resist the second transition from distress to well-being. At the point when they might make this transition they do a U-turn back into the secondary distress layer and continue to act out old patterns of emotional release that no longer have therapeutic value, and do not lead to emotional clearance; clearance is helped by finding new sources of inner nourishment as one contacts long-forgotten or newly discovered resources for hope gratification, and well-being.

In biosynthesis, through the processes described before, we try to convey a client *in each session* to this primary level of experience to some degree. The process of change is similar to the formation of the blood system in fetal development. The drops of connection to the primal stream of wellness are like blood islands which gradually coalesce to make continuous streams that organize themselves into blood vessels. The connected drops of the client's contact with his or her primary layer similarly coalesce his or her experience into new directions.

However, for this to happen the client needs to find ways to anchor somatic and psychic changes in the therapeutic session into his or her root-situation in life. This may seem a willingness to make changes in where he or she lives, who he or she lives with, what work he or she does, and how he or she organizes life time and living space. Thus the benefits of therapy need to be grounded in the life situation if they are to become secure.

This is related, in Hameed Ali's development of Reichian work, to the Sufi understanding of the difference between a 'state' and a 'station' (Almaas, 1986). The 'state', such as improvement in a therapeutic session may only be temporary. The 'station' is when the client is able, even if he or she temporarily loses touch with his or her inner direction, to recover it for himself or herself. The change has become no longer dependent on outside help from the therapist to sustain it.

CASE EXAMPLE

Instead of presenting a long case history I choose to present an example of crisis intervention using principles of biosynthesis.

A woman in her mid-twenties came to a three day non-residential therapeutic group I was leading. The organizer of the group knew a little of her history and was very anxious over whether to admit her to the group or not as she seemed very disturbed. In fact she had slashed her right wrist a few days before in a suicide attempt. Her life situation seemed chaotic: she was closely involved with a religious cult that practised ego-weakening activities (that were undermining her already weak ego). She was drinking and smoking heavily in an effort to suppress her pain.

On the first day of the group she presented the following picture: her breathing was extremely flattened and almost imperceptible. This flattened breathing I knew to be the characteristic of a pre-schizophrenic state. This feeling was supported by her greatly disturbed eye-contact which was misty and clouded in a distinctive way. She avoided looking at anyone directly, sending her gaze primarily downwards to the floor. She was withdrawn from touch, and it was possible to get some sense of her muscle tone only from her hand-contact which was limp and lifeless in a way characteristic of severe hypotonus. She could talk only in a faint voice, in a confused way.

We talked a little about the state of confusion and despair leading to the wrist-slashing a few days earlier. It was explanatory language without any emotion.

At the end of this first interaction, on day one of the group, it was clear that she was in an extremely unbounded state of severe withdrawal and I was concerned not that she would deteriorate in the group but that our resources in such a short group would not be adequate to help her step away from her suicidal feeling. She was therefore at risk, and I called a meeting of the organizers of the group to express my concern about her and to ask what kind of emergency network they might have to help people who were in severe confusion and in danger of taking their own life.

In discussion after the first meeting with her, she could talk only minimally about her situation, but she volunteered the statement 'your hands are warm'. The first contact bridge had been hesitantly established. From such threads the tapestry of change can sometimes begin to be woven.

On the second day she approached me at the beginning of the day, on her own initiative to speak about the previous night. Her doing so was already a movement towards contact, and a step out of her withdrawal. She said she had realized in the night that she had felt that her boyfriend might die. She linked this to an older fear that her father might die. She was now willing to admit fear, which had not been possible on the previous day.

I created a space for her in a small group of four people where she could continue to explore her feelings about fear of people dying. After about ten minutes she said she felt more normal and did not want to talk further. Rather she wanted to do some body-enlivening movements that I had introduced earlier. (These movements were to bring more sense of connection between the arms and the touch and were of potential usefulness to her because of the energetic withdrawal in her arms and her lifeless hands.)

She was standing, allowing her arms to loosen a little, and another member of the small group was doing similarly. Suddenly they made direct eye-contact. She had momentarily given up her avoidance in the eyes, and as her eyes met the life in the eyes of her companion, she experienced a very strong catharsis, her legs gave way, she fell to the floor, and she began screaming intensely. At the same time her body began convulsing spasmodically. For this particular group where any expression of emotion is socially difficult, it must have seemed she was having a fit or a psychotic episode. If patients in a mental hospital dare to express their distress in such a way it is normal to give immediate tranquillizers. (It is too disturbing to other people, never mind if it can benefit the person.)

For the next half an hour the therapeutic task was to contain the huge energies being released in her, not to suppress them. I, and the people of her small group, surrounded her where she had fallen, and kept an enclosure within which she was free to follow the release movements of her body, but which also gave physical security and a clear boundary. It is a womb-space for the birth of new energies. We kept this physical contact for half an hour. We could not talk to her for some time as she continued screaming, for a much longer time than usual in abreaction of fear. We could not make eye-contact with her, since it was eye-contact that had triggered her fear. But I made hand-contact and found that her hands were warm. Now we could strengthen the thread of contact established the day before. After some time her screaming subsided. Her body moved more quietly. We noticed her breathing was fuller and more relaxed. She began to speak. The first thing she said was 'I don't want to see'.

Now we covered her eyes with her hands and ours, reinforcing her right to more boundary and taking over her self-protection and affirming it. Soon she could see behind her closed eyes the dark waters of a river in which her father appeared to be drowning. She shared these images for a while. It was approaching lunch time. I gave her the choice to take a further therapeutic hour in the lunch break to continue with this theme, or to come back to this world and have lunch in which I would join her and help to integrate this exceptionally powerful release. She said, 'I think I am ready to see now, and I'll have lunch.'

She now opened her eyes voluntarily and sat up. She was now able to look at people without regressing or avoiding. Her voice was brighter and she expressed keen interest when I said I would help her to develop some practices to reduce fear.

In the lunch break we did ego-building work using language to strengthen her ability to make choice and to build better channels for facing and managing fear.

I prescribed her defence, putting her hands over her eyes. To normalize it I called it *palming* which is a well-known exercise for relaxing the eyes. Then I recommended her to take up the yoga posture of the child, in which the body takes a self-collecting fetal shape, which increases body heat and grounds the head on the earth.

Thirdly, I taught her how to reorganize her breathing so as to lead her out of a panic state, by sitting with her back to the wall, legs bent, and putting gentle pressure downwards and backwards as she breathed in.

Fourthly we created some contact links for her so that she could at least find someone to share her panic with if such a situation should recur.

Fifthly I suggested that she should paint her fears, and also the opposite of fear.

Thus I sought to offer her some life steps she could take to help her remain in better contact with herself.

For the remainder of the group she was more relaxed – in fact participated as a helper to others who were doing personal work. When the group closed she was able to express herself more warmly when she said goodbye.

I did not see her again for six months when she came to a further group. I was astonished at the changes in her. She greeted me warmly and easily. Her eyes were warm and contactful. Her muscle tone was no longer limp. She announced that she had given up smoking and drinking and had left her religious sect. And, she said, I did these paintings. She unfolded from a large folder about 30 large and very lively paintings of various members of her family and of herself, in a wide variety of moods. This is my father drowning, she said. And here is my father when I was a child and he looked happy. And here is me when I felt dead and desperate. And here is my happiness in the sunshine.

In this group she did not stand out in any way as especially disturbed. Her schizophrenic episode had been experienced and contained without the need for any drugs. In the second group she worked expressing some anger about her mother, which she expressed clearly and appropriately, integrating her eye expression, her voice and movements. In fact she was clearer than anyone else in the group.

In this case study of the crisis intervention the principle of pulsation, the emphasis on forms of expression rather than deep analysis of contents, the possibility of cathartic emotional release as a bridge from near-schizophrenic withdrawal to better ego strength in expressing and channelling expression, the understanding of the contact ground of the human body, and the anchoring of the group experience in daily life were all necessary to enable her to make these changes and to come through her crisis with better integration than she had before.

REFERENCES

Almaas, A. M. (1986) *Essence*, Almaas Editions, Berkeley, CA.

Andrade, H. (1968) *Teoria Corpusculo d'Espirito*, Instituto BioPsycologic, Sao Paulo, Brazil.

Boadella, D. (1976) *In the Wake of Reich*, Coventure, London.

Boadella, D. (1979) *The Charge of Consciousness*, Abbotsbury Publications, Weymouth.

Boadella, D. (1983) Transference, resonance and interference, *Journal of Biodynamic Psychology*, No. 3.

Boadella, D. (1985) *Wilhelm Reich: The Evolution of His Work*, Routledge & Kegan Paul, London.

Boadella, D. (1986) *Lifestreams*, Routledge & Kegan Paul, London.
Boadella, D. and Liss, J. (1986) *Terapia Corporal*, Astrolabia, Rome.
Boadella, D. and Smith, D. (1986) *Maps of Character*, Abbotsbury Publications, Weymouth.
Boyesen, G. (1985) *Entre Psyche et Soma,* Payot, Paris.
Feldenkrais, M. (1948) *Body and Mature Behaviour*, Routledge & Kegan Paul, London.
Keleman, S. (1985) *Emotional Anatomy*, Centre Press, Berkeley, California.
Lake, F. (1981) *Studies in Constricted Confusion*, Clinical Theology Association, Oxford.
Lowen, A. (1958) *Physical Dynamics of Character Structure*, Grune & Stratton, New York.
Lowen, A. (1969) *The Betrayal of the Body*, Macmillan, New York.
Mott, F. (1956) *The Nature of the Self*, Allan Wingate, London.
Olesen, J. (1974) The vein pump in sickness and health, *Energy and Character*, Vol. 5, No. 1.
Pierrakos, J. (1987) *Core Energetics*, Synthesis Press, New York.
Raknes, O. (1971) *Wilhelm Reich and Orgonomy*, Macmillan, New York.
Reich, W. (1949) *Character Analysis*, Vision Press, London.
Selye, H. (1964) *The Stress of Life*, Allen & Unwin, London.

Suggested further reading

Boadella, D. (1983) Transference, resonance and interference, *Journal of Biodynamic Psychology* No. 3.
Boadella, D. (1985) *Wilhelm Reich: The Evolution of His Work*, Routledge & Kegan Paul, London.
Boadella, D. (1986) *Lifestreams*, Routledge & Kegan Paul, London.
Keleman, S. (1985) *Emotional Anatomy*, Centre Press, Berkeley, California.
Pierrakos, J. (1987) *Core Energetics*, Synthesis Press, New York.

CHAPTER 9

THE GERDA BOYESEN METHOD: BIODYNAMIC THERAPY

Clover Southwell and staff of the Gerda Boyesen International Institute

HISTORICAL CONTEXT AND DEVELOPMENTS IN BRITAIN

Historical context

Biodynamic therapy was developed by the Norwegian psychologist Gerda Boyesen, who worked in Norway until 1968 when she moved to London. While completing her degree in psychology at Oslo University she also went into training analysis with Ola Raknes, a Freudian analyst who had been closely associated with Wilhelm Reich during Reich's years in Norway. During the analysis Raknes never discussed theory, but Gerda Boyesen's experience as his analysand convinced her of the importance of working with the body as an adjunct to verbal psychotherapy. Therefore before embarking on her career as clinical psychologist she also qualified as a physiotherapist.

From 1960 to 1968 Gerda Boyesen held posts as clinical psychologist in mental hospitals in Norway. At the same time, she had a private practice where she combined psychotherapy with massage as she judged best for her patients, and amassed a wealth of detailed observations of the relationship between psychological and bodily processes. She was particularly struck by the patients' vegetative reactions to their sessions, such as flu symptoms or diarrhoea, and the rapid changes that could occur in the quality of their facial tissue (grey and drained or puffy and swollen). She also noticed that certain patients would have loud intestinal sounds (tummy-rumblings) during psychotherapy sessions, particularly at moments of insight or emotional release, and that these were the patients who were showing the most rapid improvement. Intrigued by this connection, she began to listen to her own intestinal sounds through a stethoscope; correlating the different sounds with her immediate circumstances and mood, she arrived at her theory of psycho-peristalsis (described in the next section). Furthermore, she found that by means of massage – during which she would hear loud watery sounds through the stethoscope placed on the patient's belly – she was able to reduce the excess fluid in the patient's body tissue.

The psychological effect was remarkable: the patients might have come to the session feeling desperate or depressed; but as soon as the fluid pressure in the tissue was more normal they would feel 'light', at peace with themselves. (M.-L. Boyesen, 1974). The building up and releasing of pressure in the tissue seemed to be related to the building up and releasing of some sort of emotional burden, even if the patient had not consciously recognized it. What was the dynamic factor connecting this physical pressure and the emotional pressure?

Her own personal experience eventually led Gerda Boyesen to find her answer in the context of Freud's (1905) libido theory. At this period she was having further therapy with Raknes. She was experiencing enormous psychological pressure and also a strange pressure in the tongue and swelling in the mouth. Raknes had urged her to speak about what was troubling her, but she could only sense that it related to early infancy, before she had learned to talk. The pressure grew unbearable and she went out in the woods where she felt free to scream. With this emotional release came dramatic new sensations: the pressure in her mouth suddenly released, and she felt a flow of incredible sweetness and pleasure streaming down through her body. She then got the image of herself as a baby at the breast; she learned later that her mother had teased her as an infant by taking the nipple out of her mouth as she was sucking. Could it be, Gerda Boyesen then asked herself, that the oral libido fixation arising from the infantile traumas was now – thanks to her screaming – beginning to release? and that her exquisite 'melting' sensations were the sensation of the long-fixated libido moving, at last, through her body? Could it be that libido is not just a psychological factor but also a physiological reality?

When these streamings of pleasure were at their strongest, Gerda Boyesen would feel that she was in touch with what she called the 'oceanic wave of the universe', and so she hypothesized that this flowing libido must be some sort of universal life-force. Subsequently she saw in some unpublished writings of Reich that her own findings were supported by his theories of orgone energy.

Though often loosely referred to as neo-Reichian, Gerda Boyesen in fact developed biodynamic psychology independently. *Bio* means life; *dynamic* means force. Gerda Boyesen's theory is that the life-force moves in us as libido, its flow being intrinsically pleasurable except if it is blocked, when it causes symptoms both physical and psychological (M.-L. Boyesen, 1975). She reconsidered Freud's theories of child development, emotional repression and conversion symptoms in the light of her own experience of the libido flow (M.-L. Boyesen, 1976). In repressing our emotions we are blocking the flow of our life-force, our libido. The task of biodynamic therapy is to regain access to the life-force blocked in mind and body and to help it flow freely again.

Many of Gerda Boyesen's theoretical premises are similar to those of orgonomy and bioenergetics, but biodynamic psychology lays greater emphasis on the interrelation of psychological process with vegetative process, on the healing force of pleasure, and on the 'dynamic updrift', the intrinsic drive of the repressed libido to come to the surface and be re-integrated. This drive is seen as the bodily aspect of the instinct of self-actualization posited by Goldstein (1939).

Impressed though her Norwegian colleagues were by the clinical results Gerda Boyesen had been achieving, they were not receptive to her theoretical explanations, which they found too revolutionary. In Norway she had discussed her theories with few people outside her own family circle, but in 1968 she moved to London where she could be free of the constraints of the traditional background. Here she met with a lively response to her theories; she established a private practice, and embarked on teaching her methods. From London the training soon spread to Europe, and in the last ten years some 50 training programmes have been run in France, Germany, Holland and Switzerland. People have come to London from all over the world to study with Gerda Boyesen, and the seeds of her work have reached five continents. Biodynamic therapists trained in London are now planting the work in Australia, the USA and Brazil.

On the basis of Gerda Boyesen's theory and methods the biodynamic approach has been further extended by members of her family. Ebba Boyesen has specialized in the energetic aspects of body therapy, including birth release, auric massage and grounding, and psycho-orgastic therapy. Mona-Lisa Boyesen has specialized in orgonomy and has developed the bio-release programme, a self-help course in body-mind self-regulation; she has recently been concerned with promoting the sensitive care of newborn infants. Paul Boyesen has developed primary impulse training and trans-formational psychology, a more analytical approach to body therapy. This chapter, however, will deal only with the central theory and methods of Gerda Boyesen herself.

Developments in Britain

The London centre of the Gerda Boyesen International Institute was established in Acton Park in 1976, and provides the most comprehensive training in biodynamic methods, extended over three or more years. Some 30 students enter the programme each year, attending several times a week for theoretical teaching and practice. A variety of shorter courses are offered for people in the helping professions, and there is also a programme of courses and workshops for the general public.

The Gerda Boyesen Clinic, staffed by therapists trained at the Institute, provides a range of individual outpatient treatments, including biodynamic psychotherapy, and psychoperistaltic massage to help specific problems such as lower back pain. Many patients come referred by doctors familiar with the work. Over the years the clinic has treated many hundreds of patients, some of whom arrived in acute distress of body or mind, while others come to deepen their self-awareness through the unique biodynamic integration of 'mind- and 'body-work'. Patients generally attend once a week over a period of months.

THEORETICAL ASSUMPTIONS
Image of the person

In the biodynamic view, the functions of mind, body and spirit are totally interfused. Everything that happens in us and everything we do – our shivers, shouts, visions, actions, thoughts and feelings – all are manifest-ations of the life-force moving in us. How somebody relates to the move-ments of their life-force – inherently pleasurable when flowing freely – is central to the biodynamic image of the person.

The primary and secondary personality

We distinguish between the primary personality and the secondary perso-nality. People locked in the secondary personality have lost touch with their life-force and have thus been 'cheated of their birth-right of pleasure'; the primary personality, on the other hand, is in harmony with the rhythms of the life-force.

Most people in fact manifest aspects of both primary and secondary, and the aim of biodynamic therapy (as we shall see in the section on practice) is to dissolve the constrictions of the secondary personality and to encourage a person's true inner nature, the primary personality, to emerge and mature. Gerda Boyesen (1982, pp. 5–8) writes:

> The Primary Personality has a natural joy in life, a basic security, stability and honesty. . . . There is pleasure in work and in relaxation, a gentle euphoria and a mild intoxication in the pleasure of living. . . . He or she is in touch with the instinctual self, the primitive and animalistic urges, yet this is integrated also with the transcendant. . . . There is a sense of being at one with the universe, and not just an isolated individual . . . a natural love for humanity and, at times, a rage for those whose abuse this in others. . . . We are born with the potential for inner happiness, security and wonder. We can lose part of this as we become limited, over-rational, deprived and thus self-seeking.

When, from childhood onwards, the world presses in on us too hard and does not accept us as we truly are, we develop the secondary personality. Then, not only do we create ways to protect ourselves from the onslaughts of the outer world, but we suppress our own inner impulses, because they are too threatening to us; we block these movements of our life-force, and so limit the expansion of our true potential.

Id and ego – interplay between vertical and horizontal

The secondary personality has lost the natural harmony between the ego and the id. The biodynamic view of ego and id differs from that of Freud, who saw the id as a selfish, anarchic and anti-social force, at war with the ego (Freud, 1915). In biodynamic theory both id and ego are seen as functions of the life-force.

As a conceptual model of the relationship of id to ego, we consider the interplay between the *vertical* and the *horizontal* flow of the life-force in the person. The id, with its upsurge of raw emotion, is an aspect of the vertical flow (Southwell, 1982): the ego functions both in the vertical axis (perception, thought) and in the horizontal (action, regulation). The ego puts the force of the id into effect by carrying it horizontally out into the world, as for instance through the arms and hands (Figure 9.1). Also, the ego regulates the id's vertical upsurge by means of the horizontal counterforce (Figure 9.2) of the body musculature, which functions, as described by Reich (1950) in horizontal segments. Harmony between these horizontal and vertical forces (discussed further in the next section) is what traditional psychology calls *ego-strength*. People whose ego is well-developed can encompass and

Figure 9.2 Ego regulation of id

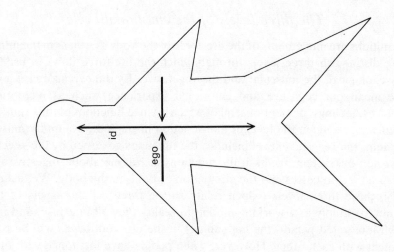

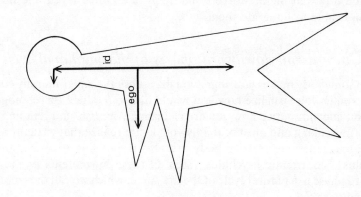

Figure 9.1 Id and ego (expression, action)

handle a strong flow of the id-force. They regard it as their ally, not their enemy, because they have found how to respect and co-operate with it.

The three levels of the emotional cycle

Emotions are movements of the life-force in the body as well as in the mind. We distinguish three levels through which the life-force flows in us: the psychological, the muscular and the vegetative. By the *psychological* level we mean our cognitive and emotional experience, such as memories, choices, feelings, perceptions, all of which involve functions of the brain; by *muscular* we mean the level of motor action through the voluntary muscle system; the *vegetative* level includes the functions governed by the vegetative nervous system, the basic life functions such as metabolic, digestive and respiratory processes and the circulation of fluids in the body. We distinguish these three levels (which relate to the three cellular layers of the embryo) simply as a working model; in reality they all interfuse, and in a well-integrated person the happenings in the different levels will be congruent with each other. However, when people have lost touch with their life-force their psychological experience will often be at odds with the reality of what is happening on the bodily levels. They may lack co-ordination, be stilted in their gestures and be physically insensitive. Also, even when reacting to a stressful situation with enormous inner tension – gut processes arrested, breathing shallow, eyes dilated, shoulders raised – they may be under the illusion that they are 'perfectly calm'. So, in biodynamic therapy we take care that the life-force flows freely in all three levels and that the person is able to integrate them.

Upward and downward phases of the emotional cycle

When somebody makes you angry you may sense the anger literally coming up in you as you visualize how you would like to retaliate (psychological); but you may not notice how you are clenching your fists and grinding your teeth (muscular); and most probably you do not realize that virtually all the vegetative functions of your body are also responding to the emotional stimulus. Biodynamic psychology sees all these movements as the first, upward phase in a natural cycle of the life-force, which we call the *emotional vasomotor cycle*.

Once the emotional incident is over, we come to the downward phase of the cycle. The feeling of anger subsides and we begin to come to terms with what has happened (psychological), the contractions in our limbs begin to relax (muscular) and the whole metabolism of the body tissue slowly returns to normal (vegetative) (Figure 9.3).

Figure 9.3   Emotional vasomotor cycle

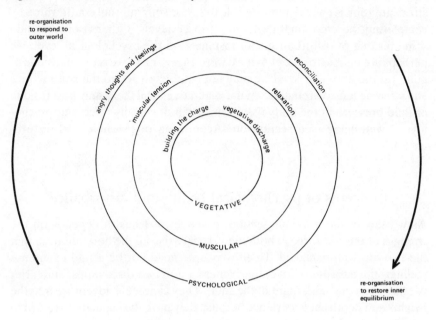

In the upward phase of the cycle the psycho-organism went through a massive disruption as it prepared to deal with the outer world. In the down-going, 'returning' phase we must then clear up this disruption inside ourselves, assimilate the experience, and restore our inner equilibrium.

The 'emotional canal': psychoperistalsis

In the upward phase of the cycle, the actual force of the emotion (the *charge*) is born; according to biodynamic theory, this occurs in the alimentary canal, which Gerda Boyesen refers to as the 'emotional canal', or 'id canal'. Our feelings are expressed at the top of this canal, through the mouth, by our words and voice, smiles or grimaces. According to Gerda Boyesen's theory, the intestines, in the lower part of the canal, digest the remaining emotional stress. Through this function, which she terms *psychoperistalsis*, we literally clear out of the body – ultimately through excretion – the vegetative after-effects of emotional stress.

The digestion of emotional stress: completing the cycle

Stress is part of the fabric of life, inherent in the dynamic interaction between a person and the environment (Selye, 1978). But once the external stress situation is past we must be able to restore our internal equilibrium, by completing the emotional cycle on all three levels. Otherwise, we retain some residue of disturbance. For instance, on the psychological level, we perhaps are unable to accept that we were angry and so we retain a residue of guilt; on the muscular level we may not completely let go the contractions and so some tension remains; on the vegetative level there may be a residue of fluid pressure in the body tissue which can drastically affect our psychological well-being (see section on 'Acquisition of psychological disturbance').

Concepts of psychological health and disturbance

As we saw in the previous section, psychological health depends on the strength of our life-force in both the vertical axis and the horizontal, so that the two are well-balanced. Healthy people need not be afraid of intense feelings: the passions of love, the excitements of new discoveries, and furies of rage, even the 'dark night of the soul'. They can safely adventure into the heights and depths of experience because they have the capacity to return to equilibrium, as surely as a swinging pendulum will always return to centre. These people can complete their emotional cycles and so restore their inner balance.

We distinguish this 'dynamic equilibrium' of the healthy adventurer from the 'neurotic equilibrium' of people who pride themselves on 'letting nothing upset them'. Such rational, 'well-adjusted' and socially acceptable people may – in the biodynamic view – be sadly limited in their range of experience. This is one aspect of the secondary personality. These people have achieved rigid control of their feelings at the cost of the richness of their inner life, and they may be totally out of touch with the life-force.

Excess of the horizontal over the vertical force

Biodynamic theory regards this neurotic equilibrium, where the horizontal is overweighted against the vertical, as a form of psychological disturbance. The opposite imbalance – the vertical in excess over the horizontal – is found in the people regarded as disturbed or pathological also by conventional psychology. These people lack the (horizontal) ego capacity to direct the force of the id in an effective way, and so are easily overwhelmed by the vertical upsurge of their feelings. This imbalance may manifest in thought disorder, emotional chaos and bizarre behaviour, which, in the biodynamic view, are essentially symptoms of unresolved pressure.

Indeed, many of the disturbances we suffer, with psychological symptoms such as chronic anxiety or with physical symptoms such as headache, are essentially symptoms of pressure. This pressure arises when the life-force does not complete its movement through all three levels of the emotional cycle, but is interrupted in its path and so accumulates in the body tissue.

When, on the other hand, the flow along both horizontal and vertical axes is too weak, people will suffer from apathy, sluggishness, resignation and lack of assertion.

Acquisition of psychological disturbance

Biodynamic psychology follows psychoanalytic theory as to the effect of emotional trauma on psychological development, particularly in children. Yet even more significant than such specific traumatic events, past and present, is – according to biodynamic theory – the *atmosphere* in which we are living. Given an atmosphere of security and trust we can – thanks to the inherent healing force of the emotional cycle – recover even from severe trauma. For instance, a baby who has just had a hard struggle through the birth canal will recover unscathed from the trauma if it can then rest and recuperate on its mother's body; a child who has had a violent quarrel with its parents will recover completely from the trauma, provided it knows that the episode has not shaken the parents' love. The stress then can melt away: no trace of the trauma is left in the body.

Without this atmosphere of security the cycle cannot be completed and the child stays on the alert, partly locked in the emotional experience. The earlier in life this happens the more devastating for our development. Thus the seeds of much psychological disturbance lie in the patterns of childhood experience.

The atmosphere conducive to the primary personality

Children are full of exuberance, curiosity, noise, and, when frustrated, of rage. If parents can bear with the full liveliness of their children, can listen to them, respond to them and provide a structure of clear limits, then these children will feel met, recognized and accepted. There is then a proper balance between the life inside them and the life around them: support and challenge, space and security. These children will know they have the right to be who they are. They will learn to shape their life-force, but will not have to stifle it.

The atmosphere that leads to the secondary personality

'We can become ill', Gerda Boyesen says, 'simply from the repression of joy.' If all children hear is 'Sit still!' 'Be quiet!' Be quick!' 'Do it right!' then they may begin to feel that there is something inherently 'wrong' with them, and they may even feel guilty for existing. So they start stifling their impulses, hiding their feelings: in biodynamic terms, interrupting their emotional cycles and compromising their primary personality. These children will not necessarily suffer specific severe traumas, but the whole atmosphere in which they live is thwarting to their evolution.

Puberty is a critical period, when the child's self-expression may not at all suit the male and female images of the parents. Some children will then rebel, in a desperate effort to assert their primary personality; others, in the attempt to make themselves acceptable, will diminish themselves, developing a bodily system of weak muscles, wan smiles, lethargy, and depression. Others, in a strategy of passive resistance, become phlegmatic, unresponsive and – at the extreme – may become catatonic.

The secondary personality becomes a fixed structure

The older we get, the more the patterns of our society impinge on us. 'Men don't cry.' 'Women don't shout.' We swallow more and more frustration, absorb more and more distress, while 'putting a brave face on it': the face of the secondary personality.

In so doing we also distort our body functioning. If you do not want anyone to know how excited or angry or miserable you are, you will not let a sound escape you, not even a sigh. So you hardly breathe out at all. Or, if you do not want to be overwhelmed by the feelings coming up in you, you hardly breathe in. So we disturb the natural responsiveness of the diaphragm, our main muscle of respiration. This is part of the 'armouring' process described in the next section and in earlier chapters.

Perpetuation of psychological disturbance

When our capacity for self-regulation is functioning well, we can 'catch up with ourselves' and recover from psychological disturbance. But the more we lose our self-regulation, the more armouring we build up, which then holds fast the patterns of disturbance within. This happens on both the psychological level and the bodily level.

Each time we fail to complete an emotional cycle a trace of the stress remains in the body. The posture we repeatedly distort will rigidify into 'muscle armour'. Also, when insecurity repeatedly prevents us from completing the cycle, we develop 'visceral armour': the intestines lose their sensitivity to the subtle pressure which should activate the psychoperistalsis. The more armoured we become the less we can digest the stresses of living. So we suffer more pressure; so we build more armour.

The pressure comes from inside us and from the world outside. Our culture is biased towards external achievement and rationality, 'getting on in the world', 'being reasonable in all things', 'not letting your heart govern your head'. Already as children we learn not to pay attention to our own sensations and experiences. As we lose touch with the life-force and identify with the secondary personality we may win social approval. But, not respecting our own basic rhythms, we lose the capacity for self-regulation, we build up armour, and our patterns of disturbance become chronic.

PRACTICE

Goals of therapy

Biodynamic therapy can be used at many different levels. Short-term treatment may relieve persistent psychosomatic symptoms such as digestive disturbances or headaches, or can help people return to a level of psychological clarity when their vegetative self-regulation has been upset. As a longer-term process biodynamic therapy is a journey of profound self-exploration, to become who we truly are. The client's vision of what is possible often changes along the way, as we shall see in our case example.

Biodynamic therapy is not a goal-oriented, problem-solving process. It is not our concern to 'improve' the secondary personality or to challenge the particular ego defences. We try to get under the secondary personality, to help the client reach into the depths of the unconscious and contact the life-force bound in those depths, so that the emotional cycles interrupted in the past can now be completed. Regression and catharsis may occur in biodynamic therapy, but this is not an end in itself. In the biodynamic view, the healing lies in completing the emotional cycle, with special emphasis on the down-going, inward phase in which we digest and assimilate our experience. When the cycle is complete we can enjoy the full benefit of the life-force. Whether we are working with people over a period of years or just for a couple of sessions, we will always aim to increase their capacity for pleasure and *self-regulation*, so that they find their own harmony with the life-force, their own *independent well-being*.

Accordingly, we aim to harmonize the flow through all levels of the cycle – psychological, muscular and vegetative – so that these functions will nourish and support each other. We want to balance the ego with the id, and the active 'male' functions of the left brain hemisphere with the receptive 'female' functions of the right hemisphere, and to integrate our animal nature and our higher nature. We want people to be able to achieve equilibrium while enjoying the richest possible range of experience.

In distinction to the genital character postulated by Reich, Gerda Boyesen speaks of the developed individual as the *ethical personality*. Rather than being constrained by the superego dictates of the disembodied will, the ethical personality lives in harmony with the universal values through being in touch with the inner life-force.

The 'person' of the therapist

The basis of biodynamic therapy is the trust in the life-force, our reverence for its potential in each person. Only when we are in touch with the life-force deep inside ourselves can we perceive the workings of the deeper forces in our clients, and help them contact those levels in themselves.

It takes a deeply receptive, non-judgemental therapist to create an atmosphere in which the client feels safe enough to give up at least some of the self-protection of the secondary personality and begin to let the primary speak. The specific biodynamic techniques, if used only in a mechanical, non-expansive way, simply will not work. The quality of the 'therapeutic presence' is all-important.

Therapeutic style

The key factor in biodynamic therapy is time. Time enough to feel safe, time to explore; time to follow your own rhythms, time for these stimuli to begin to impinge.

Inviting and encouraging

We follow the movement of the life-force, rather than a therapeutic programme of our own devising; this is the *ripeness* principle. We work with the dynamic updrift of the life-force in the client, watching for any tiniest movement from the primary level, then helping it grow stronger and clearer, till at last it says whatever it has to say.

The client may have kept the primary impulse buried for so long that he or she simply does not recognize it when it impinges, or thinks it 'wrong' and fears it. We now have to 're-educate' people to help them feel that what is moving inside them is fascinating and significant. Accordingly the style of biodynamic therapy is inviting and encouraging rather than probing and critical. Interpretation is used sparingly, if at all. It is a person's own sense of what is moving in them that is so valuable. Biodynamic therapy is a process of deep self-recognition.

As people contact their life-force more and more strongly they will often come to experience the spiritual dimension of life. Again, biodynamic therapy gives support and confirmation but no esoteric teaching, so people develop their own understanding on the basis of their own direct experience.

Resistance

We recognize that there will naturally be a tussle between the expanding primary force – which brought the client to therapy – and all the contracting, self-defeating fears of change. So while, on the one hand, we are calling on the primary personality to emerge, we are trying, on the other hand, to melt whatever obstacle is standing in its way. Is that immediate obstacle some process of the body? or is it some restrictive attitude of mind?

Characteristically, we speak of 'melting' the armour rather than of 'breaking through', and the wide range of techniques at our disposal means that we seldom run into a total impasse. We may try to melt the resistance: we do not battle with it. Sometimes, indeed, we encourage people to explore that side of themselves which is silently saying No. Finding one's strength in opposition to someone else may need to come before one can reach the pleasure of simply existing in oneself, for one's own sake.

Pleasure, harmonization and healing

Biodynamic therapy works with the essential pleasure of existence. Fear of pleasure – ultimately, fear of surrender to orgasm – is, we find, present in almost everyone. Yet pleasure is a naturally expansive force, infinitely healing. So, at many junctures of the work we will invite the client simply to 'see what feels good right now', 'explore the pleasure of the moment'. Or, we may suggest simple movements (similar to Reich's orgonomy exercises) which help the life-force to stream through the body with vibrations so fine they are scarcely perceptible to the eye, yet creating an internal 'buzz' that is exquisitely pleasurable. This is the physical reality of the healing power of the libido flow.

Fundamental personal change may involve some uncomfortable periods of 'healing crisis'; but biodynamic techniques of harmonization let us minimize the pain and disruption which can occur. Towards the end of most sessions, when the life-force is moving to complete its cycle, we may leave time for the client simply to rest. During these minutes of rest, healing and integration will get under way, from the vegetative level through to the conscious. The process works on throughout the week.

Major therapeutic techniques

We shall consider biodynamic therapy under three headings:

1. Biodynamic massage – a range of techniques serving various specific therapeutic purposes, such as to harmonize, to vitalize, to provoke the dynamic updrift, to strengthen the client's sense of bodily form
2. Biodynamic vegeto-therapy – in which we encourage clients to explore their bodily sensations and impulses, as a way of bringing unconscious material to the surface
3. Organic psychotherapy – verbal work 'rooted' in the dynamic processes of the body.

Which technique we will choose for a particular session depends partly on the client's horizontal/vertical balance, partly on how much the client is already in touch with himself or herself. For instance, in some people the muscle armour is so rigid that it literally encages them, limiting their sensitivity and stifling the movements of their life-force. Such people are incapable of feeling what is going on inside, and so are not 'ripe' for vegeto-therapy or organic psychotherapy. We must first disrupt their neurotic equilibrium by using more provocative exercises or special forms of biodynamic massage to loosen the grip of the horizontal defences.

Biodynamic massage

Massage to melt the muscle armour

We work week by week, over a period of perhaps several months, using deep systematic massage to soften the armour. At first the body may feel almost like concrete under the hands, but slowly the apparently solid mass will soften and we can differentiate the individual muscles. The muscles will not all soften at the same rate, and when one muscle lengthens, another will take more strain, so the process is one of constant adaptation. As the ripening proceeds, more fluid comes into the tissue and the muscles become tender. This is a sign that the emotional dynamic is nearing the surface.

Every muscle tension is connected with a disturbance in the breathing pattern. As we work on the muscles we adjust the rhythm of our touch so as to encourage the sudden, spontaneous deep 'emotional in-breath'. Then at last the dynamic updrift of the repressed emotions can begin to impinge.

This technique is deeply provocative: we are restimulating the upward phase of old, incomplete emotional cycles so that the dynamic process of resolution can get under way.

Massage to encourage the downward flow

Sometimes our therapeutic intention is just the opposite: to restore the client's equilibrium by encouraging the downward flow of the life-force. When the client is excessively agitated or confused we may work with *energy distribution*. Using a series of strokes, some deeper some lighter, we draw the life-force in the client to flow down through the body from the head towards the feet, and also encourage it to surface from deep in the bones, through the layers of muscles and fascia, until it radiates out through the skin, as it naturally should in the healthy person. At times we will hardly touch the physical body but work directly with the life-force in the aura.

The psychoperistaltic sounds. As we work we will be listening through a stethoscope to the movements in the client's belly, to hear in precise detail how the psychoperistalsis is responding to the various movements of our hands. (Indeed, psychoperistaltic massage is sometimes seen as the 'trademark' of biodynamic therapy.) The psychoperistaltic sounds come in an astonishing variety. Dry, percussive sounds tell us we are softening some fibres in the chronic muscle armour; sounds like thunder tell us we are moving excess fluid out of the tissue; gentle continuous sounds like a babbling brook tell us that the life-force is flowing harmoniously. The more watery the sounds the riper is the life-force that we are mobilizing; the drier the sounds the more deeply the dynamic is buried. The language of the sounds tells us, from second to second, what effect our work is having and guides our hands in the most effective way of approaching the client.

Massage to deepen the client's self-awareness

Through biodynamic massage a client can gain a deep sense of his or her inner substance. The pattern of the breathing wave shows how emotionally free the client has become. Our ultimate aim is to help the diaphragm become so flexible and responsive that the breath comes in spontaneous, unbroken, harmonious waves. Gradually the client will become aware of his or her own inner movements, of the rhythm of his or her 'inner ocean', and eventually of the cosmic rhythms of which he or she is part. At first this is hardly a conscious sense, but rather a vegetative sense, a sense in the viscera: literally, a gut sense. With it comes a sense of his or her own inner richness and power, his or her own libidinous flow. The client finds his or her independent well-being.

Through the massage we are 'speaking' to the client at a deep, unconscious level and the effects continue long beyond the session, with repercussions in all aspects of the client's life, including the client's dreams. Biodynamic massage is not just 'body work'; it speaks to the whole person, bearing an invitation to profound change.

Biodynamic vegeto-therapy

The technique of biodynamic vegeto-therapy is particularly valuable for discovering the psychological content of the dynamic updrift and for deepening the client's awareness of his or her emotions.

We ask the client to lie down and close the eyes, to take time simply to feel the body and to 'let it breathe'. The very tone and rhythm of the therapist's voice help the client to sink below the level of the bodily defences and contact the inner depths. We invite clients, should they feel any impulse to say anything or to do anything, simply to let it come; we do not ask them to 'make sense' of it. Biodynamic vegeto-therapy has been described as a technique of 'free association through the body'. A session might, typically, develop in the following way.

The client, a middle aged man is lying quiet and still; breathing is regular. As he relaxes more deeply we may see a fluttering movement in the region of his diaphragm. This tells us that the breathing defences are letting go and that the vegetative charge is mounting.

Soon we may notice a tiny movement in the fingers of one hand, as the pressure of the life-force impinges from within. We ask him to 'feel what the hand is doing', and 'let the movement grow'. At this stage the client may recognize no emotional significance in the movement: it is simply 'happening'. We let the movement evolve and grow stronger without, at first, having to be named or defined in any way. As the movement intensifies it may develop the character of a particular emotional action, such as angry hitting. Even now the client, who is a passive, self-effacing character, may 'have no idea why' he is hitting. In the early stages of the session we deliberately avoid engaging the client's ego, as his rationality could block or predetermine the course of the emerging life-force.

When the signs of anger become more apparent in the client's face and in the rest of the body, we may invite him to let out a sound, and to speak any words which come into his or her mind. To the client's own surprise, he may hear himself shouting 'I hate you!' Gradually the old scenario emerges as we ask 'How old do you feel?' 'What's happening?' 'Whom are you shouting at?' The client is temporarily in regression, reliving an occasion – perhaps typical of his childhood – when his emotional cycle was traumatically interrupted. For example, perhaps, as a boy, his father had hit him for something that was not the boy's fault, giving him no chance to explain. We now encourage the client to complete that old cycle: to vent his anger physically and to say to his father what he could not say then – and indeed has never been able to express since. The therapist's support makes it possible for the client to overcome his inhibitions of guilt.

This effort leads to deep satisfaction, as the client resolves that old conflict between his indignation and his sense of inadequacy.

Once the anger is expressed, waves of love will often follow, and as the client rests after the session, psychoperistalsis completes the final phase of the emotional cycle.

The purpose of such a session is not to 'make believe' that the original situation in the past had a 'happy ending'. Rather, it is to acknowledge and accept the reality of the emotions, impulses and frustrations which were occurring at that time, and now – at long last – to help the life-force complete its natural cycle so that it can flow through muscles and consciousness in a new-found pattern of vigorous self-assertion.

Organic psychotherapy

We may use organic psychotherapy when someone is already very open to the movements of the life-force and does not need the more physical techniques, or when the dynamic updrift is already very strong in its pressure towards resolution, so we want to avoid increasing the vegetative charge.

Sitting comfortably, the clients can explore whatever comes to mind, ruminating on difficulties in present life or perhaps on events in the past. They are not simply talking *about* these issues: thoughts and feelings are literally moving them as they speak.

We give clients 'all the time in the world' to express themselves without interruption or comment, simply offering the occasional word to encourage the flow of speech. Meanwhile we are watching for minute physical changes, uneven rhythms of breath, varying tones of voice. If we see that nothing is actually changing inside them as they speak, and that they have slipped into disconnected generalizations, we may ask them to pause a moment and register how they are sitting, how they are breathing. This will help people reconnect with what is really moving them.

Eventually, in most such sessions, the client will arrive at a simple sentence which encapsulates the essence of the matter. On the level of consciousness the emotional cycle has now reached completion; we hear a sigh of relief, often followed by rumblings in the belly, as the psychoperistalsis completes the discharge on the vegetative level. The psychotherapy has been an organic process of change.

The change process in therapy

The dynamic updrift is the key to change in biodynamic therapy. As the repressed life-force presses nearer the surface of consciousness the pressure will get more intense. The stronger the pressure the stronger the symptoms and – paradoxically – the stronger the healing potential. At such a time a person may – in the eyes of conventional psychology – appear to be 'disturbed'. Biodynamic psychology sees this phase as a healing crisis: the very intensity of the symptoms is a sign that the person is getting nearer to genuine psychological health. The buried conflict is now ripe to be recognized and resolved.

We take care that equilibrium is not disturbed for too long. Our motto is 'provoke and dissolve, provoke and dissolve', layer after layer, until the neurosis is progressively cleared out of the psycho-organism. Phases of upheaval will alternate with phases of harmonization, as the updrift is first liberated and then re-integrated, completing its cycle.

As we develop a sense for the emotional cycle we grow to trust it more and more. Once we find that we can live *through* pain and reach pleasure again, we become less afraid of intense feeling. We reach a certain basic security and can dare to open ourselves to the streamings of the life-force both in ourselves and in the world. We no longer feel victim to ourselves or to outer circumstances. We discover that it is good to live; the world is no longer 'flat'. Our inner treasury of joy, love and spirit is open to us again.

The following account of a client in therapy for some seven months shows how biodynamic methods were able to help one woman who had been locked in a 'neurotic equilibrium' to become more open to her own emotional processes and discover more of her inner resources.

CASE EXAMPLE

Betty, aged 43, comes for biodynamic massage 'as a last resort', to see if it can relieve the recurrent headaches for which her doctor finds no physiological cause.

Betty regards her life as 'very satisfactory'; she is comfortably off in a 'good marriage' to a successful business executive; her two sons (by a former marriage) are at university. Five years ago Betty had a hysterectomy following two miscarriages and an ectopic pregnancy, but she has 'completely recovered from all that'. She would never think of herself as needing psychotherapy, but a friend had suggested that biodynamic massage might help the headaches, and she agreed to give it a try.

Early memories surface

It is no surprise to Betty's (woman) therapist to find that her neck, shoulders and upper back are as hard as wood, and the muscles at the top of her right arm somewhat swollen. As the therapist is working down to the fingers of Betty's right hand, Betty starts to smile. She is remembering how her piano teacher had spread her hand over the keyboard in her very first lesson, and the first piece she learned at the age of six. She hums a phrase of it to herself and draws a sigh. A wave of sadness comes over her, and she tells how she had dreamed of being a concert pianist but had left the Royal School of Music early because she 'had to get married'. She had then got submerged in a rapidly deteriorating first marriage, with two small sons and never enough money.

At the end of the session Betty gets off the massage table looking young, and a little bewildered. She is amazed that these old memories should suddenly have surfaced, but says she feels 'light' and relieved and decides to come for a further three months' treatment at least.

Massage releases the dynamic updrift

With this commitment her therapist now feels free to work more strongly, and for the next few sessions she uses deep systematic massage to loosen Betty's chronic muscular tensions and so release the repressed life-force. Betty dreams vividly during this period. After the sixth session she dreams that she is wandering in a strange town and cannot find her children: this theme of the 'lost child' recurs over the next weeks. During the sessions Betty gradually confides more of her feelings to her therapist, telling of the 'nuisance' of not having been able to have a child with her present husband, and how their sexual relationship has dwindled. She also begins to report 'uncharacteristic' incidents such as 'just standing there laughing' when she found she had left her husband's treasured suede coat out all night in the rain.

Abreaction of protest

During the ninth session, as the therapist is working on the deltoid muscle of the right arm, she sees that Betty's jaw is tightening and her legs stretching out as if she were 'digging in her heels'. Betty is remembering how, one day when she was 12, her father had called her to put away her bike, but she was immersed in a book and had not done it right away; that evening her father had been cold and silent. The therapist then invites Betty to get down off the massage table and lie on the big mattress on the floor. Betty's whole body stiffens, feet and fists in an attitude of defiance. The therapist encourages Betty to express whatever she is feeling. In a thin, hesitant voice she brings out 'No, I won't!' Gradually she gains courage, she begins to kick, and her protest escalates to the sort of temper tantrum seen in small children. Exhausted at last, memories of childhood pour into her mind as she rests.

Completing the emotional cycle

When Betty arrives for the next session her face is distended with fluid, she appears depressed and her manner is abstracted and distant. When she starts to speak it is not about her feelings but about the trivia of the day. The therapist recognizes the signs of the uncompleted emotional cycle: the energy which had come up so forcefully last time had not been fully integrated and there is again massive fluid pressure in the tissue. The therapist returns to massage, now not with the aim of loosening more of the muscle armour, but to empty the tissue of the excess fluid. At first she hears few sounds in the stethoscope and recognizes that something on Betty's mind is preventing the psychoperistalsis. Betty is not feeling secure enough to move into the downward phase of the emotional cycle. So, as she massages, the therapist gets Betty to talk about how she has been feeling since the 'temper tantrum' last week. Betty is reluctant at first: 'What's the point? it won't do any good.' The therapist coaxes her to say more about this, and it gradually emerges that Betty used to have similar feelings of helplessness and hopelessness as a child, when 'the grown-ups didn't understand'. As soon as she says these words the psychoperistalsis starts.

Deepening contact with the emotions

The dynamic process is now well under way. In further powerful vegeto-therapy sessions more childhood material emerges. Then at last Betty begins to speak about her miscarriages, and the horror of the ectopic pregnancy. She feels as if she had not merely lost the babies she should have borne, but had, in a sense, lost touch also with the child-being in herself. Grief is mixed with feelings of inadequacy and guilt and also of blame. 'It's all my fault' alternates with 'It's all his fault', and during this period she has outbursts of disproportionate irritation against her husband.

To help maintain Betty's equilibrium her therapist works intermittently with emptying or harmonizing massage, encouraging Betty to talk the while. The tension patterns in her back are changing from week to week, and as the armour dissolves Betty is becoming more expressive, verbally and physically. In the vegeto-therapy sessions, it's 'Men don't care!' 'Men never understand!'

The animal instincts emerge

The next major turning point comes in the fifteenth session. Betty is lying on the mattress. Her torso starts to writhe in a blend of sensuousness and aggressivity. She gets up on her hands and knees, snarling. She is like a tigress protecting her young. Soon the sensuality outweighs the hostility and she stands up, the libidinous movement continuing through the whole body. Her therapist encourages her to overcome her hesitation at 'displaying herself' and Betty begins to giggle like a teenager, enjoying the movement more and more.

The Oedipal triangle

This session too has a backlash. Next week Betty is reluctant to meet her therapist's eye, and eventually admits she's been anxious about meeting her after the last session. It emerges that Betty's mother disapproved if ever Betty 'made an exhibition of herself' or did anything to win Daddy's attention. It is a shock for Betty to see her 'perfect' mother in this light. Now the can of worms is opened and a host of tiny incidents come to mind where mother had somehow sabotaged the child's pleasure. Betty's relationship with her mother now plummets and she cancels her Easter visit. As so much material is now mobilized the therapist works with organic psychotherapy for the next two sessions, to let Betty talk it through without increasing the dynamic updrift.

Transition to pleasure

The nineteenth session – vegeto-therapy again – brings a change of heart. Betty comes into a strong abreaction and pounds angrily on a cushion (her 'mother'). But as the fury of the outburst passes Betty's hands cautiously begin to caress and clutch the cushion, though with much ambivalence, as she begins to reconnect with the longing and the love she had for her mother.

In the next session too these tender feelings are in the ascendant. Holding the cushion to her breast, Betty reaches deep pleasure and her breath comes in long slow waves of unprecedented fullness. She lets go of the cushion, and libidinous streamings pour through her body. For many minutes she lies quiet, only the subtlest waves of movement visible as she breathes. Betty has reached the place of independent well-being.

Independence

Betty is now out of the regression stage of her therapy. Impulses to stretch out her body, and to 'take her place in the world' are encouraged by her therapist, and Betty develops more self-assertion. She sees that her stance in the marriage has been rather like that of child to father, and she now – sometimes! – takes a more adult stand with her husband. She also puts a long-dormant ambition into practice and gets in touch with some experimental musicians; they meet together each week for improvisation sessions. Her relationship with her sons becomes more enjoyable for all as she lets go of the compulsion/burden of 'looking after them'. The headaches are a thing of the past.

Termination

Although Betty is still vainly hoping for more from her husband than he is willing or able to give, she has reached a plateau of well-being in herself, and decides to stop therapy. Although she has by no means reached her full individuation, the quality of her living has already improved substantially. If, later on, she felt moved to explore more deeply they would probably – her therapist foresees – be able to uncover and resolve more of the conflicts of Betty's early years while her father was away at the war and her mother under great strain. But the therapy to date has far more than met Betty's original hopes.

REFERENCES

Boyesen, G. (1982) The primary personality, *Journal of Biodynamic Psychology*, No. 3, pp. 3–8.

Boyesen, M.–L. (1974) Psycho-peristalsis I: the abdominal discharge of nervous tension, *Energy & Character*, Vol. 5, No. 1, pp. 5–16.

Boyesen, M.–L. (1975) Psycho-peristalsis V: function of the libido circulation, *Energy & Character*, Vol. 6, No. 3, pp. 61–8.

Boyesen, M.–L. (1976) Psycho-peristalsis VII: from libido theory to cosmic energy, *Energy & Character*, Vol. 7, No. 2, pp. 38–47.

Freud, S. (1905) *Three Essays on the Theory of Sexuality*. Reprinted in Pelican Freud Library Vol. 6, Penguin, Harmondsworth.

Freud, S. (1915) *The Unconscious*. Reprinted in Pelican Freud Library Vol. 10, Penguin, Harmondsworth.

Goldstein, K. (1939) *The Organism*, Macmillan, New York.

Reich, W. (1950) *Character Analysis* (3rd edn), Vision Press, London.

Selye, H. (1978) *The Stress of Life*, McGraw-Hill, New York.

Southwell, C. (1982) Biodynamic massage as a therapeutic tool, *Journal of Biodynamic Psychology*, No. 3, pp. 40–54.

Suggested further reading

Boyesen, G. (1985) *Entre Psyche et Soma*, Payot, Paris.

Journal of Biodynamic Psychology, Nos. 1, 2, 3, especially The biodynamic theory of neurosis, No. 1 (1980), Biodynamic Publications, London.

The Collected Papers of Biodynamic Psychology, Vols. 1 and 2. (1980), Biodynamic Publications, London.

Liss, J. (1983) The systems model as applied to the field of bioenergetic therapy, psychology and psycho-somatic medicine, *Energy & Character*, April.

CHAPTER 10

PSYCHOSYNTHESIS

Jean Hardy and Diana Whitmore

HISTORICAL CONTEXT AND DEVELOPMENTS IN BRITAIN

Historical context

Psychosynthesis was founded by Roberto Assagioli, an Italian psychiatrist who lived from 1888 to 1974. As a young doctor training in psychiatry in Italy in the early years of the twentieth century, he attended some of the early international conferences in psychoanalysis, and became known to both Jung and Freud for his commitment to new research into unconscious material, and his enthusiasm as a practitioner. But from his earliest writings, he asserted that exploration of unconscious material is concerned not only with the solution of personal problems, but also with the growth of human potential. Creativity and strength as well as difficulty and pain spring from the unconscious and the true potential of a human being may be involved with his or her willingness to explore that pain, and use it towards growth.

The roots of psychosynthesis are in the world's mystical and spiritual writing and experience, as well as in the growth of personal psychotherapy as it has developed this century. Assagioli was concerned not only with the individual human being, but also with the fragmentation of the world which he saw as related to the struggle of each person to become more whole. The word *psychosynthesis* conveys the meaning. It is in accepting and relating to our own brokenness and fragmentation that we can accept ourselves, and the potential in each of us can be released.

Thus psychosynthesis was conceived by one man, in Venice and Florence, during the years before the First World War. It was developed in practice in Rome through the 1920s and 1930s, and was then only known to the world through articles in Italian psychological journals during that period, and through two articles published in the *Hibbert Journal* in England in the 1930s (Assagioli, 1933; 1937). The first psychosynthesis institute was founded in Rome in 1926 – the Instituto di Cultura Terapia Psichica. This not only was a centre for practice, a clinic, but also offered a series of lectures annually on the developing therapy, particularly on the application of human potential in education and medicine.

The intellectual roots of the early development of psychosynthesis lay in Assagioli's own lifelong convictions. Growing up in a cultured upper middle-class Jewish household, where Italian, French and English were all regularly spoken, and where he was encouraged to read and travel extensively, he was deeply versed in European culture. Throughout his whole life, he was influenced by his childhood reading in Plato and Dante Alighieri and their classic symbolic pictures of the spiritual journey of the individual. And as his knowledge developed, his library – which is presently open to the public in Florence – extended into spiritual and philosophical material from Eastern as well as Western cultures. The household in which he grew up was spiritually aware – his mother became a Theosophist, and so later did his wife. Whilst he was training to become a doctor, he was also involved in philosophical and mystical work, and attended conferences in moral and educational philosophy.

So psychosynthesis from the beginning was based on the conviction that human beings are deeply spiritual creatures, that individuals and the human race as a whole are in an evolving spiritual process, and that our growing knowledge of unconscious processes is a key in this continuing journey. Assagioli, like Freud and Jung, regarded himself as a scientist: he was investigating, diagnosing and treating illness, on a medical and clinical basis, but this was always in a spiritual context. Psychosynthesis developed separately and independently on this basis, though Assagioli, through all the difficult years of Mussolini's rule in Italy during which he was imprisoned briefly and became a refugee for a time, was in touch with a wide range of thinkers and philosophers as well as practitioners in Europe. These included Carl Jung, Martin Buber, Hermann Keyserling, Alice Bailey and Tagore.

Until the 1950s, psychosynthesis was thus practised only in Italy. It was only at that time, when Assagioli was already in his sixties, that it began to be known internationally, and work was published in the USA and France.

The Italian Institute was transferred to Florence after the war; the Psychosynthesis Research Foundation was opened in Valmy near Delaware in the USA in 1958, and in 1960 the Greek Centre for Psychosynthesis was founded by Triant Triantafyllou. In 1959 and 1960 conferences were held in Paris and London, with Assagioli attending and speaking.

In the 1960s, this extension into the modern psychotherapeutic world continued. Assagioli learned of the work of such congenial writers as Maslow, Fromm and Frankl in the USA, and incorporated their findings into his publication of the book *Psychosynthesis* (Assagioli, 1965). His main concerns in the 1960s were with individual psychotherapeutic work; work with children, particularly gifted children, and their parents; work with couples of many kinds – marriages, friendships, parent–child relationships; and work with groups, and awareness of the fragmentation of the earth and the nations within it.

Developments in Britain

It was in the 1960s that psychosynthesis was first introduced to England on a lasting basis. In 1959, Assagioli held three meetings in London, and he visited again in 1962. Weekend conferences were held in August 1964 in London, in October 1964 at Attingham Park. In May 1965 the Psychosynthesis and Education Trust was founded, being registered as a charity in August of that year. This held several successful series of lectures, and involved such people as Sir George Trevelyan and Geoffrey Leytham (who are still both trustees of the Trust), Dr Bill Ford Robertson, Dr Martin Israel and Dr Cirinei from Italy. This first attempt lasted for four years but lapsed in 1969.

At the invitation of the trustees, the Trust was revived again in 1980 by Diana Whitmore, who had trained with Assagioli in Italy. The Trust now produces an ever-growing number of psychosynthesis therapists, as well as graduates from the more general education stream. In 1974, the Institute of Psychosynthesis was founded in London, particularly by Roger and Joan Evans, who had trained in California. Trainees come from all over Britain, and indeed Europe, to learn at the two establishments, and there are currently about 300 or 400 people registered as trainees in London. Courses, especially introductory courses, are already developing through the rest of the country.

THEORETICAL ASSUMPTIONS

Image of the person

In 1933 Assagioli published a map of the person in the *Hibbert Journal*. This is the 'egg-shaped diagram' (see Figure 10.1) which is still used in psychosynthesis. He wrote in this article that this is a

> crude and elementary attempt, that can only give a structural, static, almost anatomical representation of our inner constitution, while it leaves out the dynamic aspect, which is most important and essential . . . it is important not to lose sight of the main lines . . . otherwise the undominated multiplicity confuses the mind, the wealth of particulars hide the picture as a whole and prevent one realising the respective significance, purpose and value of its different parts.

The domination to which he refers is the fundamental importance of the spiritual, the Self and the transpersonal elements. The personality is essentially seen within the context of this Self, a centre of identity and being. In most, the Self exists in a more or less veiled and confused way. Assagioli's view is that many people are only aware of the field of consciousness (4). This is everyday reality; what the person is aware of day by day, minute by minute. This is however in his view only the tip of the iceberg of the potential that is open to us all. The potential, and the problems of the personality and indeed of the human race as a whole, are contained in the various areas of the unconscious. These are the areas that people can become gradually aware of in their lives, as being the source of their being. This awareness may spring first of all from crisis, from pain, and from problems. But these may also be the source of longings, of a search for meaning and purpose, of glimpses of another reality from that of everyday mundane living.

The lower unconscious (1) has been systematically studied by Freud and other psychoanalysts. This is the area from which the personality springs, the drives, the energy, the maturing development. It is also the source of many manifestations perceived as problems by people who experience them – childhood defences that become inhibiting, accretions of patterns that fail to serve the adult, illnesses that the body expresses for a personality that does not acknowledge the tensions and contradictions built up within its structure. The middle unconscious (2) is closest to consciousness – the material is relatively available to the person through memory. It is the area in which day-to-day experience is routinely processed by the individual.

The higher unconscious, or superconscious (3), is the realm of transpersonal or spiritual awareness. It is, in psychosynthesis, the context for the personality. Within this sphere are the qualities which we see as good –

Figure 10.1 Our psyche: 1. 'lower' unconscious; 2. middle unconscious; 3. super-conscious; 4. field of consciousness; 5. personal self or 'I'; 6. transpersonal self; 7. collective unconscious.

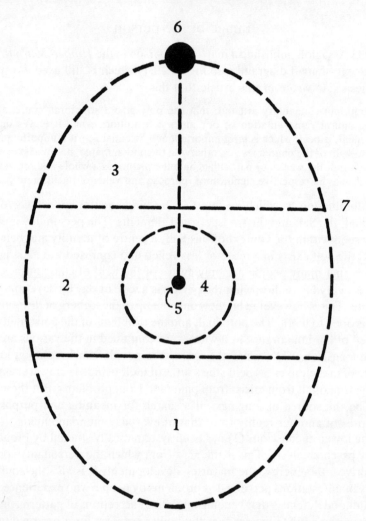

beauty, truth, will, love, harmony. Whereas the personality as it matures is complex, fragmented, struggling, the higher unconscious is simple, clear, at rest. In this model of the individual, the personal aspects are contained within the collective unconscious (7), which holds all the innate experience of the human race, the situation into which we are born. Assagioli uses the concept of the *archetype* here, an ancient Greek formula brought into depth psychology by Jung, which expresses the great myths and symbols of the human spirit occurring in every civilization – for example the mother, the father, the searcher. We are born with human expectations that are already strong and formed in the collective unconscious.

Thus the field of consciousness is contained within a much larger reality, of which people are differentially aware. To be truly alive is to grow into these areas, to acknowledge both our potential as the context for growth, and to be prepared to work through the difficulties each one of us has accumulated over a lifetime.

The key to growth is consciousness of the 'I' (5). This is the permanent centre of experience, without content, observant, integrating. Many people are not in touch with the I: they are fragmented, without a steady sense of identity, alienated from themselves, living out perhaps the social roles that are expected of them but dependent upon other people and external structures for a sense of reality. A person who is prepared to grow to his or her true potential during his or her lifetime needs to experience this sense of sureness and integrity, the true centre. In psychosynthesis terms, it is only in being constantly centred in this way that one is able to contact the higher self (6), which is both the true source of transpersonal qualities, and the soul, the context, the unity in which the person can be most truly himself or herself and at home in the world, at one with living existence. This is why Assagioli was so anxious to point out the relationship of the conscious and unconscious areas of the person to each other, and the predominance of the spiritual. He said that the Self is latent in people, it must be searched for and experienced and recognized: but also 'the Self is one; only it manifests itself in different degrees of consciousness and self-realisation' (Assagioli, 1933).

This process is ever changing, complex and lifelong. If growth occurs, a person can come to live nearer the soul than the personality, can begin to detach from the struggles of everyday living and reflect and act with more clarity. This does not mean that such a person detaches from ordinary life; rather he or she comes to be more active in living, but from an experience of centredness and stillness.

One further concept in Assagioli's image of the person is central to therapeutic work: this is the notion of subpersonalities. His view was that we are all many people: that through childhood and adult development we come to group and structure our experience into constellations of behaviour, each of which could be seen as a separated personality – for example, the frightened child, the teacher, the mystic, the parent. This was a nineteenth-century idea, which enables the therapist to work explicitly with the parts of the whole person, and which provides a language in which anyone can discern internal conflicts, motivations and energies. Most of these subpersonalities will be consciously known to the person – some will be very familiar, others recognized only more slowly. But some are quite hidden, usually in areas of the lower unconscious, and only slowly come to be recognized by the I.

Concepts of psychological health and disturbance

The concept of psychological health in psychosynthesis is essentially seen along a spiritual dimension. Assagioli, later in his life, came to accept Maslow's distinction between self-actualizing people who are effective at living successfully in the world, able to work and to love, to achieve and to cope with failure; and those he came to call 'transcending self-actualizers' – people whose lives are seen by themselves as existing in a greater spiritual context, who are prepared not only to take responsibility for themselves and those nearest to them, but for the whole human situation. This sense of responsibility can of course arise from anger, hurt and bitterness, but such driving forces are not the qualities of the 'transcenders'. People who are driven may have a glimpse of the possibilities of transcendence but without the wholeness of personality to cope with this vision. The true achievement and vision, in the view of both Maslow and Assagioli, occurs where the personality is integrated around the I and the Self, from a still and clear centre.

A source of psychological disturbance may be having a glimpse of the transpersonal but without the integration of the personality to cope with this. Many people who are seen as mad have visions of God or the devil, spiritual or evil forces, but have not achieved enough self-knowledge and conscious awareness to sustain such experiences. Psychological health in psychosynthesis terms is always seen as balance: a balance of the different areas of the personality and soul, and health is essentially centred around the integrating I. Health is about acting consciously, about not being driven by inadequately understood processes, and about living lovingly and pur-posefully.

In psychosynthesis those who are self-actualizers without any awareness of spiritual reality would be seen as healthy, but limited. On the other hand, although therapy is always undertaken from a spiritual context, there would be no attempt to induce a client to acknowledge the spiritual context unless he or she naturally wished to do so. It is always assumed that people create their own natural limits and these need to be respected. Psychosynthesis is not an evangelizing therapy, and is always prepared to go along with the client's reality until he or she wishes to change.

Many clients come, of course, to psychosynthesis with problems based entirely in the lower unconscious: issues that have often stayed with them for many years, defences that have become inhibiting, or pain that has become too great to live with. Often a life crisis will be the precipitating cause, or a sense of meaninglessness and unsatisfied potential. Facing death or loss with what seems to be insufficient resources may bring a client to therapy. The pain or crisis and the person's anxious response to this will be seen as a possibility of growth, of a person being prepared to look at old patterns and try out new. Paradoxically therefore, the *disturbance* itself may be seen as a symbol of potential growth. Disturbance is not seen as something to be avoided, but as a possible threshold to the next stage of life. The theory of psychosynthesis expects that a healthy life will go on changing, there is no achievable 'steady state' or 'normality': on the contrary, the healthy person will continue to experience disturbance throughout his or her life, but hopefully will be prepared to see this crisis' as opportunity rather than danger. Growth and healthiness mean living with whatever life may bring with consciousness, self-knowledge, from the centre, and ever nearer to the soul. This is an essentially dynamic concept.

Acquisition of psychological disturbance

Life itself then is seen as essentially disturbing. But the disturbance may be experienced as debilitating and impossible to live with without a broader, spiritual framework.

Human beings are born into a difficult existential situation. We carry with us, in the collective unconscious, much of the past – the pain of the past, the human concepts that Jung called the *archetypes* which hold expectations of mothering and fathering, of searching and of God, and what Wordsworth defined as the 'still, sad music of humanity'. Alienation can arise at any time in life if the child or the adult cannot cope on his or her own terms with these major themes. For instance, he or she may be brought up in an inhibiting and reserved environment, not seeing himself or herself loved or understood in a way that is compatible with these unconscious expectations. Many people face danger, death or cruelty in their early lives, or grow up in an environment where there is little sense of meaning. These factors are experienced personally but the roots seem deep in the whole human situation and the unconscious expectations with which we seem to be born.

Also great pain may lie in the child's original relationships, with the mother or father or their equivalents. Almost all adults seem to have 'unfinished business' with their parents, and this is almost inevitable, as any child needs to grow up in a nurturing environment which he or she sees as understanding as well as loving, and then needs to leave it. Anything can go awry at any one of these points. The parents themselves may not have grown enough to enable them to parent in a way that is appropriate for a particular child; the personalities of parent and child may be incompatible in ways which they both experience as quite destructive. People who are parents have their own lives to live and their own crises to meet; and loss of parents may occur. The conditioning that any child receives and the culture in which he or she grows up, especially in a society such as our own which is class-ridden, sexist, competitive, materialistic, and achievement-orientated may bring great traumas. Any adolescent is likely to have to struggle to attain independence and his or her own integrity.

In childhood and adulthood, there are *passages* to be lived through, as we strive towards independence, attempt to make satisfactory relationships and find a contribution we can make in the world. Death, one's own and others' has to be faced: Eliott Jaques (1970) has writen well on 'the midlife crisis' which is about facing death and from that awareness the possibility of creativity. And, as Jung indicates in many of his writings, there is the potentiality and the problems of the second half of life, which can become far richer that anything that has preceded it, or alternatively can be an experience of disintegration and depression if meaning is lacking. Many people also experience the hardships of world events – war, emigration, being a refugee, harsh political regimes. There are many situations in which people can become victims, which are partly a sociological and partly a psychological condition.

Defences are likely to be built up in any of these circumstances. These defences first of all serve the person well, but afterwards may restrict growth and change. Roles have to be filled which may give little freedom to the person who has to undertake them. An identity may emerge which is dependent upon others, which has little sense of self-worth. A person's inner life may be very different from the outer life he or she may be required to lead, and the integrity which comes from feeling at home in the world may be lacking in many ways.

So disturbance may be acquired at any point, and may go underground. The problems of the personality may be so great that there is little possibility of acquiring a sense of a deeper or higher self or of the I, the centre of oneself. But in the view of psychosynthesis it is precisely in acknowledging and working with disturbance that many people find or rediscover a spiritual context to living. In contacting the pain it may be possible to find the transpersonal quality behind it. Paradoxically, in facing death, depression and loss, life and energy of the soul may be tapped and opened in a completely new way.

Perpetuation of psychological disturbance

As has been indicated, it is not the 'psychological disturbance' itself that is destructive to a person's growth: rather the pain and inhibition spring from its perpetuation. Defences of fear, withdrawal and aggression may be useful and almost inevitable in any particular situation. It may be most appropriate to be afraid of a parent who is perceived as harsh, or to be terrified of an army in occupation in a country. But if the fear persists, if what is built up is a frightened child subpersonality which remains with all its inhibitions, automatic defences and overriding wish to avoid difficult or frightening situations through adolescence and into adulthood, then the whole life of the person may be dramatically restricted by its presence. It may be appropriate and almost inevitable for a small girl to learn her concept of femininity in early childhood from the values of her parents and the surrounding adults. However, if this concept is restricting, debilitating, making her feel constantly inferior to men in the things she wants to do as she grows older, then this role learning could create a sense of psychological disturbance, of deep disjuncture at some point of her life. Again disturbance depends on a mixture of outer constraints and inner experience, the mix particular and unique in each case.

Thus patterns spring up in all human beings that are not of their own making. With awareness and self-perception, which may begin at almost any time in life, we become conscious that what we are is largely the product of others, either individually or collectively. Much important and fundamental conditioning happens in childhood, before we are aware of it: by the time we become conscious then we are already formed. It thus seems that we might almost entirely be the product of our environments, genetics and conditioning. The patterns that are already built into a person's personality structure seem permanent, inevitable, made by early reactions to the conditions of life.

It is this assumption that psychosynthesis questions. The source of freedom for any individual is awareness of the I, and of the potential within arising from the Self. These perpetual patterns may be tackled if there is the will to do so, so that the source of a person's strength can be acknowledged as lying within, integrated and always growing, rather than without on the old structures, patterns and relationships. A person may continue with these, but from a clearer, freer place; and he or she may change from choice.

Within this process, the spiritual dimension is crucial. In the psychosynthesis view, psychological disturbances may persist without hope if there is no sense of centring, of being the still observer, and through this observation able to experience oneself within a spiritual context. The suffering, pain and alienation may be similar whether or not there is spiritual awareness: but to perceive oneself and one's clients within a wider transpersonal perspective, gives a proportion to and a detachment from the struggle which is crucial. It is the difference, in classical terms as depicted in Dante's *Divine Comedy*, between the hopelessness of Dante's hell and the strivings of his purgatory where the higher self can see that a paradise is possible and attainable; this vision needs both reason and faith, and is seen in psychosynthesis as being part of each person's essential journey through life.

The spiritual dimension of therapy is essentially about meaning – about each person's meaning in life, about the possibility of finding, perhaps helping to create, one's soul; and about the possibility of fulfilling the vision of a peaceful, centred life for the human species. It is about the necessity of working through suffering to contact our spiritual context.

PRACTICE

Goals of therapy

What are the aims of psychosynthesis therapy? They are many and varied: to alleviate suffering, first of all, but also to facilitate understanding of its significance; to clear the way for a greater and more objective knowledge of one's own weaknesses as well as inner gifts and concealed potential; to move towards congruence between the inner and the outer world; to help the individual create his or her own life and express himself or herself in the world; to raise the quality of life and evoke hope and optimism; finally to evoke one's own inner authority so as to render the therapist obsolete. On the psychological level it aims to build a personality which is free from emotional blocks, has command over all its functions and has a clear awareness of its own centre. On the transpersonal level, it enables the individual to explore those regions full of mystery and wonder beyond our ordinary awareness, which we call the superconscious – the wellspring of higher intuitions, inspirations, ethical imperatives and states of illumination. This exploration culminates in the discovery of the self, our true essence beyond all masks and conditions.

The therapeutic process focuses both upon pathology and psychological disease as well as upon the evocation of latent potential. In psychosynthesis there is no normative definition of the healthy, fully functioning individual. And there is no straightforward recipe for the therapist or guide to follow. The questions therapists must ask themselves are: 'Does the client have the inner freedom to deal with his or her particular psychological reality in a way he or she deems appropriate and meaningful? Is the client increasingly able to be responsible for his or her inner development and outer behaviour?'

Western culture emphasizes the importance of being a strong individual, intelligent and fully able to invest oneself in one's activities, functioning well and effectively in everyday life and society. Most of those seeking therapy have ample room for growth along this dimension. They may have conflicts or psychological obstacles to effective functioning. They may have had difficult or traumatic childhood experiences which have limited and distorted their adult life, or have in some way damaged the full development of their personality. They want to attain what Freud claimed were the goals of therapy: to love, to work and to play.

All of this is a fine and worthy goal but, in the perspective of psychosynthesis, it is not enough. Psychosynthesis too seeks to enable the client to function at his or her best. But, supposing the client has attained a reasonable measure of well-being and competence, what is he or she going to do with that? What are the deeper values he or she wants to live for? What is the ultimate meaning of the universe he or she lives in? And what is the place in his or her life for such issues as creativity, intuition, inspiration and the interconnectedness of all life? These are the questions worth asking, and on them may depend the success of therapeutic work.

In fact, at some time during one's existence, an individual may feel a lack of meaning, both in his or her existence and in the world in which he or she lives. This existential crisis is a central element in psychosynthesis therapy. It often occurs when an individual finds that the satisfaction he or she gets from achieving goals is less than he or she expected. At other times, a specific event such as the death of a loved one, the loss of a job, the vanishing of a cherished goal may evoke a similar problem. This crisis of meaning is increasingly occurring in young people today who are saturated with the glitter of material goods and superficial sensory stimulation, or who are troubled by current social or global issues. Everyday life turns empty and grey and normal activities no longer bring fulfilment: this is the existential vacuum.

As a transpersonal psychotherapy, psychosynthesis does aim not only to solve particular problems but to create the conditions in which problems may be solved or transcended. The therapist is concerned that the client learns how effectively to recognize and overcome psychological blocks or problems as they arise. In the transpersonal dimension lie all the resources which can provide the experience of meaning, creativity, intuition, insight and inspiration necessary to enable the client to develop beyond ordinary functioning. This is essential to fulfilment and true psychological health.

Psychosynthesis places much value upon work with potential, with creative possibilities and with the talents each person has, which are universal in their essence, but unique in their expression.

Psychosynthesis therapy aims to clear the way for and encourage transpersonal experience and to enable a person to use the resources of those experiences in an ordered way for growth. Some of the meditative and imagery techniques of psychosynthesis may directly evoke transpersonal awareness. However, this transpersonal awareness may emerge in so many different ways that the psychosynthesis therapist can have no prescribed recipe to follow. The therapy is a co-operative interplay and the course of the work will be dictated by the client's own experience. A rich spiritual life, peak experiences, a vision of one's potential and a sense of unity of all life may, however, lead only to despair unless the individual is capable of bringing this consciousness into manifestation in his or her daily life. In fact, the goal of psychosynthesis therapy is not only the *experience* of the transpersonal dimension but also its *expression*.

The 'person' of the therapist

The therapist's presence and his or her relationship with the client is seen in psychosynthesis to be the single most important factor in facilitating growth. It is the human relationship which nourishes and evokes psychological health and determines the subsequent outcome of therapy. In psychosynthesis the therapist is often called *guide*. This change in term reflects the view which psychosynthesis holds of the therapeutic process and the relationship involved therein. It assumes that each individual has within a unique hidden blueprint of his or her personal and spiritual development. A working hypothesis is that, given the opportunity, the wisdom of the self will emerge as a guiding, healing and integrating force. The psychosynthesis therapist is trained to trust this inner potential, to provide therapy from this context and to actively encourage the emergence of inner knowing.

The guide must be familiar with and learn to skilfully travel the terrain of his or her own path of development, and knows something of the hazards and pitfalls along the way. The guide will offer his or her knowledge or skill to the client, but will not carry the client up the mountain on his or her back, nor walk right behind. The guide also will not presume to know what is right for the client, what the solutions to the client's problems are or where the client's potentials lie. The client must ultimately make his or her own decisions. In psychosynthesis the guide approaches the client with a belief in the client's capacity to understand his or her life, to make choices and to transcend apparent limitations. The client is seen to have the resources (although sometimes deeply hidden) to solve his or her own problems.

These attitudes offer a different perspective to the diagnosis and treatment of mental illness and totally reject the adjustment of the client into some prescribed way of being. Going one step further, the psychosynthesis guide undertakes therapeutic work with clients from a perspective of bifocal vision. Not only must the client be perceived as being more than his or her pathology, but also as a self with a specific purpose in life, as well as challenges and obstacles to meet in order to fulfil that purpose.

To provide this wider and more positive context for the therapy, it is essential that the psychosynthesis guide has worked on and found his or her own path of development. It is only when the guide is available as a whole person that he or she will be able to facilitate the whole person of the client. Consequently the heart of training for becoming a psychosynthesis therapist constitutes a confrontation with one's own depths and shadows, as well as the exploration of the transpersonal dimension. Martha Crampton (1977) sums up the role of the therapist as follows:

> The quality of the helping relationship, based on unconditional love and close attunement to the client, is the indispensable context without which the techniques are mere mechanical gimmicks which lack true healing power. The level of the guide's personal integration is a crucial element which determines the amount of clarity and love he or she is able to bring to the traveller on the path.   (p. 16)

Therapeutic style

The therapeutic style of psychosynthesis is not necessarily neutral, objective or logical, but it requires the full involvement of the therapist. There are several dichotomies with which the guide must feel at ease.

Verbal vs experiential

There are times in therapy when active dialogue and discussion leading to true understanding are appropriate. However, understanding and rational analysis may not create deep and lasting change. In the case of certain psychological issues it may be wise to explore the client's deeper realities through the use of experiential techniques designed to evoke the unconscious levels of the psyche. For example, guided imagery may be used to bring to the surface unhappy childhood experiences, or emotional abreaction can release repressed feelings.

Directive vs non-directive

Active listening, acceptance and unconditional positive regard can do much, especially in the earlier phases of therapy, to facilitate growth. A non-directive approach traditionally builds a mutual bond and allows the client to find his or her own answers within. However, at times, clients may find themselves caught in vicious psychological circles which require active intervention and direction from the therapist.

'Hard' vs 'soft'

A love-oriented, *feminine* therapeutic style is frequently used in psycho-synthesis therapy. Here the guide adopts a more motherly function, of caring, accepting, nourishing, healing, and building trust. Not until trust is established can effective therapy take place, and generally the more disturbed client will require longer to develop trust. This trust building phase creates a safe environment in which the client may open up and explore his or her depths.

At a certain point in the therapy, the guide may begin to adopt a more confronting and provocative, *masculine* style. Here the guide may challenge the client to look deeper, take greater risks and more positive steps forward. With certain issues it may be appropriate to confront and encourage the client to go beyond his or her self-imposed limitations. The guide here may be seen to be acting in a traditional fatherly way of stimulating the pursuit of goals, opening the client's perspective, and reminding the client of what he or she can feel and do.

It is the responsibility of the psychosynthesis guide to choose an appropriate therapeutic style for his or her own personality and temperament and for that of the clients. Since the work may be on any level, emotional, mental, physical or imaginative, a good guide should have mastery of all modes of style and a wide range of therapeutic tools. The psychosynthesist will increasingly restore responsibility to the client. The guide would not interpret while the client passively listens but rather act as a facilitator to what is trying to emerge from within the client. He or she also assigns the client exercises and work to be done away from the session.

In the initial phases of therapy transference and also countertransference are likely to take place. The client responds to the guide in a way which may be more or less connected to his or her parental relationships. These relationships and the corresponding fantasies are lived again in the therapeutic setting either in the original or in a modified form. Often the client will have regressive tendencies, unconsciously wishing the guide to be a

loving parent and to provide him or her with the security and l[e]
never had. After a positive phase of transference, its opposi[te]
emerge. Negative patterns of relating will be transferred o[r]
which are a historical repetition or a revised edition being unco[n]
enacted. It is important that the guide adopt a behaviour and style whicn
does not directly react to the transferred patterns of behaviour, but rather
helps to understand them. The guide must be fully aware of his or her own
reactions to the client and from whence they come. The departing point
from psychosynthesis here is that the transference rather than being the
pivot of therapy is dealt with only when it blocks the therapeutic process.
Psychosynthesis guidance is based on a warm, genuine, human relationship
between client and guide in the here and now.

Major therapeutic techniques

The psychosynthetic approach is primarily pragmatic. The actual *work* of
the therapy is both *discursive*, in terms of understanding and analysing
currently existing psychospiritual blocks, neuroses and complexes, and
experiential, going deeper or beyond the rational assessment of a situation or
problem. Experiential work has the purpose of exploring the deeper reality
of both roots or historical beginnings of a problem as well as the creative
possibility for change which that problem contains. Thus the client actively
participates in working through his or her blocks.

There are a great many techniques employed in psychosynthesis, because
no one technique fits all purposes or all persons. A lot depends upon the
client's psychological makeup and temperament, level of development and
personal preferences. Moreover, new methods may be adopted, using
psychosynthesis as the ground from which all techniques are applied.

The techniques used in psychosynthesis can be better understood by
looking at the various aspects and stages of therapy.

At first one must assess both the blocks and the potentials of the
personality, enabling the exploration of the underworld of the unconscious,
and reaching the roots of psychological complexes. Here the history and
earlier life experiences of the client are systematically explored with emphasis on the impact they are currently having on the individual's life. Imagery,
free drawing, writing, critical analysis and subpersonality work are used for
these purposes. Subpersonality work is a technique of psychosynthesis
which gives form and content to various *subselves*, or 'parts', of the
personality. These subpersonalities are recognized as valid aspects of the
individual, each with its own organismic need as well as having a part to play
in his or her life.

Eyes-closed imagery reveals in a symbolic way conflicts and contents which may be otherwise unavailable to the conscious self. All sorts of images may emerge: of natural and artificial landscapes, people and beasts, demons and healing entities, sometimes also cosmic and visionary scenarios. In imagery the myth-making property of the human mind has the opportunity of creating stories and events which pictorially represent the client's inner situation. Free drawing (which does not require any expertise) has a similar function. Writing also facilitates insight. Critical analysis has the aim of attributing meaning to the unconscious material thus surfaced. Subpersonality work further helps in establishing a general geography of the psyche.

Full awareness and understanding of harmful images and complexes may help to disintegrate them, but do not necessarily produce permanent change. The cognitive work needs to be completed by the active and gradual training of all psychological functions (sensations, desire, impulse, feeling, imagination, thinking, will). In this way we coach and develop the archaic immature elements of our being. Special emphasis here is given to discovery of the I, or centre of awareness, and to the cultivation of the will as a skilful agent, capable of harmoniously regulating and co-ordinating the various aspects of the personality.

For this kind of work, specific exercises have been devised for the client to repeat on his or her own: the *self-identification* exercise, for example, in which one learns to withdraw attention from the peripheral aspects of the personality, and becomes fully conscious of his or her own I, or centre; *will* exercises, for developing the capacity for choice and self-affirmation; *visualization* exercises, in which, rather than letting images emerge spontaneously, the client is instructed to imagine vividly a previously chosen, specific subject.

Higher states of consciousness are not by themselves a guarantee of effective psychological functioning, and when improperly handled, can cause a wide variety of problems, a true pathology of the sublime. Therefore psychosynthesis attempts to harmonize the personal with the superconscious realm in the client and to enable free and effective expression. This task may be fulfilled with any of the methods previously described, depending on the situation and the characteristics of the client.

Healthy interpersonal relationships are the natural counterpart to individual growth. Clients can learn to deal with the common obstacles to relationship, to cultivate interpersonal qualities such as openness, love and empathy, and to acquire new communication skills. Particular emphasis and techniques are used here to foster both awareness and the integration of clients' love and inclusion needs with their healthy assertion and autonomy needs. There often exists a conflict between deep needs for unity, for being accepted and liked by others and healthy urges to affirm oneself, to be autonomous and whole. Also, during the course of psychosynthesis therapy, a spontaneous concern may arise for ways of coping with social issues and concerns. The therapy may evolve through a period of addressing these issues and evoking an awareness of belonging to a greater whole. The client may work to find his or her relationship to and part in the larger society.

The change process in therapy

In psychosynthesis, pain, crisis and neurosis are seen as creative opportunities rather than negative manifestations to be dealt with. The process of change in psychosynthesis therapy involves the creative use of suffering and failure. This context does not deny the value of systematically exploring the unconscious, both the lower or past and the higher unmanifest potential, nor does it belittle, ignore, or explain away the reality of pain. Rather, it requires a consciousness able to perceive any problem as a step forward along the path of unfoldment, and an opportunity for growth – a blessing of the obstacle.

Every psychological problem may be seen to have three levels, which are intimately involved in the process of change. The first level is the presenting issue the client wishes to bring in and represents the present. How the problem is felt, when, where and with whom it emerges brings it to therapeutic attention. Most often psychological pain is what draws attention to the existence of the presenting issue and motivates one to ask for therapy.

However, in facilitating the process of change it is often necessary to explore the second level of the problem: its *past*. Every psychological difficulty has a history, often going back to early childhood. There may be an initial more or less traumatic core experience, generating an unhealthy psychological pattern which later emerges, as a painful difficulty. To foster deep and effective change it is often useful to work with the unconscious and find the roots from the past, to release the emotional energy contained within them, and to facilitate the understanding necessary to transform them. Here cathartic work may be useful for releasing painful and negative emotions, which, if unredeemed, inhibit and block life energy and free expression.

The third level of work in the process of change is transpersonal. Inherent within the problem is its future, its evolutionary unfoldment. Psychosynthesis hypothesizes that every psychological difficulty also contains the seeds of what we may be, or are indeed becoming. In every problem lies a creative opportunity to leap forward. In fact we could see every problem as a distortion of some higher aspect. For example, anger can be perceived as a distortion of healthy self-assertion; insecurity is an immature form of sensitivity; dependency is an improper manifestation of the capacity to love. The transpersonal aspect in the process of change involves the capacity to perceive something new trying to be born *through* the difficulty, or some higher integration or identity seeking to emerge.

As a snake sheds its old skin, so the client outgrows the identity contained within a problem, but because of the nature of psychological identification, he or she is seldom conscious of this. The client will experience pain and the need for change in those areas where a new and more inclusive identity is trying to be born as the next level of integration and development. The more an individual is conscious of this process and collaborates with it, the more there will be a natural process of change. The more one is unconsciously and blindly lost in any particular way of being and living, the more there will be pain and crystallization. Much suffering is generated through *holding on to* old identities and the resistance to change.

The will is a central function of the process of change in psychosynthesis therapy. Rather than viewing the will as the forceful, dictatorial striving of Victorian times, it is seen as a predominant function of the self. A natural outcome of increasing psychospiritual health is an increasing experience of identity and autonomy. This autonomy is more than a wilful spurt of energy: it is a journey from dependency to independence. When the process of change has taken the client to the point of being autonomous in relation to life circumstances, interpersonal relationships and whatever psychological problems he or she is working with, he or she will accrue the experience of the true will, no longer operate as a victim to circumstances and environment, and become a *cause* in his or her universe.

Finally, in the psychosynthesis view of change, there is a recognition that there will always be *contents* of consciousness and that the process of self-realization is a process of death and rebirth – of things coming together and breaking apart, a continual evolutionary disruption of the personality. And yet there is some invisible, higher principle operating, the *self*. At times the process of change in an individual may take a quantum leap towards this type of contextual change involving a deeper reorientation of both personal existence and transpersonal awareness.

CASE EXAMPLE

When Sarah, a 48-year-old mother of three, started therapy, by outward appearances nothing seemed to be wrong. She appeared healthy and well cared for, she expressed herself effectively, and she presented herself in a convincing, integrated manner. However, beneath the surface a deep shattering crisis was taking place. Little in her life made sense any more, and she experienced despair much of the time. In this weakened state several other disturbances arose: a lack of concentration and an inability to take charge of the situation, hearing voices and other paranormal experiences, a sense of depersonalization, an embarrassing and intense feeling of shyness that made her feel, when she was in public, that she was 'invisible'. The implicit belief that she was going to live in this state for the rest of her life further increased her feelings of hopelessness and helplessness.

We started, as usually is done in psychosynthesis, by examining the life process that had brought her to the present crisis, to unravel the knots and recapture the thread of her development. This process of understanding which in psychosynthesis we call *critical analysis* aims to discover the causes of the client's difficulties and is in itself healing: the diagnosis is the first step of the cure.

Sarah's drive for achievement had led her to become a successful business executive in a large American corporation. But behind it lay a childhood heavy with traumas and difficulties; at three years old the death of her mother, persistent physical and emotional abuse by her stepmother and the increasing withdrawal of her father's care and concern.

Understanding that her overachieving style was a compensation and a cover-up for her deep insecurity was central to her therapy. Also it was essential that her despair be recognized as a crisis of meaning, not just as pure pathology: 'The fact that when I described what had been happening in me someone could understand and identify that as a spiritual crisis was a tremendous source of relief and joy.'

As we kept looking at Sarah's life story, we met with another phase: her inauthentic striving identity and lifestyle had to collapse. 'I had proved that I could be independent, and in control of my life,' Sarah wrote in her autobiography, which is another essential tool in the initial phase of the work. But as she reached the culmination of success and achievement, difficulties started to emerge: severe allergies, a general decline in physical health and a lack of motivation in her job. She tried to solve the problem by changing her outer situation; she got married and moved to Paris with her new husband. Having left her job, she would now be supported by her husband within a traditional family structure. This was a turning point, a painful but decisive moment. Her high achieving identity crumbled, and this inner death led her into two years of pain and confusion which culminated in divorce from her husband. At this point Sarah came to live in England in the country. Again she thought that by dealing with the concrete aspects of her problem she would surmount all difficulties. But again her problems became worse: 'From the momentary sense of joy upon arrival, I now felt as though I was tumbling down stairs, occasionally hitting a "landing" and thinking that that was the end of the descent and chaos, only to tumble down again. This experience lasted for eighteen months until I came into psychosynthesis.'

After the first stage of critical analysis, we started working on subpersonalities. The aim here was to recognize the various forces that were tearing Sarah's inner world apart, and making order out of emotional chaos; it was also to create distance between the conscious I, the observer, and the various psychological contents. Sarah, for instance, recognized the 'golden girl' subpersonality – the part of her that was able to function well in the practical world and to succeed; the 'critical witch' that spewed anger and destruction at anything and anyone including herself; or the 'lost lonely little girl' a remnant from her past, the child in her that felt powerless and victimized.

Dis-identification from controlling forces leads to freedom. However, we must be ready for that freedom, and Sarah, although already stronger, was not. After a wave of very real relief and a period of spiritual seeking and transpersonal experiences, she met with new difficulties. In dreams, imagery, and everyday experience Sarah recurrently felt the contrast between herself as a wanting to hold tight, anxious control of herself and the environment, and, on the other hand, a sense of vastness and void to which she was not able to surrender and towards which she felt ambivalent. It was a conflict between regression and growth.

The 'ideal model' exercise, in which one is invited to visualize oneself as one wants to become in the future, evoked in Sarah a negative reaction, the image of a black hole capable of devouring her. During an imagery session, she saw a wonderful golden light but was unable to let herself go to it. In another session, she visualized a whirling formless void, but was not willing to enter it. Dreams of being imprisoned became recurrent.

At this stage there was another turning point in Sarah's life: she was offered a safe and rewarding job in her old company which provided security, but it also meant returning to the old way of living. The therapy helped her to understand the meaning of her choice: taking the old job meant re-adopting her masculine style of affirmation in the world; refusing it meant cultivating her feminine values, the openness to contemplation and, simply, the ability to *be*. When asked during a session to visualize herself in the job, she understood that this was the time to move forward, to explore new territories, to challenge the unknown. She decided to refuse the offer.

An important and conscious decision, an act of will tends to dissolve blocks and strengthen the psyche. Now, although she did not know it yet, Sarah was ready to let go. The void, which in previous sessions had frightened her so much, now lay open to exploration. Sarah presented a nightmare she had had recurrently since childhood: she is floating in space lying in a saucer of wet cement; the saucer moves towards planet Earth, where she is pressed down on the surface and unable to move forever. At this point she wakes up in terror. This was the starting image for a subsequent guided imagery session.

All took place as in the worst of her nightmares: totally involved in the process Sarah wanted to vomit, cried desperately and felt that her head and heart were going to be crushed. But as she was pushed into the surface, she felt herself going through to the other side of the planet and into space again. Going into the darkness, surrendering to the void brought about a powerful catharsis. Sarah had entered fully into her helplessness and had emerged again liberated.

The session, a basic one which Sarah remembers as the culmination of her death and rebirth process, did not end here. When asked what was the force pushing her against the surface she answered it was a powerful, ruthless, dark hand. Sarah imagined herself – a minuscule being – climbing up the hand, then the arm, and all the way to the head of a gigantic dark person. Reaching the top of the head, she raised her arms in triumph and cried 'I did it? I did it!' This was an immense symbolic victory. In her ascent through the body of the dark person (a metaphor for her dark destiny, persecuting her), Sarah had employed her anger, all her determination, and all of herself. Alone and unaided, she had triumphed over an adverse situation. She had affirmed her right to exist and her will to be.

After this imagery, followed by a few sessions of grounding, Sarah gained a clear and stable sense of what she wanted to do in her life; she was able to be centred even in difficult circumstances; and she felt capable of regulating herself and dealing more effectively with her relationships. She seemed to have reached a stable plateau. Her therapy continued for some time, working on areas of her life that she wanted to improve, confronting new dilemmas as they arose and further integrating her personality. She continued to have a sense of meaning and purpose in her life; establishing herself in a new career which reflected more of her values. She also found ways of re-owning her past skills and talents in a new manner which strengthened her sense of continuity. It is now a year since the *key* session in this course of therapy and the stability that Sarah created remains with her today.

REFERENCES

Assagioli, R. (1933) Dynamic psychology and psychosynthesis, *Hibbert Journal*, Vol. 32, p. 184.

Assagioli, R. (1937) Spiritual development and its alternative maladies, *Hibbert Journal*, Vol. 36, p. 69.

Assagioli, R. (1965) *Psychosynthesis*, Turnstone Press, London.

Crampton, M. (1977) *Psychosynthesis: Some Key Aspects of Theory and Practice*, Canadian Institute of Psychosynthesis, Montreal.

Jaques, E. (1970) *Death and the Midlife Crisis: Work, Creativity and Social Justice*, Heinemann, London.

Suggested further reading

Assagioli, R. (1965) *Psychosynthesis: A Manual of Principles and Techniques*, Thorson Publishing Group, Wellingborough, Northamptonshire.

Assagioli, R. (1974) *The Act of Will*, Thorson Publishing Group, Wellingborough, Northamptonshire.

Ferrucci, P. (1982) *What We May Be*, Thorson Publishing Group, Wellingborough, Northamptonshire.

Hardy, J. (1987) *A Psychology with a Soul: Psychosynthesis in Evolutionary Context*, Routledge & Kegan Paul, London.

Whitmore, D. (1986) *Psychosynthesis in Education*, Thorson Publishing Group, Wellingborough, Northamptonshire.

CHAPTER 11

TRANSPERSONAL PSYCHOTHERAPY

Ian Gordon-Brown and Barbara Somers

HISTORICAL CONTEXT AND DEVELOPMENTS IN BRITAIN

Historical context

Transpersonal psychology is an umbrella name. While its formal establishment is very recent (1969) its roots lie in the far distant past. The religions of the world with their systems of spiritual training; mystery schools and esoteric movements; symbolic systems such as alchemy, tarot and the I Ching; all have been custodians of the approach to the self.

Similarly some of the most 'transpersonal psychologies' of the modern era antedate by many years the establishment of the *Journal of Transpersonal Psychology* in 1969. We would include analytical psychology (C. G. Jung); psychosynthesis (R. Assagioli) and logotherapy (V. Frankl) in this category.

The formal emergence of transpersonal psychology is also part of a wider world movement of thought. In his letter of invitation to the 7th Annual Conference of the International Transpersonal Association in Bombay in 1982, Association President Stanislav Grof wrote of 'the increasing convergence of western physics and eastern metaphysics, of modern consciousness research and eastern spiritual systems'. He emphasized that

> The image of the universe and of the human mind emerging from modern science shows this increasing similarity to the descriptions offered by various systems of Yoga, Vajrayana, Zen Buddhism, Taoism, Sufism and Kabbalah – to name just a few ancient spiritual systems.

Transpersonal psychology, as a distinct branch or force within psychology, was conceived and nurtured in the period 1966–69. Its birth is marked by the first issue of the *Journal of Transpersonal Psychology* (1969) and the establishment of the American Association for Transpersonal Psychology (1971).

The originators of these initiatives were Abraham Maslow and Anthony Sutich, who was the journal's editor until his death in April 1976. Maslow and Sutich had played central roles in the development of humanistic psychology during the 1950s and in founding the *American Journal of Humanistic Psychology* in 1961. Sutich was that journal's first editor until 1968.

Both men, who first met in 1949, were deeply interested in the spiritual dimensions of the human psyche. They had hoped that *third force*, or humanistic psychology, would provide a channel through which this interest could be expressed and integrated into the main stream of psychological thought.

By the mid 1960s this seemed increasingly unlikely, so they proposed the *Journal of Transpersonal Psychology* as a vehicle for these topics. (It is interesting that the term *transpersonal* seems first to have been coined by Carl Jung in 1917.) Sutich (1976) gives a fascinating account of the creation of the new journal and the genesis of transpersonal psychology.

This history is important. It led to defining the transpersonal orientation as a fourth force in psychology, in contrast to *first force* (classical psychoanalytic theory), *second force* (positivistic or behaviouristic theory) and *third force* (humanistic psychology). *Fourth-force* psychology, as the *Journal of Transpersonal Psychology* defined it, was to be concerned with 'articles and studies in meta-needs, ultimate values, unitive consciousness, peak experiences, ecstasy, mystical experience, B values, essence, bliss, awe, wonder, self actualisation, ultimate meaning, transcendence of the self'. The list goes on. The primary emphasis *at that time* was on inward and transcendent experience and on self-realization. *Transpersonal Psychology* by Tart and others (1975) explores the psychology of growth and consciousness expansion in eight spiritual traditions and reflects a similar orientation.

This early emphasis led many to an 'other worldly' image of transpersonal psychology which is far from true. Subsequent developments in the United States have stressed the actualizing dimension. There are now undergraduate and postgraduate programmes in a number of universities and research institutes. The California Institute of Transpersonal Psychology has offered a doctoral programme since 1975, combining professional training in psychology with spiritually focused inner work. The association's conferences became international in 1973, with a conference in Iceland. Major conferences have been held in Australia (1980), India (1982), Switzerland (1983) and Japan (1985).

Developments in Britain

In the UK the Centre for Transpersonal Psychology, which we founded in 1973, has been a prime mover in the development of transpersonal psychology.

Our approach has differed in a number of respects from that of the Americans. For example we started at the grass roots, developing a continuing *series of workshops* that combined structured experiential work with some theory. From these workshops demand grew among interested professionals and semiprofessionals for *training in transpersonal perspectives and techniques*. We began to meet this demand in 1977. Our ninth training group for counsellors, psychotherapists and allied professionals (orthodox and complementary) started in January 1986. This training, which is part-time and lasts two years, has created an informal network of *counselling/therapy practitioners* who work from a transpersonal orientation.

While we have not sought to 'storm' the citadels of the establishment, their members come to us individually in growing numbers. Numerous colleagues in the network can be found working within establishment organizations, in the various complementary fields, and in private practice. Recently, a sister centre, the Transpersonal Psychology Study Centre, was established in Devon by Joan and Reynold Swallow, providing its own professional training programme.

To complete the statistical picture, we have in the last 13 years held over 500 workshops on our centre's programme. Over 50 per cent of those who now attend these public workshops are from the caring, healing and teaching professions.

We see the real dividing line between what is transpersonal and what is not, to be *an acceptance of the reality of the self*.

In the beginning was the *self*, in potentia.

At the end there is also the *self*, realized and actualized. (This is spelt out more fully in the next section.) The practical consequence is that, depending on a client's need or problem, we have no difficulty in using the perspectives or techniques of the first, second or third forces – but always from the standpoint of the self.

Brief histories must always be incomplete and out of date as soon as written. So we end this section with some footnotes:

We wish to underline that transpersonal psychology *is a perspective, not a system or doctrine*. We can only tell you how we see it. Others may tell it differently. And why not?

We speak here from the experience of the Centre for Transpersonal Psychology and those associated with it. Others in the UK should be mentioned: John Heron who down the years has held a torch for transpersonal psychologies and altered states of consciousness research; John Rowan whose writings in *Self and Society* have helped to bring thinking in humanistic and transpersonal psychology close together; and Alan Bleakley who for some years ran a two-year Institute for the Development of Human Potential course with a transpersonal orientation. And there are others.

In a meeting in July 1985 between Ian Gordon-Brown and Jill Mellick, a faculty member of the California Institute of Transpersonal Psychology, it became clear that American and British thinking and practice were following closely similar lines, and are on a converging course.

THEORETICAL ASSUMPTIONS

We have some discomfort writing under the heading of theoretical assumptions. Good theory is essential, and it provides a framework to our teaching and work as therapists. Nevertheless, we believe therapists are useful only to the extent that they have integrated their experience of life with their being as a person. Theory can help this, but it cannot replace experience.

No single theoretical framework or model of the psyche can possibly fit everyone who comes through our door. Every major movement in world history – political, religious, social, artistic – has ultimately had to come to terms with the infinite diversity of human nature. Our trade is no exception.

Image of the person

Our experience in therapy is that *the image of the person that matters is the one that is most meaningful and creative for the client*. For most of us there will be a number of images, representing the characters in the drama of our life, our inner family. Images for subpersonalities; for body, emotions, mind and intuition; images for the wise person within us, for the child, for anima and animus, and for our own shadow side. At some stage images will appear that represent processes of integration, and the beginnings of an approximation to the self. We will write more of this later when dealing with therapeutic techniques and change process in therapy. Such images are present in the unconscious at each stage of our growth, waiting opportunity to surface. They grow and change as we grow, change and become more conscious. To recognize them can greatly aid the therapeutic process. *The image of the person with which we work is the client's own self-image.*

To introduce our own image of the person/self we offer three concepts fundamental to transpersonal psychotherapy.

The collective unconscious

First is the collective unconscious – *collective* because it encompasses our macrocosm, our psychic environment; *unconscious* because none of us can be aware of more than a fragment of its reality at any one time. This is the world which the self inhabits, of which we become increasingly aware as we grow into the consciousness of that self. Past, present and future are contained within it. It embraces all levels of awareness from the instinctual to the transcendent; the fundamental building blocks and patterns of the psyche, which Jung called archetypes, are found there. It may also be regarded as a continuum of energy and consciousness because it is a realm where fundamental life impulses to meaning, wholeness and fulfilment reside.

The theme and meaning of identity

Second is the theme and meaning of identity – the answer to the perennial question *Who am I?* Transpersonal psychology, in common with many of the world's religions and philosophies, asserts that for practical purposes we have (or are) two fundamental centres of identity. The *primary centre* is called the self (Jungian psychology); the transpersonal centre (psychosynthesis); atman (Hindu philosophy); the soul (in many traditions). It is our essential being.

The *secondary centre* is the ego (Jungian); personality or personal centre (psychosynthesis); the not self (Eastern traditions); the everyday 'I'.

Most of us normally live in and around this secondary centre or ego. Ego-centred concerns are personal concerns: human ambitions, worries, and loves: natural and right enough in their own place, but limited and limiting if they are all we are capable of.

By contrast the experience of the self, the transpersonal centre, the soul *includes* the personal but goes beyond it. It focuses on the whole, and with the welfare of the collective. It is associated with experiences and consciousness that are deep or transcendent, in which the individual is 'taken out of the little self' into the wonder, awe and unity of the cosmos. See Maslow (1964); also White as editor (1972).

The Chandogya Upanishad (1932) says:

> Verily the Soul *extends* from below, the Soul *extends* from above, the Soul *extends*

from behind, the Soul *extends* from before, the Soul *extends* from the South, the Soul *extends* from the North, the Soul *extends* from the East, the Soul *extends* from the West – of a truth the Soul is all this. He, who is aware of this, seeing the Soul thus, thinking it thus, knowing it thus, becomes (even in this life) *one* whose entire devotion is to the Soul, whose recreation is in the Soul, whose helpmate is the Soul, and whose felicity is the Soul. (In after life) he becomes self resplendent. He is able to accomplish whatsoever he desires in all the regions of the universe.

It is generally said that each of us 'has a soul'. The transpersonal perspective turns this statement on its head: 'The soul has us – the personality is a reflection and a fragment of the soul.'

The journey

The third key concept is that of the journey. The transpersonal view is that birth is not the beginning and death is not the end. We come from somewhere and we go to somewhere.

In the East many regard birth into this world as the true death, and our death from this world as a release and liberation. Most Westerners reverse this view. Perhaps we should see truth in both perspectives.

The transpersonal therapist sees life in this world as a journey through which the ego, the personal I, gathers experience, grows in consciousness and moves towards fulfilment.

One type of journey is travelled by those whose search is consciously chosen and directed. Jung called this journey *individuation*. Here, after its encounters with the external world, the ego hits crisis, or a period of crises, and eventually turns within to discover the meaning of what has been happening. So it explores the shadow (that which is not in the light of consciousness); its inner opposites, polarities or contradictions (especially the feminine and masculine) and eventually travels the world of inner meaning and archetypes towards the self.

Religious traditions, esoteric and mystery schools, have often described this same fundamental journey in terms of initiation into ever-expanding dimensions of consciousness. The symbolism of certain great lives depicts similar stages and processes, for example, the initiations of Christ: birth, baptism, transfiguration, crucifixion, resurrection and ascension.

Alchemy provides another map of this journey, in its four stages of *calcinatio* (burning), *solutio* (washing), *coagulatio* (cohering) and *sublimatio* (transcendence). By whatever names, these symbolic systems express the same testing journey to the self, involving constant recapitulation, apparently covering the same ground but at different levels, so that the work of psychological transformation is truly done and the lessons of the journey thoroughly learned.

We can hardly help feeling that the unconscious process moves spiralwise round a centre, gradually getting closer, while the characteristics of the Centre grow more and more distinct. Or perhaps we could put it the other way round and say that the Centre itself virtually unknowable – acts like a magnet on the disparate materials and processes of the unconscious and gradually captures them as in a crystal lattice . . . Often one has the impression that the personal psyche is running round this central point like a shy animal, at once fascinated and frightened, always in flight, and yet steadily drawing nearer. (Jung, 1953, para. 325)

An encouraging sign of our times is the growing number of people who are consciously choosing to travel this journey to the self.

Another way of looking at life's journey is its mythic dimension. Myths, legends and folk tales have power because they express profound truths about the human psyche. To discover our 'myth' or 'myths' – for most of us have different myths for different stages of the journey – can be profoundly enlightening. It links us to the collective human story and provides psychological insight about the journey and how to meet its tests and challenges.

Concepts of psychological health and disturbance

Discussion of the collective unconscious, the nature of identity and the journey has been an essential preliminary to a transpersonal view of psychological health and disturbance. We can now summarize some central ideas, as follows:

1. *We are cautious about labels.* We trust in the wholeness and wisdom of the self. Thus we would never say: 'he is schizophrenic' or 'she is manic-depressive'. At the most we might say 'part of him is schizophrenic' – 'an aspect of her is manifesting manic-depressive symptoms'. This attitude allows people to retain their dignity and let their health work on their sickness. To deny them this sense of self-worth is to remove one of the fundamental requirements for healing.
2. *We identify three main classes of psychological change on the health/ disturbances axis*:
(a) Breaking up to break down.
(b) Breaking up to break through.
(c) (a) and (b) together, happening at the same time in the same person.
(a) Breaking up to break down. In this category the individual's ego is not strong enough to withstand the pressure to which it is subject. Such pressures may arise from within the psyche, or from the environment, or both. The individual (or part of them) breaks up and regresses to an earlier developmental stage. Supportive therapy and treatment may suffice, or they may have to be taken into care and helped to rebuild.

(b) Breaking up to break through. Here the symptoms are often similar to (a) above, but the cause and treatment are quite different. In break through cases the pressure is to grow and break free of existing limitations, whether inner or outer or both. This is the wine of new life splitting old wineskins; it is the butterfly breaking out of the chrysalis; it is the process of transformation.

(c) Breaking down *and* breaking through. It is common to find people in whom one part of their nature is breaking down and another part is breaking through. Here the breaking down part will need support, containment and caring, while the breaking through part will need help to establish and ground emergent new life-patterns.

3. *The meaning of health and disturbance.* Before deciding whether a state or symptom is healthy or disturbed, or both, we must explore its meaning. Psychological disturbance is often a by-product of the transformation process. Chiron, the centaur, was renowned as a teacher and healer, but had an unhealing wound. It is commonplace that an individual's defect, wound or failure becomes the source of their creative gift to humanity. Disturbance may be a necessary part of the journey to the self. It may not be pathological. Health may equally be part of our destiny. One is not necessarily better or more desirable than the other; both may be needed for growth.

4. *Collective health and disturbance.* In times of great change certain conditions of ill health and malfunction cannot be avoided – they are part of collective destiny. We suffer not always through personal failure but because of our common humanity and connection to the collective. Similarly some people may act as 'lightning conductors' for the collective, attracting and catching the fire so that others may be saved. We need to watch for such cases.

5. *Symptom as symbol.* Every symptom (physical and psychological) conveys a message, but similar symptoms can arise from quite different causes. What is the *meaning* of the symptom, what does it *symbolize*? Take the example of a heart attack. Is the heart really 'attacking' and threatening death, or is it signalling the need and opportunity to live more appropriately? By helping people to dialogue with their own heart we can help decode the message of the symptoms. Until symptoms are explored and understood in this way we cannot know whether they represent healing or disturbance. We return to this theme later as a central theme of transpersonal psychotherapy.

Acquisition of psychological disturbance

In common, we suspect, with most therapists in the Western world, we find that the majority of psychological disturbances emerging in adult years have their primary origin in some early childhood trauma or traumas, commonly in the first seven years of life.

The causes are many and various. While particular incidents will have their place, including accidental events over which the parents may have little control, our attention is drawn again and again to the subjective atmosphere of the home and early environment. The young child lives close to the unconscious world and is therefore extraordinarily sensitive to what lies beneath the surface. Tensions in the environment, particularly between parents; inappropriate expectations and failure to understand the basic needs of the child, can cause apparently minor incidents to have quite disproportionate effects within the child's psyche.

Thus maladaptive patterns can become fixed, or natural development blocked. The child may adopt some coping device, inner or outer, which serves its temporary needs – for example protecting its vulnerability by suppression of feeling – but which proves quite inappropriate in adult life.

Such effects can be particularly marked when the child is born into an 'alien environment', where its nature and gifts are neither understood nor valued. This is the ugly duckling syndrome – the artist set down among parents and siblings who cannot understand his or her needs or temperament; or the extraverted child born into an introverted family.

People drawn to a growth path in adult life are *not* exempt from these early difficulties. Indeed our impression is quite the reverse. Early problems and conflicts often seem to trigger the search for something different/better in later life. For such clients the question 'Why did you choose your particular parents?' though from one standpoint totally irrational seems to have a very pertinent meaning. If we come from somewhere and go to somewhere, if the self chooses its journey . . .

Finally we wish to re-emphasize that while there *are* general rules and conditions relating to the acquisition of psychological disturbance, the treatment is, first and last, *a matter for exploration with the person concerned*. As Jung says (1928):

> I say to any beginner – learn your theories as well as you can, but put them aside when you touch the miracle of the living soul. Not theories but your own creative individuality alone must decide.   (para. 361)

Perpetuation of psychological disturbance

Just as we identified three main classes of change on the health-and-disturbance axis namely:

Breaking up to break down
Breaking up to break through
And these two happening together

so do we find three related categories in the perpetuation of psychological disturbance.

In the break-down category it is intensely difficult to let go of the hard-won coping patterns that enabled us to survive early trauma, even though they now block change. Better the devils we know than the ones we do not! So we remain in that soul-destroying job because we fear insecurity more; the sensitive, hurt inner child who hid feelings rather than risk rejection, continues to gag the adult person; partners who make each other's lives a misery unconsciously collude to stay together for fear of a worse prospect apart.

In sum, the damaged part in us holds on out of fear and because there is benefit as well as pain. The deeper the damage, the stronger often are the defence mechanisms and the longer does it take to repair the psyche.

Where our client is breaking through there is often a fundamentally different factor at work. It is as if the self holds us in the process, and will not let us go until the necessary stages of development are firmly established and there can be no going back. It often looks like resistance to change, but it is in fact a quite other process of preparation for new birth or transformation. This is the *calcinatio* stage in alchemy. By analogy, in steel-making the melt in the furnace goes on until every impurity has been brought to the surface and skimmed off: only then is the steel without flaw. So it is within the psyche.

Finally these two contrasting processes can be found working within the same person, each needing its appropriate treatment.

PRACTICE

Goals of therapy

Ideas of therapy are changing. No longer is it seen just as untanglement and working through past traumas. For many it is essentially a growth path, and this is particularly true of transpersonal psychotherapy. With this in mind the following are some central goals of therapy.

1. *To discover the client's need.* The problem(s) clients present are often not the real issues. An early task of therapy is to discover what these are.
2. *To provide a contained place* and framework wherein pain can be released and wounds healed, and the processes of repair, growth, change and discovery be safely made.
3. *To help clients to become in actuality what they are in potential.* Inevitably this means looking at outer effectiveness and relationships, as well as inner awareness and consciousness.
4. *To travel part of their journey with the clients*, to help them discover the meaning of that journey and its various stages.
5. *To help clients become more conscious and creative* – to be in charge of their lives.

The 'person' of the therapist

A therapist is first and above all a human being. Head and heart should be in balance. Quality of being and livingness are primary. Skills, though essential, take second place to this. *Thus transpersonal psychotherapists*:

1. Seek to become more whole and avoid lopsidedness. To this end, personal experience of one or more growth paths and disciplines is essential.
2. Know life in its broadness, roundness and depth. Their interests and activities are varied, their perspective eclectic. Narrow and dogmatic people make bad therapists.
3. Recognize their limitations and work within them, while seeking always to enlarge both understanding and capacity. They will have been, and often remain in therapy. They will seek experienced supervision of their work, knowing that even the Pope has his confessor.
4. Enjoy the contrast of different styles and approaches to therapy. They often seek training in such other modes to give counterpoint to their own natural preferences.
5. Rarely enter the transpersonal branch of their trade before their thirties. Mid-life seems to be the norm and deep and varied life experience the essential prelude.

Therapeutic style

Transpersonal psychotherapists come from diverse personal and professional backgrounds. Typically, they already have expertise within the broad spectrum of work in the helping professions. An initial task in training is to find appropriate ways of blending these different styles with the transpersonal perspective. Thus therapeutic styles in transpersonal work span a considerable range. Ultimately every therapist must find the style natural to themselves and flexible enough to adjust to the differing needs of their clients.

Different therapeutic techniques dictate and require their own distinct style

In the use of imaging for example the pace is slow and the mode evocative, in quite sharp contrast to the conversational mode which has its place in all counselling and therapeutic situations.

Different again is the transpersonal use of gestalt and body work, where the style is likely to be more extravert, vigorous and at times even directive. We illustrate these differences in the next section, Major therapeutic techniques.

Two practical matters are intimately connected to style: *space and time*. Transpersonal work needs space – physical and psychological. If the therapist is too close some clients experience invasion of their psyche. Most transpersonal psychotherapists sit facing their clients, with relaxing chairs angled so as to allow for natural making and breaking of eye contact.

On session time, we find one hour to one and a quarter hours more appropriate for transpersonal psychotherapy than the 50-minute 'analytic hour'. The 'analytic hour' suits a situation where clients come from two to four times a week. More time is needed when clients come less frequently.

Major therapeutic techniques

To describe the full range of techniques used in transpersonal work requires a substantial book. They come from multifarious sources and traditions, including many invented *mid-session*. We can give only brief descriptions of some of the main techniques with indications of their specific transpersonal application.

Techniques using symbols

Our lives are full of symbols and symbolic events, both inner and outer. The power of the living symbol comes from its spiritual roots. Events and relationships; visual images; feelings and emotions; body language and body energy; illness and accident; 'chance' encounters; can all carry the magic of an archetypal imprint. The unconscious psyche communicates its intentions and wishes, its needs and goals, through symbols. We have largely lost the art of reading symbols and need to relearn these languages in which the self speaks to us. *Symbolic work thus has a central place in transpersonal psychotherapy.*

The transpersonal therapist has to discover *which* symbolic languages the client can use. There are generalized meanings for many symbols, but these are indications only. Each client has his or her own idiom or dialect. We must always ask the clients for *their* association. Invariably the golden rule is: 'What does it mean to you?'

The best and most useful books on symbolism come out of the Jungian field.

Dreamwork

The preceding comments all apply directly to transpersonal work with dreams. Apart from dreams which only reflect the undigested froth of the previous day, the dream is a message from the inner world of the psyche, even from the self.

To unravel their meaning we have to encourage our clients to treat their dreams seriously, live with them, and discover by association the links between dream motifs and the motifs of their life. The outer context of life when the dream came will often provide a key to its meaning. As therapists, we watch for dreams as they mark the stages of therapy – dreams of transition, endings, new beginnings, wholeness, etc. Especially we watch for the 'big' dream, with its numinous quality, remembered down the years. Such dreams often appear in the lives of those who may appear to be breaking down, but are in fact breaking through. Dream images invariably give a clue to the real nature of what is happening. Imaging, body work, gestalt and active imagination are also used in dreamwork.

Inner dialogue

Inner dialogue is a central technique of symbolic work. Broadly it has three parts. One, to discover what the different aspects of our nature are telling us. This calls for a specially receptive inner listening, a fine-tuning to what is happening at different levels of psyche and body.

Two, how we communicate back to these aspects of ourselves. The dialogue sometimes takes the form of a two-way conversation with our inner figures. More often it is non-verbal.

Three, inner dialogue is a means by which self and ego may communicate. The self may manifest in many ways – through symbol or inner figure, by sound, voice, scent or a heightening of energy. In time we may come to know where self and ego meet.

Inner dialogue comes most naturally to intuitive/feeling people. It works best when thinking consciousness adopts a receptive mode. This can be learned, and transpersonal therapists often teach clients its uses early in therapy. Once learned, it becomes an invaluable self-monitoring device, in everyday life as in therapy. Modes of imaging work now to be described depend in large part on the inner dialogue process.

Spot imaging

'Spot' imaging – means catching, on the spot, the moment when our client offers some graphic image, phrase, body gesture, or is in touch at the feeling/energy level with an experience, usually recent, which carries shades from the past.

On the spot, therapist asks client to go within himself or herself and enter a state where inner dialogue becomes possible. Therapist then gently encourages client to allow the memory track evoked by the recent experience to play-back through time (like turning the pages of a photograph album), picking up other occasions when the same quality of experience had been present.

Spot imaging is based on the fact that each part of our nature – instincts, body, emotions, mind, intuition and so on – has its own distinct memory track. The art in using it is to help the client stay true to the quality of the recent experience, and so take the right memory track. It calls for a slow pace and a soft voice. Mirroring, leading questions, and interpretation usually disrupt the process.

Spot imaging helps the client to get back to crucial and forgotten experiences and repressed memories, joyful or painful, and to experience them vividly and directly, sometimes after only a few minutes of the process.

Spot imaging can be for a few minutes or a whole session. Short periods of imaging can be very effectively interspersed with discussion and interpretation of what is going on. The session then becomes a creative blend of 'rational' and 'non-rational', of left and right brain modes of therapeutic work.

Long guided daydream

A long guided daydream is a journey of inner exploration using the imaging mode. A powerful and time-consuming technique – the daydream itself can last up to one and a half hours – relaxedly lying down. Early pioneers include Hans Carl Leuner's *Guided Affective Imagery*, Robert Desoille's *The Directed Daydream*; Ira Progoff's *Twilight Imaging*; and psychosynthesis practitioners. Leuner and Desoille used structured situations to get at specific material. We encourage the psyche of the dreamer (client) to provide its own structure and find this technique extremely useful for raising material in early therapy, for dealing with blocks, and for integrating material towards the end of therapy. The therapist's role is to facilitate the dreamer's journey and ensure, from wide knowledge of symbolism, that important moments/themes are explored.

A central transpersonal component of this technique is the use of the *talisman*. At the start of the journey the dreamer chooses a talisman as guide, helper and friend. Talisman often represents a less conscious side of the dreamer, or the self. By encouraging dialogue between dreamer and talisman the therapist can ensure, without being directive, that major issues are confronted. The client remains in the dreaming mode throughout. Discussion and interpretation come afterwards.

Imaging exercises

In recent years numerous psychological exercises have been developed, using imaging, to help people explore the inner structure and dynamics of their psyche. The best of these exercises (we prefer the term *journey*) are based on mythological and archetypal themes and have the power, when given appropriately, to throw strong light on what is moving beneath the surface of our lives.

At the Centre for Transpersonal Psychology we use a range of exercises to explore such themes as images of the self; subpersonalities; masculine and feminine energies; life as a journey; growth and initiation; exploring the elements; discovering the self; and so on.

Such exercises are normally designed for group use, but can be equally effective in therapy. The therapist uses the mode of a structured long guided daydream, intervening to describe each stage of the journey and to facilitate detailed exploration.

Maps

There is a strong 'effort after meaning' within the psyche. Many people want to understand their lives in terms of general principles of human behaviour. This placing of their personal experience within a wider human context often satisfies a fundamental and valid intellectual need. So, remembering that 'the map is not the country', we use maps and models of consciousness as explanatory tools in transpersonal psychotherapy. The effect can be to re-inforce and sharpen clients' insights and bring them into unforgettable focus.

The chakras and astrological maps (see below) are good examples of helpful explanatory tools. Jung's four functions of consciousness map throws a clear light on many relationship difficulties. In the section on the Image of the person, the paragraphs on the *journey* provide some useful additional examples. We frequently use other maps – Assagioli's egg diagram (Figure 10.1); planes of consciousness; Jung's conscious/unconscious map with the self at the centre.

Chakras

Chakras is a Sanskrit term used to describe centres of energy and consciousness within the psyche, each with a fairly specific bodily location. The main centres are base of spine, sexual centre, solar plexus, heart, throat, brow, alta major centre (back of head) and crown (top of head). Each has its central energy point just behind the spine, though often experienced in the front of the body. There are also 21 minor centres in various bodily locations, for example the palm of each hand.

In our view the chakras system is the most sophisticated map of consciousness available. It is particularly useful for identifying and working with:

Energy imbalance within the psyche
Early warnings of health difficulties of psychological origin
Impending transitions/transformations
The need to take up some spiritual discipline or path
The centre where the self can be most fully experienced

It works best in therapy with clients who experience energy at the body level alongside different states of consciousness. Here is a very brief example.

> Male client, solar plexus tension of long standing, no organic cause. In spot imaging, got image of unhappy inner child for the tension. (The damaged child often lives in the solar plexus area – the healthy/divine child in the heart.) Client finds his heart is closed to this child; child does not want to go there anyway. Client asked whether he could invite damaged child to visit his heart centre and child whether he could accept invitation. Child went to heart for a few minutes. He and client found it good. In subsequent sessions child went willingly to the heart, and rediscovered his happiness, client accepting him. Solar-plexus tension largely disappeared, except as a warning signal.

In the final section, Case example, we illustrate further how a therapist can work with the chakras.

As to literature, we advise caution. Most Western material is highly simplistic. Our recommendations are: Bailey (1953), Woodroffe (1918) and Mindel (1984).

Meditation

Symbolically therapists sit at a crossroads in the life-journey of their clients.

It often becomes clear that the next stage of that journey should include some regular form of meditative or contemplative inner practice.

In such cases we may use session time to talk about various types of meditation, suggest some reading, and to give names of helpful groups or organizations. The most valuable aid however is to meditate *with* the client. Direct experience takes clients to a place that no amount of talk can reach, and the combined energies often give a preview of what can be accomplished in focused inner work.

Elements of meditation which we suggest clients can use if they wish include:

Alignment– stilling and linking the personality and its vehicles to the self
Visualization – a simple heart centre exercise
Reflection – on some seed idea or symbol
Linking with the collective and concluding invocation or mantram

Astrology

The creative frontier in this area is how to be both psychotherapist and astrological consultant to the same person. Today a number of skilled practitioners trained in both disciplines are pioneering this area.

We and many colleagues find an astrological chart a useful adjunct to transpersonal psychotherapy and welcome it if the client raises the question. We use the chart, not for 'character analysis' but:

1. To highlight a client's cyclic rhythms, and timing of events in his or her life, both inner and outer
2. To indicate potential mythological themes, derived from the placement of zodiacal signs and planets (Greene, 1986)
3. To help clarify component elements of crises and tests
4. To point to possible unconscious factors – for example, when a strong aspect in a chart is not expressed in life

The self per se, the soul, is nowhere shown on the chart. The self uses the chart, and may even have chosen it, but it remains the X factor, the unknown element in the equation.

Analysis of the transference

Analysis of the transference is a technique which focuses on the interaction between therapist and client and forms a central part of Freudian, Kleinian and Jungian therapeutic work. It assumes, correctly, that many clients will project a complex range of feelings and expectations on to the therapist (transference), many of which originate in childhood. The therapist will 'use his own responses and countertransferences as sources of information about the responses and transferences of the patient' (Lambert, 1984). As the analysis proceeds the client's projections are seen for what they are and can be withdrawn. There is profound meaning here. Individuation is a process of internalizing our projections.

Transpersonal psychotherapists work with the transference in this mode, when appropriate. In many cases, however, there is a critical difference, which arises from the use of imaging. Often the client's images cut quickly through to show that 'The world out there is not my problem. My problem is that one part of me is in battle with another' (as in the case quoted in the *chakras* paragraph). The transference/countertransference analysis must then shift to the inner conflict. Projection will continue – since old habits die hard! – but the recognition which imaging provides shifts the therapeutic ground from looking at the problem towards exploring solutions.

Gestalt in transpersonal work

We commend the admirable account of gestalt by Faye Page (1984). Our primary debt to gestalt is the 'chair' technique which we use, and train therapists to use, and which we find extraordinarily effective.

Apart from normal variations in style, the main difference between our practice and that described by Page is that we establish an *observer* position. This is where client can become the wise and compassionate observer, in touch with the self. (We believe it was first introduced into gestalt by psychosynthesis practitioners.)

In one sense the therapist is always the observer. But clients also need to develop observer consciousness. Many find that they have to lose their observer awareness in order fully to become the person or figure in another chair. Or they carry the feelings that belong in one position to another. So we ask them to return to the observer position and clear their consciousness of the previous position before moving on.

We also ask our clients when in the observer position to function as co-therapist. It is they who decide who the main actors are to be (numbers are not limited to two), where to be placed, and when to appear.

Gestalt with objects

Gestalt with objects is a graphic way of mapping the dynamics of relationship, conflicts, and decision-taking areas. If, for example, a client wishes to explore family patterns the therapist will indicate a range of objects – small decorative items, equipment from the top of the desk, objects from the client's pockets or handbag – and ask the client to choose one for each family member and important other figures, including the client.

Client lays out the first pattern – perhaps of family relationships before client's birth. Client is then placed in the pattern, and what is the result? Then client and therapist look at changes in the pattern at critical points in time: birth of younger sibling; death of a grandparent; moving house; wartime evacuation; older siblings leaving home; etc. Some key questions are: Is there a pattern in the patterns? Are any early patterns being repeated in present-day relationships? This technique has multiple uses, and can greatly aid the client to make choices and break redundant patterns.

Body language

We return to the theme of the body as a marvellous symbol of the total psyche which can tell us much if we learn its language.

We observe how the body stands, and moves, how it reacts to challenge and stress, how it tells us by gesture and posture when some inner figure (child, adolescent, frustrated breadwinner or loser) has taken over.

We need to know where the body reveals a split or unbalanced consciousness – the head/feeling split in the neck; the 'higher' and 'lower' consciousness split around the waist; the masculine–feminine/right side–left side split, vertically down the middle of the body.

If the body is held too tight to give us the information it contains, we can 'turn it on its head' and get it to adopt postures that will trigger long-locked feelings. We must see that the body has enough freedom to signal its messages.

Supportive techniques

In fact, a number of supportive techniques have become major therapies in their own right. Most techniques can be used in session, but more often form a part of homework. We have space only for a few of our favourites. Homework is anything that helps to anchor and express the insights of therapy in daily living. The client, with the help of the therapist, chooses a task or tasks to try out before the next meeting.

Drawing and painting: sculpting and modelling – of symbols, images, subpersonalities and dreams; helps to amplify, clarify, develop and anchor

Writing of many kinds: creative work; letters to discover what one would really like to say, though not necessarily to send; diaries, leading on to the kind of journal or day book that becomes a creative record of one's life

Active imagination – a stage beyond spot and guided imaging, wherein the full power of the creative imagination can be safely released to carry forward a chosen theme

Play – anything done purely for its own sake, just for fun; as much a prescription for therapists as for clients.

The change process in therapy

Psychotherapy is a co-operative venture. It changes, or should change, both therapist and client. There is of course the problem of how you know whether a client has changed and, we hope, been helped. And as the French say, cynically and realistically, 'Plus ça change mais c'est toujours la même chose.' Or as one analyst put it: 'At the end of a course of therapy your life may still be the same, but you feel differently about it!'

There will always be those for whom therapy is at best a holding operation. They are either so damaged, or the circumstances of their lives are so raw and intractable that we can do little more than stand by and help them manage things better and build in times of relief and respite. Doing this can even bring a kind of transformation in the long term.

At the other end of the scale are those, perhaps already on the cusp of change, for whom therapy provides the trigger for growth that seems both rapid and permanent. In these people creative energy is released in abundance, and they are quite literally never the same again.

Between these poles we find the infinitely variable possibilities for change, growth, development and transformation of the human psyche.

There are a number of measures which we have come to value down the years, measures which indicate that a real change has taken place:

1. Clients move towards wholeness. Imbalance and one-sidedness are redressed, and we increasingly see whole people before us.
2. Clients discover or rediscover meaning in life. The wonder of having something to live for, even a goal and purpose, is in some degree found.
3. Clients become more authentic, more real. The signs of this are often increased spontaneity, greater enjoyment of life, and no longer being run by other people's expectations, whether these are present in outer living or internalized deposits from the past.
4. Clients actually *listen* to what is happening in life, both within and without. They can therefore respond and adjust to the need for change at the time it is required.
5. Clients develop a positive and healthy self-image. They come to love themselves appropriately, to accept their limitations as natural and right,

and can embrace their darkness as well as their light.

6. They take charge of their life, and increasingly make and implement their own decisions. They recognize that they no longer need therapy, and can in large measure become their own therapist.

We need to remember that real and enduring change is normally slow and that a sense of fulfilment is perhaps the ultimate criterion of the change process. We find that the fear of death often disappears when the individual feels fulfilled.

Finally the process of therapy and the process of change require and are based on love. The processes we have outlined in this chapter are ultimately all about love. The atmosphere of the counselling room, the being and energy of the therapist, the interaction between therapist and client, must be expressions of and be grounded in love. Without this nothing will endure.

CASE EXAMPLE

The client

When he first came to see me John was 46. He had been married for 22 years, had a daughter aged 19 and a son of 17. He described his marriage as 'good', but said that in the last year there had been tension and irritation between himself and his wife, whom he described as 'bossy'. His daughter had just gone to university. His son was in his 'A'-level year and appeared unsettled and uncertain of his career direction.

John heard of me (Ian Gordon-Brown) from a business colleague in whom he had confided. John was a management consultant and said he enjoyed his work and had been with his firm some six years. But he felt tired much of the time, he was not sleeping well, and was experiencing a lot of throat tension. He had been having rheumatic type pains in his left arm and leg, and had recently had a series of minor accidents to his car ('not all his fault, but all on the left side') and he felt these were connected in some way with how he was feeling. He said he felt that something was going on underneath the surface and notwithstanding that he had been passed fit at a recent insurance medical, he decided to seek help.

Therapist's initial view

I rarely attempt a detailed assessment at a first meeting, unless the potential client is severely damaged. I prefer to let the client's psyche unfold its own story and leave reactions and questions at the back of my mind, for future reference. John's symptoms suggested a fairly typical midlife crisis, with suppression of feelings and the feminine side of his nature. I guessed it might not take too long to handle the immediate problems of fatigue and disrupted sleep – John was nowhere near exhaustion. But if he repressed his feelings in close relationships as well as at work, the implications of going deeper could be radical and affect the whole pattern of his life. I outlined some of these initial reactions to John, explained how I worked, and suggested we should try four to six sessions at weekly intervals (my normal practice) and see how they went. We could then review the situation.

The first six sessions

As I suspected we started with John's sleep and body-tension problems. They were for him the most urgent as they were affecting his work.

On sleep, John was waking regularly at 4 a.m., with anxiety symptoms in his stomach and solar plexus. We started to map these, getting John to describe them and feel into them. I went from this into spot imaging, and John came up with an image of a schoolboy self, aged 15 to 16, saying he seemed 'to live in his solar plexus'. At one point John came out of the imaging into his head to explain that there was no special significance to the schoolboy's age. But as he went back to the feelings and imaging a flood of memories loaded with fear and anxiety around career choice surfaced. How would he do at 'O' levels? Could he satisfy his mother's standards and high expectations? John admitted that his current worries at work had an identical 'feel' to these early anxieties of the 15/16-year-old.

We spent the next two sessions exploring early home life. John was the eldest child of three. His mother wore the trousers, and father, a gentle man who worked in local government, was not ambitious enough for her. Here John felt there was a connection between his ambitious mother and his 'bossy wife', who wore the trousers in *his* home.

As we talked, John had an acute attack of throat tension, and when I asked him to stay with the tension and attend to what it might be saying, he got a picture of himself at nine years of age, listening to rows between his parents, where mother berated father and the nine-year-old self held back his tears and anger and did not say what he felt.

We moved on and spent two sessions using gestalt and gestalt with objects to explore connections between John's present situation and his childhood, especially the connections between mother and wife and the similarities between John's behaviour and that of his father.

It became clear that both of John's inner figures played powerful roles. The 16-year-old in the solar plexus was still seeking 'to please mother/wife' and avoid any form of confrontation, while the nine-year-old managed John's emotional expression from the throat.

I suggested some homework – that John should start telling his wife about his feelings, especially on emotionally toned but relatively unimportant issues, and that he should spend time getting to know the nine- and 16-year-old inner figures better. John was already feeling and sleeping better and he decided to continue in therapy.

The next six months

We met once a week for the next six months, exploring in depth the themes opened up in the first six sessions. Soon after the beginning of this phase John had a dream. He could remember little, except that he was driving in his car. So we talked about his car and his early run of accidents.

John said that he loved driving, particularly in the country. (The nine-year-old in him was, he felt, a nature lover.) His car meant privacy, the opportunity to be by himself, where no one could get at him. He was fascinated when I told him that all forms of transport have important symbolic meanings, and that cars, for example, often represent portable psychic space. I suggested that since he remembered little of the dream, I could give him our 'Road of your life' exercise. This has three stages: *first*, driving on the present road of your life; the *second* stage, continuing to drive along the present road, but this time into the future; and stage *three*, driving into the future, but along a different route. John readily agreed.

John's images for the present road, and continuing that road into the future, were virtually identical – motorway driving with a lot of traffic and too many dangerous drivers. In stage two, driving the present route into the future, John was unable to get out of the fast lane, being constantly overtaken on the inside by faster cars. They bumped him on the left side, back into the fast lane, whenever he tried to get off it. John said it felt just like work. He enjoys being a management consultant and gets pleasure from the firms he visits and the people he meets there. But he likened many of his colleagues to 'fast-car consultants', cutting him up on the inside and setting company targets that were not only unrealistic but compelled him to skimp what he felt were important parts of his assignments.

Stage three, the alternative journey into the future, was quite different. He turned left, and found himself in the same car, but travelling along a country road at a comfortable pace. At one point he stopped and found himself going out on short trips from a central building (a kind of base), sometimes by car, sometimes on bicycle and sometimes on foot.

We had already discussed the meaning of the left and right side in symbolism and that for many people movements to the left could represent shifts towards the feminine, receptive, feeling and intuitive sides of our natures. John said that the third-stage journey, when he turned to the left, felt far closer to his feeling side than the first two. He saw that he had suppressed this aspect of his being for many years, and that it had insufficient opportunity for expression in his working life. He described himself as having been a sensitive and idealistic youth who had wanted to study biology, English and religious studies for 'A' level, but had given in to family pressure (mother) to do something practical and safe. Engineering just won over accountancy. He said that the third journey to the left felt closer to his essential nature than the other two.

John now knew that he could not stay much longer in his job. I asked if he could talk with his wife about how he felt. Adult John was very reluctant, but the nine- and 16-year-old inner figures were keen that he do so! By now his physical symptoms had virtually disappeared and John felt more in charge of his life. So after some gestalt work to prepare the ground he agreed to try.

To his surprise his wife was both understanding and sympathetic. She said she also felt at a crossroads, and had been thinking of seeking work in a year or two when the children left home. They agreed to continue talking. John managed to tell his wife he sometimes found her 'bossy'. She said it was mostly because he did not stand up to her.

The process of therapy had reached the point where I suggested I should give John a long guided daydream, to search for symbols of integration. Two main symbols came up. The first was the place (the base or central point) which he had found on the 'road of your life' exercise. John sensed that he had a task or responsibility there, caring for the land. Later he came to a church, which took him back to the religious interest of his youth. He felt deeply at home in each place.

As I had hoped, there were practical consequences. John started a part-time course in environmental studies, to do with land use and care, and began to look for a church which he might join.

Shortly after this John got a consultancy assignment that took him away from home. He was able to see me occasionally, but we had to stop our regular meetings. Eventually he and his family decided to move to the country, and nearer to his assignment. Later he wrote to say that he was in good health, the family were enjoying their new life, and he was determined to change his job in the next two or three years.

Up-date

Some three years later we bumped into each other at a National Trust meeting. John greeted me warmly and I met his wife for the first time. He told me that arising from his environmental studies, he had got a job with his new local authority as an Environmental Health Officer. He loved the work, both his engineering and consultancy experience were relevant and he felt socially useful at last. Much of the work took him into the country. He also said that he and his wife had found a local church where the vicar was progressive, and full of creative ideas for community welfare. He felt that the religious impulse which had been blocked so many years ago was now finding creative expression.

REFERENCES

Bailey, A. A. (1953) *Esoteric Healing*, Lucis Press, London.

Chandōgya Upanishad (1932) *The Twelve Principal Upanishads*, Vol. III, Raja Rajendralal Mitra and E. B. Cowell (translators), Theosophical Publishing House, Madras.

Desoille, R. (1965) *The Directed Daydream*, Psychosynthesis and Education Trust, London.

Greene, L. (1986) *Astrology for Lovers*, Unwin Paperbacks, London.

Jung. C. G. (1928) *Contributions to Analytical Psychology*, Routledge & Kegan Paul, London.

Jung, C. G. (1953) *Psychology and Alchemy*, Collected Works, Vol. 12, Routledge & Kegan Paul, London.

Lambert, K. (1984) Psychodynamic therapy: the Jungian approach, in W. Dryden (ed.) *Individual Therapy in Britain*, Harper & Row, London.

Leuner, H. (1984) *Guided Affective Imagery*, Thieme-Stratton, New York.

Maslow, A. H. (1964) *Religions, Values and Peak Experiences*, Ohio State University Press, Columbus.

Mindel, A. (1984) *Dreambody*, Routledge & Kegan Paul, London.

Page, F. (1984) Gestalt therapy, in W. Dryden (ed.) *Individual Therapy in Britain*, Harper & Row, London.

Progoff, I, (1963) *The Symbolic and the Real*, Coventure, London.

Sutich, A. J. (1976) The emergence of the transpersonal orientation: a personal account, *Journal of Transpersonal Psychology*, Vol. 8, No. 1, pp. 5–19.

Tart, C. T. (ed.) (1975) *Transpersonal Psychology*, Routledge & Kegan Paul, London.

White, J. (ed.) (1972) *The Highest State of Consciousness*, Anchor Books, New York.

Woodroffe, Sir John (1918) *The Serpent Power*, Ganesh, Madras.

Suggested further reading

Jung, C. G. (1978) The Collected Works, Routledge & Kegan Paul, London.

Journal of Transpersonal Psychology. Published twice yearly since 1969 from P.O. Box 4437, Stanford, CA 94305.

CHAPTER 12

NEURO-LINGUISTIC PROGRAMMING

Eric Robbie

HISTORICAL CONTEXT AND DEVELOPMENTS IN BRITAIN

Historical context

NLP began in the early 1970s when John Grinder, then an associate professor of linguistics, teamed up with Richard Bandler, a mathematician, computing student, and gestalt therapist. The task they gave themselves was to study such therapeutic 'wizards' as Fritz Perls, Virginia Satir, and later, Milton Erickson to find out how each could use seemingly different methods, and yet all get 'magical' results.

At that time Bandler and Grinder were primarily interested in making this magic comprehensible. 'We never had the intention of starting a new school of therapy,' they wrote (Grinder and Bandler, 1976, p. 195), 'we wished rather to start a new way of talking about it.' Moreover, they described what they were doing as *modelling*, and the distinction, they maintained, is crucial in that a model is different from a theory. 'A theory has to talk about what's truth, what's real,' says John Grinder (taped seminar, 1983), 'it has to be internally consistent.' A model just has to produce the same results as the person or process being modelled.

Which they did. After months of observing Perls, Satir, and Erickson – both in person and on video tape – Bandler and Grinder presented what they found. In a series of books and seminars they claimed 'to show some of the many patterns that therapists of every school have in common' (*ibid.*, p. 195). Using linguistic analysis and mathematical notation, they presented the sequences that make any therapy work.

It's probably fair to say the study of Erickson proved the most fruitful (Bandler and Grinder, 1975b; Grinder, DeLozier and Bandler, 1977). From their analysis of Erickson's language patterns – which later became known as 'the Milton Model' (Grinder and Bandler, 1981) and which they described as 'artfully vague' – and from Satir's work on clear communication (Satir, 1967), they described how therapists can be the opposite of vague, and use the clients' language to build a model of their world.

In fact, central to *The Structure of Magic* is Bandler and Grinder's (1975a) model of how we all make models of the world. Since *their* model is 'meta' to – that is, is a logical level higher than – our ordinary models, they called it 'the Meta Model', and it is the linguistic cornerstone of NLP.

In 1976, Grinder was still teaching at Santa Cruz University, and at one point he asked his undergraduate class to find and name something in experience they had not previously paid attention to. One of his most diligent students was Robert Dilts, and it was he primarily who delineated the famous 'NLP eye movements' (see p 255), fitting them in with work (Sperry *et al.*, 1969; Ornstein, 1972; 1973) on the differing functions of the right and left brains.

Indeed, systematic study revealed other connections between internal experience and external behaviour, and these, plus the split-brain patterns, make up the neurological part of NLP, as well as re-inforce the notion that mind and body are part of the same interlocking system. (The programming part owes more to cybernetics than computers.)

In the period 1975–79, Bandler and Grinder attracted a group of co-developers including David Gordon, Judith DeLozier, and Leslie Cameron-Bandler, and through workshops began making their approach more widely known. Initially, these were 'seminars in hypnosis', but as techniques streamlined, they began publicly calling them NLP. (The term 'neuro-linguistic programming' was first used in the spring of 1976.)

In 1978, the Society of Neuro-Linguistic Programming was formed, offering three levels of formal training and certification – Practitioner (the lowest), Master Practitioner, and Trainer. In the USA, over 50,000 people have attended some kind of NLP seminar, and there are over 6,000 certified Practitioners.

In terms of 'roots' the paradox is NLP can embrace the modified be-haviourism of Miller, Galanter, and Pribram (1960) – John Grinder studied psychology with George Miller – and the radical ethnology of Gregory Bateson (1972; 1979) – for a time Bandler and Grinder were neighbours and thus friends with Bateson, and it was he who arranged for them to visit Erickson.

The paradox is perhaps resolved by remembering NLP is a model, not a theory – 'it is an attitude more than anything else, and a methodology,' says Richard Bandler (taped seminar, 1984), 'it is not the trail of techniques it leaves behind.' And as NLP spills over into educational and business applications, new therapeutic developments are still being made – most notably by Bandler himself. His book, *Using Your Brain — for a Change* (1985) promises to be as influential in the 1980s as *The Structure of Magic* was ten years before.

Developments in Britain

NLP first came to Britain in 1979 when Gene Early, who had trained with Richard Bandler and Leslie Cameron-Bandler, presented a paper at the ITA conference in Brighton, and met Eileen Watkins-Seymour. Throughout 1980 and early 1981, she brought him over to give workshops, and ran a small study group in her North London home. Meanwhile, Judy Maul, Ian Cunningham, and Graham Dawes had quite independently invited David Gaster, who trained with John Grinder, to give a workshop in May 1981.

The two sets of sponsors learned about each other in August 1981, when Graham Dawes, in Santa Cruz to do Practitioner training, met Gene Early, and was told of Eileen's interest. Shortly after, the two groups joined forces, and in March 1982 Gene, David, Eileen, Ian, and Graham met round Eileen's kitchen table to plan the first British Practitioner-level course – the UK Diploma in NLP.

That course took the bold and expensive step of insisting all training should be done by certified Trainers, each of whom had to be flown in from the States, and was administered by Eileen and Graham, both of whom put in enormous time and energy, initially for very little reward. But their concern for standards paid off in the quality of the training.

The UK diploma ends its fifth year in May 1987, while the newly-formed NLP Training Program ends its first year in August 1987. There should then be over 250 British people qualified at Practitioner level. Meanwhile, British developers are making contributions – for example, the author's 'submodality eye accessing cues' take eye movements one step further on – and the next year should see the first properly certified British Trainers, and the opening of other training centres.

THEORETICAL ASSUMPTIONS

Image of the person

Richard Bandler is fond of saying that when people come for therapy, it is not because they are broken – in fact, they work perfectly. It's just that the thing they succeed at is not what they want. So in order to interrupt old patterns and teach new ones, we need to understand the *structure* of the client's subjective experience, and to do that, we need to answer the question: how do people make models of the world?

To begin with, the world 'out there' is much richer and more detailed than what we normally experience. With the exception of certain altered states, our nervous systems act to filter out much of that richness and detail. In NLP what we experience is called the *primary representation* of the world, to distinguish it from words, which are a *secondary representation* of the world.

As you may appreciate, in that distinction there is already some 'slippage' between the two ways we represent the world, that is, between raw experience and the words we use to describe it. Just think for a moment of all those arguments about whether a particular colour 'is or is not a purple', or attempts to put words to a particular taste in wine.

Primary representation can be broken down into the five senses – sight, sound, touch, taste, and smell. In NLP these are called *representation systems* (or 'rep systems' for short), and are given the formal names of visual (V), auditory (A), kinesthetic (K), gustatory (G), and olfactory (O). (Kinesthetic includes both sensation and emotion.)

Except for cases of neurological damage, people are born with equal awareness in all five senses (Aldrich and Aldrich, 1947). But by five or six, they experience only one system in consciousness at any one time. Certainly, by the time they are fully grown, most people have a distinct preference for visual, auditory, or kinesthetic as their secondary representation system (McCormick, 1975; Falzett, 1979; Pantin, 1982). Although there may be brief forays into other systems, they express themselves in terms of one.

So one individual will say 'I see what you mean' or 'Can I make something clear?', another will say 'I hear what you're saying' or 'Can I explain?', while a third will say 'That feels right to me' or 'Can you grasp that idea?' – when all three mean 'I understand you' and 'Can I get you to understand me?'

As well as the slippage that occurs between primary and secondary representations, there are the differences which occur when people use words such as 'love' or 'trust'. These abstract words need to be traced back to what a person would see, hear, feel, taste and smell when using them. In

Figure 12.1   Eye 'accessing' for a normal right-hander

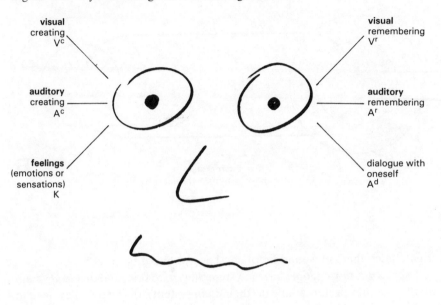

(straight ahead and defocused is also visual)

NLP terms, there is a *complex* of sensory system experiences which is *equivalent* to each word (Grinder, DeLozier and Bandler, 1977).

A non-verbal way of identifying a person's preferred representation system comes from neurological observations. There had been research through the early 1970s associating eye movements with the functions of the right and left brain (Kinsbourne, 1972; Kocel *et al.*, 1972; Galin and Ornstein, 1974). The co-developers of NLP took this research a step further by showing that eye movements are related to representation systems (Grinder, DeLozier, and Bandler, 1977; Dilts, 1977; Owens, 1977), and Figure 12.1 shows where the eyes of a right-handed person move to as they 'access' or find different kinds of experience.

So for example, if you asked that person 'What is the colour of your front door?' he or she would have to remember seeing it in order to answer, and his or her eyes would typically move up and to the left, while 'What does Mrs Thatcher sound like speeded up?' ought to produce a horizontal shift to the

Figure 12.2   A two-person communication system

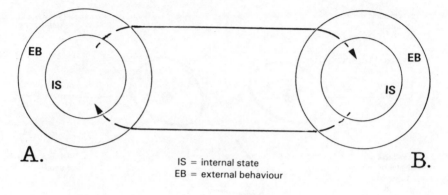

IS = internal state
EB = external behaviour

right, since that is a sound he or she has not heard before.

In practice, most people have a system they go to first, and that *leads* them to the one they prefer talking in (their *main* system), or the one they need to be in to respond to the question (Thomason, Arbuckle and Cody, 1980). So with the second example above, a 'mainly visual' person would first make a picture of Mrs Thatcher before adding in the sound.

It's worth stressing that these eye accessing cues are only one aspect of the systematic connection between internal states and external behaviour (Dilts *et al.*, 1979; Lewis and Pucelik, 1982). And if you like, the system involving others is shown in Figure 12.2.

Based on his or her internal state, A utters words and shows external behaviour to B. B takes in those words, and if they refer to direct experience, easily makes sense of them, otherwise she or he has to search across her or his 'store' of experiences for a meaning. B is also aware of A's external behaviour, which may or may not match up with what A says, and as a result of the combined messages, B's internal state will change.

B may not reply at first, but will show a behavioural manifestation of his or her internal response, since it's a principle of NLP that *a person can't not respond*. So if B does reply, her or his words and external behaviour will have an effect on A.

This rather detailed analysis of what only takes a few seconds explains, for example, how two people can get stuck in a 'loop' (Bandler, Grinder and Satir, 1976), so that when A 'comes on' one way, B 'just has to' say something back, which in turn stimulates A, and so on. NLP believes not only that you can make people feel, but also that you will always elicit *some* response – and that elicitation is something you are responsible for.

This leads to a second principle in NLP, that *the meaning of what you say is the response you get*. In the culture of humanistic psychology, which places such a high value on 'authenticity' and 'self-expression', this is possibly the most provocative statement to come out of NLP. What it means is that, even more important than 'being yourself' is being responsive to other people.

At a larger level of organization, NLP shares with other approaches the notion of subpersonalities, but prefers not to give them such specific names as 'Topdog and Underdog' or 'Parent, Adult, and Child'. Naming sub-personalities not only gives them unwanted permanence but also introduces connotations which may be inaccurate or irrelevant to the client.

Instead, NLP uses the notion of *parts*. Thus, an NLP therapist will say to a client, 'There is a part of you which is scared, and there is a part of you which is curious . . .' bearing in mind that a 'part' doesn't actually exist – it is merely a useful description (Russell, 1905), a way of organizing the client's experience at one particular time.

The division in awareness NLP makes the most use of is the one between the conscious and unconscious minds. The conscious is 'whatever is in consciousness right now', and as demonstrated by Miller (1956), it has limited 'channel capacity' and can only process seven plus or minus two 'chunks' of information at any given time.

The unconscious is not so easy to define. One version is 'everything which is not in consciousness right now', but this does not explain how the other-than-conscious creates 'reality', or how we edit and select from reality so that it matches our expectations. What is undeniable is that it is possible to change those expectations in trance *without the conscious knowing* (Bandler and Grinder, 1975b), and without pain, distress, or seeming effort.

Another process that is undeniable is that the unconscious quite readily responds to 'commands' that are 'embedded' in, or hidden in, otherwise indirect conversation – such as 'most people are able to *sit down and relax* . . . and as they continue to *breathe in and out* . . . pretty soon they begin to *feel comfortable*' – especially if these instructions are 'marked out' by a tiny shift of the head, or a slight change in voice. In general, people are much more suggestible than some humanistic psychologies would like to believe.

Concepts of psychological health and disturbance

One basic premise of NLP is that people 'are not bad, crazy, or sick – they are, in fact, making the best choices . . . available to them in their model [of the world]' (Bandler and Grinder, 1975a, p. 14). And so psychological health is about adding choices, and creating a richer model of the world.

Another basic premise is that *most people already have all the resources they need* to solve the problem – it's just that they do not know they do. For example, someone who presents with a phobia or anxiety has almost always had the experience of being unafraid or competent at some time in his or her life. Within this general frame, psychological health is 'the client setting goals and getting what she or he wants', and in this respect NLP is clearly actionistic. That is, NLP therapists value the client behaving differently over having insight or gaining understanding – neither of which, on its own, guarantees change. And because *behavioural flexibility*, or having a range of new behaviours, is so highly valued, several NLP techniques directly install patterns that will enable the client to solve other problems, problems that may come up after the therapy is over. In NLP this is called *generative change* (Bandler and Grinder, 1979; Bandler, 1985; Cameron-Bandler, 1985, p. 162).

However, the most important premise in NLP to do with psychological health is that *there is a positive intention behind all our parts and all our behaviour*. This belief, which originally comes from reframing, may or may not be true. But as Leslie Cameron-Bandler (1985) says, 'When I organize my behavior as though it were true, positive change becomes easier to accomplish' (p. 161).

In terms of psychological disturbance, NLP practitioners believe that when people feel denied, consider themselves stuck, or experience a lack of choices, this is misperception. In reality, the world is rich and varied enough for them to get what they want, but their model of the world is limited.

The acquisition of psychological disturbance

When people have a limited representation of the world, it shows up, or announces itself, or makes itself felt in the language that they use. And the journey from experience to language involves three universal modelling processes:

1. *Deletion*: which is the 'process by which we selectively pay attention to certain dimensions of our experience and exclude others' (Bandler and Grinder, 1975a, p. 15). If you like, we leave bits out.
2. *Generalization*: which is 'the process by which elements or pieces of a person's model become detached from the original experience and come to represent the entire category of . . . experience' (*ibid.*, p. 14). Or, once is always.
3. *Distortion*: which is 'the process which allows us to make shifts in our sensory data' (*ibid.*, p. 16), and which permits us to form and maintain

unwarranted beliefs. Thus, 'I know what you're thinking' and 'When you look at me like that I feel ill.'

This model of how we all make models (the Meta Model) is useful in that it allows therapists to deal with the *form* of clients' experience, as much as with the content. And it's worth noting that it is neutral with respect to time – that is, it may describe the present, but it can only *imply* the past.

For this and other reasons, I take issue with the model of therapy implied in the format of this book. The words *acquisition* and *root causes* come from a limited, and possibly limiting, model of personal change. As Leslie Cameron-Bandler puts it:

> Most psychotherapies . . . psychoanalysis, transactional analysis, primal therapy, and rebirthing, as well as the 'pop' psychotherapies such as est, Lifespring, and Scientology, are designed to deal with the past as the source of problems. . . We agree with this to a certain extent. What we don't agree with is the assumption that you are trapped by the past, an assumption that is held explicitly or implicitly by all of the approaches listed above.   (Cameron-Bandler *et al.*, 1985, p. 40).

In general, NLP would classify these approaches as 'past history' models, and is cautious about them for two main reasons.

Conceptual: The central motivation of past-history models is *discovering the secret*. That is, people think, 'If I could only find out what really happened,' with the implication 'then I would be free'. NLP's developers believe this search to be misplaced. As Richard Bandler says, '*Nothing* ever *really* happened. The only thing that happened is that you made a set of perceptions about events' (Bandler and Grinder, 1979, p. 97).

Practical: Most NLP practitioners would say that 'all this talk about the past does not do anything to change it'. And some NLP trainers (David Dobson, for example) who use a lot of hypnosis would go even further. Since people are so suggestible, and can be talked *out* of their problems, while in trance, they can just as easily be talked *into* them, while in therapy.

Perpetuation of psychological disturbance

A similar caution extends to the concept of *perpetuation*. And an NLP practitioner will seek from the beginning to 'challenge' the client's limited model of the world.

1. If the client *deletes*, and says 'I'm no good', the therapist might say 'At what?' or 'In what way?'
2. If the client *generalizes*, and says 'I'm no good at everything. It always turns out wrong,' the therapist might say 'Everything? Has there never been a time when it didn't turn out wrong?'

3. If the client *distorts*, and says 'That isn't the point – I'm no good because such-and-such . . .' the therapist could ask 'How does that experience "cause" you to be no good?'

What distinguishes this kind of questioning is that it is impossible to gather information about the client's limited model without implicitly directing attention to a richer, fuller one. The three challenges above (which come from the meta model) get to the nub of the problem, while implying 'that isn't the way it has to be'.

At the neurological level, NLP is similarly positive. How the problem was originally acquired *may* be of interest, but what matters is how to change it now. The question then becomes 'What structural patterns does the client have?' For example:

1. If there are limiting beliefs, how are they represented? What pictures, sounds, or sensations are the 'bedrock' for those beliefs?
2. When the client is communicating a particular experience, are there any external behaviours which suggest there is a representation system to which the person is reacting *out of awareness*?
3. Does the person habitually go through a sequence of V, A, and K which gets him or her into the problem? For example, when faced with external visual input (V^e) – say, an untidy bedroom – the client may remember past untidinesses (V^r), then hear his or her mother's voice saying he or she is 'awful' (A^r), and then feel bad (K^{i}–ve). This whole sequence can be undercut if, at the second step, the client makes different pictures (V^c) instead.

So rather than ask 'How do we perpetuate problems?', NLP therapists prefer 'How can we eliminate them?' instead. If 'the most pervasive paradox of the human condition is that the processes which allow us to survive, grow, change, and experience joy are the same processes which allow us to maintain an impoverished model of the world' (Bandler and Grinder, 1975a, p. 14), then such a move does seem the better choice.

PRACTICE

Goals of therapy

The goals of therapy – in NLP jargon, the *outcomes* of therapy – are 'what the client wants', but with the qualification that the outcomes need to be *well-formed*. This is another jargon word, and its origin is unknown even to some NLPers, although what it means is actually quite simple. The term 'well-formed' comes from mathematical logic, and it describes any formula that is written out properly, so that you can use it in an orderly fashion, and there will not be any mistakes later. In NLP, it means much the same, and being well-formed is what makes outcomes worthwhile.

This concern for worthwhile goals is central to NLP. As far back as 1978, Bandler and Grinder began to stress that, because NLP techniques are so powerful, the real task is to make change that fits with the whole life context, or 'ecology', of the client, and which they called *ecological change*. And in keeping with the basic principle of NLP, the key steps of this approach were modelled out by Robert Dilts and Todd Epstein as a series of questions to ask the client (Dilts *et al.*, 1979, p. 161) and a set of conditions to be satisfied in the process (Cameron-Bandler, 1985, p. 85). To be well-formed an outcome should be:

1. *Stated in the positive.* Many clients come into therapy saying what they do not want – 'I don't want pain', 'I don't want my girlfriend to leave me' – and therapy is begun without them saying what they *do* want. Not only is time wasted in endless explorations of the past, but the client does not have a clear representation of where to go in the future.
   So the question is: '*What do you want?*'

2. *Demonstrable in sensory experience.* Many therapists actually get the changes they want but do not notice them, while some clients blithely report 'I feel much better now', when patently they're not. This requirement is that both the client and the therapist are satisfied that the client has what he or she came for.
   So the questions are: '*How will you know you've got it?*' and '*How will I know you've got it?*'

3. *Appropriately contextualized.* These long words simply mean that the proposed change is thought of in the context of the client's life, and some consideration is given to how it would affect his or her personal and professional life and close relationships. NLP does not want the effects of change to be worse than the presenting problem.
   So the questions are: '*When and where do you want it?*' and '*When and where don't you want it?*'

4. *Initiated and maintained by the client.* This is the requirement that the client be agent in his or her world, which NLP shares with many other therapies. A typical example is the client who asks for a change in someone else's behaviour, or who says 'I want my wife to be more considerate.' An alert therapist would direct attention to what the client

can do differently. This requirement also entails the accessing of resources that the client already has, as well as demonstrating that the obstacles the client thinks are external may really be internal.

So the questions are: '*What do you need to get it?*' and '*What stops you from getting it?*'

5. *Preserves the positive by-products of the client's present state.* The classic cases involving a positive 'by-product' are smoking and over-eating. The exchanging of cigarettes and the mutual lighting up is a ritual many people feel they need to start a conversation, while much socialization takes place over food. If the client is to successfully give up smoking or overeating, she or he will probably need to find other ways of relating in those situations.

So the question is: '*What will happen if you get it?*'

It's worth noting that, in spite of the mathematical metaphor of 'well-formed', these questions do not in themselves constitute a formula for doing therapy. And while novice therapists may need to ask all eight explicitly, more experienced practitioners may not ask them at all, being content if they get the answers in a seemingly casual interview.

The 'person' of the therapist

Whatever outcomes the client wants, the basis for coming to therapy is that he or she has exhausted all the existing choices or ways of getting them. And if the therapist is convincingly to add more choices, he or she needs to have access to a greater range of experiences than the client. Another way of saying this is: If greater flexibility is useful for the client, it's vital for the therapist. Indeed, it is an axiom of NLP derived from cybernetics – where it's known as the 'law of requisite variety' (Ashby, 1956) – that *the person with the most flexibility controls the situation*, whether that control be for good or ill.

As an example of how that control can be utilized for the benefit of the client, we can consider Ericksonian hypnosis. In a typical session, Erickson might have said:

Sometime in the last five years you had a very powerful experience . . . which was of great significance to you . . . but whose meaning you didn't fully consider . . . at the time . . . but if you begin to think about it now . . . you can realize . . . there was something very useful . . . and beneficial . . . for you to learn from that experience.

What gives this its power is not just the sequence of 'find a past experience, think about it now, and learn from it', but the way Erickson continuously responded to the client. So he would pause meaningfully at 'very powerful experience' and look over to see if the client had in fact found one, and again at 'great significance to you' to see from the response if indeed it was. Then again, he would look over at 'you can realize' for the tiny head-nods which would tell him the client was beginning such a realization.

There are two points to notice here, whether the NLP therapist is doing formal hypnosis or not: one is that the therapist needs to have extremely refined sensory awareness to be able to detect such subtle shifts in the client's external behaviour as skin colour changes, tiny head-nods, and changing lip thickness. It's another axiom of NLP that *you will always get an answer to your questions in so far as you have the sensory acuity to notice the response you get.*

The second point to notice is that, if at any of the pauses to look over and 'read' the client Erickson did not get the response he wanted, he would artfully change – often in mid-sentence – what he was saying. This flexibility of syntax generalizes out to a third NLP axiom – *if what you do doesn't work, do something different.*

(One of the most basic ways for the therapist to be more flexible is to become equally proficient in all three main representation systems so that he or she can switch his or her own verbal output to match that of the client. Just this one manoeuvre can profoundly affect the level of communication [Falzett, 1979; Brockman, 1980; Hammer, 1983].)

In addition to sensory acuity and flexibility, NLP maintains that the therapist needs to be believable to have any effect, and this brings up the question of what it is to be convincing, or *congruent.* To begin with, Bandler and Grinder wrote about incongruence as it revealed something about the client, but thinking since then has concerned itself with the congruence of the therapist. And in NLP there are now two schools of thought on the subject.

One is the strict definition of congruence, which says, 'If all my output channels – the way I look, the way I sound, the way I move – convey the same message, then I am being congruent.' According to this definition, being believable is a matter of consistent external messages (Bandler *et al.*, 1976, p. 45).

A more recent, and much wider, definition of congruence includes having the appropriate internal representations, feelings, and beliefs as well (Cameron-Bandler, 1985, p. 79). So *for therapy*, being congruent means not only caring for the client but also having the belief system that says 'people are valuable', 'change is possible', and 'there is a positive intention behind all behaviour' amongst other criteria.

In this respect, NLP hardly differs from other approaches – and the best NLP therapists (Gene Early, Barbara Witney, to name but two) embody warmth, empathy, and unconditional positive regard – although, using NLP, they might give them a more precise formulation. For example, warmth is both the internal feeling (K^i) and the external expression of it (A^e, K^e), while empathy comes from the therapist having had a requisite variety of emotional experiences, or 'whole body states'.

To sum up, the personal power of the therapist comes from flexibility, sensory acuity, and congruence, and from remembering that the most significant interventions in therapy often come when you learn to trust your unconscious.

Therapeutic style

For NLP, therapeutic style means *rapport* – what one person 'carries back' to another. And NLP's most significant contribution could well be that it has analysed what makes up this desirable state. As with flexibility, getting rapport is a skill that anyone can benefit from acquiring, but again, while deploying it is useful for the average person, having it is vital for the therapist. It is unlikely that anything meaningful will be done in therapy until rapport has been attained. So the NLP practitioner is taught to:

1. Unobtrusively move into the posture of, and minimally copy the gestures of, the client
2. Imperceptibly match the voice tone and tempo of the client
3. Subtly drift into breathing at the same rate as the client

All of which has a profound effect, even if they seem unnatural to do at first.

(If you observe people who already communicate successfully, you will find they are doing these things all the time. And after a period when you make these things part of your conscious behaviour, you should find they become automatic, and quite unconscious.)

Rapport should not be confused with mimicry, which carries an ulterior, often mocking, message, nor should it be confused with empathy, which is an entirely different thing.

As defined by Stevens, empathy is 'understanding' (Stevens and Rogers, 1967), and by Egan it is 'communicating understanding' (Egan, 1975). These are both primarily about content – what one person thinks or feels about another – whereas NLP's rapport is precisely about form. In terms of our previous discussion, empathy is primarily about the therapist's internal state, *and his or her description of it*, while rapport is mainly about the client's and the therapist's non-verbal behaviour, and is about the relationship as a whole (Maurer, 1982).

The concept in the literature (e.g. Rowan, 1983) that comes closest to rapport is Watkins's 'resonance' (1978). Since mind and body are part of the same cybernetic system, the therapist will often – *once rapport has been established* – 'pick up' some of the client's internal states. Indeeed, NLP practitioners are taught the sequence of: taking in a picture of the client (V^e), moving one's own body into an exact copy of the client's posture (K^e), asking internally 'What would have to be true for me, if I were always like this?' (A^i), naming the feeling that comes up (K^i, A^i), and then checking it out. With practice, this sequence can speed up, or 'streamline', and can even be done largely in the imagination – at which point it is resonance by any other name, and with the metaphor made explicit.

The point about rapport is that it offers undeniable and convincing evidence to the clients, in the way it speaks directly to the unconscious, that someone cares enough to join with them in their dance, their model of the world.

On the form-of-language level, rapport is also about tracking and matching representation system words (Falzett, 1979; Schmedlen, 1981), and about *pacing* – that is, going along with – the client's belief system (Rossi, 1983; Dolan, 1985). NLP therapists are taught to *respect all messages from the client*, and if this is done, there is no such thing as 'resistance' (Lankton and Lankton, 1983). Such resistance when it occurs is a sign of insufficient pacing.

The purpose behind all this matching and pacing is to establish the kind of rapport wherein the therapist can irresistibly *lead* the client to a desired outcome, and it is probably this which has gained NLP the reputation of being 'manipulative', while another common criticism is that it is 'remote' – which criticisms NLP would both agree with, and deny.

It is remote in the sense that it is the job of the therapist to keep his or her model of the world separate from the client's. And it is the *least* manipulative of therapies precisely because it does not impose the therapist's meanings on the client. And yet some people will not be convinced by this argument, seeing it as mere sophistry. Usually, these same people have concerns about manipulation meaning 'being made to do things they don't want to do'. In short, they fear NLP precisely because it is so effective. But if the notions of 'respecting all messages', 'adding choices', and 'making ecological change' have any validity, then 'being manipulative' means 'getting people where *they* want to go'.

To sum up, since the therapist cannot *not* influence people, he or she might as well influence with integrity, and with a full awareness of what he or she is doing, and how he or she expects the client to change.

Major therapeutic techniques

NLP can be used to make the techniques of other therapies work better – for example, re-enactments are more effective if done in all representation systems, 'contracts' can be made clearer using meta-model probes, and out-of-awareness messages recovered using external accessing cues. Indeed, Lankton (1980) has analysed several major approaches in terms of the NLP processes they employ. The following, however, are technqiues that are explicitly NLP.

Anchoring

Anchoring is the process of associating a touch, a word, or a visual signal to a complete representation of an experience so that it can be brought back into consciousness later (Dilts *et al.*, 1979; Cameron-Bandler, 1985). The advance it represents on straightforward conditioning is that NLP describes:

1. What's inside behaviourism's 'black box'.
2. How a link can be established after only one association.

(As with rapport, anchoring was going on long before NLP gave it a name. It explains, for example, how phobias are developed – and hints at the dissociation needed for a cure.)

One use of anchoring is to bring two experiences together – called Collapsing Anchors – so forcing integration, and giving the client a choice of which to have. Another is to combine experiences into a sequence – called Chaining Anchors – that the person has not had before.

Changing personal history

NLP has several ways of dealing with personal 'history' and of changing perceptions of the past, including:

V/K Dissociation, which deals with traumatic memories and phobias, and separates what was *seen* then from what is *felt* now. The separation allows a re-evaluation to be made (Cameron-Bandler, 1978; 1985).

Change History, which deals with unattached and recurrent negative feelings by tracing them back to some early memory, and then forward through a series of similar experiences, adding positive resources to each in turn.

Re-imprinting, which seeks to install new 'belief reference experiences' in place of ones that are already there.

Changing patterns

As mentioned before, the NLP practitioner looks, listens, and feels for patterns in experience, and there are patterns of representation systems, patterns of language, and patterns of beliefs. The first of these, a sequence made up of V, A, or K is called a *strategy* in NLP (Dilts *et al.*, 1979).

One of the simplest strategies is exhibited by people with depression. Typically, a depressed person has the sequence of: feeling bad (K^i-ve), then blaming themselves for feeling bad (A^d), then feeling bad because of that (K^i-ve), which only 'proves' they were right to think 'I'm bad' (A^d), and so on. And what they have is a *loop*, a cycle of limited choices.

An NLP therapist would want to turn this sequence into a more productive strategy – that is, one that every-so-many steps checks with external reality, and which involves each representation system at least once.

Working with parts

A good example of working with parts is the technique originally called Six-step Reframing (Bandler and Grinder, 1979), which was invented by John Grinder, and which is really a dialogue between parts. It is used when there is some behaviour the client wants to change.

The overlap this technique has with hypnosis is that the change is really made at an unconscious level – indeed, Grinder originally ran this sequence with the client in trance – and using this technique may give the client a greater respect for his or her unconscious processes.

Other forms of working with parts include the client negotiating between two parts in conflict (Bandler and Grinder, 1982, p. 45), and the 'parts party', borrowed from Satir (Grinder and Bandler, 1976, p. 76) for dealing with several parts at once.

Working with submodalities

The techniques using submodalities are the most recent, and possibly the most powerful, in NLP. Developed and refined over the last four years by Richard Bandler (1985), they include the Swish Pattern for changing troublesome thoughts and behaviour, the Threshold Pattern for interrupting compulsions, and the Submodality Belief Change.

(A *modality* is another name for what this chapter has been calling a 'representation system', and a *submodality* is just a distinction within any one of these – for example, brightness or colour in visual, and loudness or pitch in sound. The point is that simply changing one submodality can have a remarkable effect on an experience.)

If, for example, you think of a time that was extremely pleasant, and see it now – what happens if you make the picture brighter? Or more colourful? Does it change the way you feel? If you recall the voice of someone that you like, and hear it now – what happens if you speed it up? Or make it lower and more mellow? Does that change your internal response?)

Like rapport and anchoring, submodalities have always been there, and all NLP has done is draw attention to them. The interesting speculation is that maybe submodalities are involved in *every* form of change.

Changing frames

Reframing is the process of changing the frame in which a person perceives events, and was first defined by Watzlawick, Weakland and Fisch (1974). The events in question are content, and *content reframing*, to give it its proper name, divides into:

Meaning reframing, which assumes there is another, positive meaning to the behaviour offered in this context

Context reframing, which assumes there is another context in which this offered behaviour would have a positive meaning

The emphasis on content is important. Even though reframing has formal aspects, 'successful reframing needs to take into account the views, expectations, reasons, premises – in short, the conceptual framework – of those whose problems are to be changed . . . [it] presupposes the therapist learn the *patient's* language' (Watzlawick *et al.*, 1974, p. 104).

Using metaphor

Metaphor is the technique of prompting change in people by telling them seemingly innocuous stories, and the master of it was Milton Erickson (Haley, 1969). What makes metaphor work is that 'a person can't not respond'. When people hear a story, they have to access their own meaning and experiences just to make sense of it. And a carefully constructed metaphor (Gordon, 1978; Lankton and Lankton, 1983) allows people to apply their own resources to the problem.

Metaphor is profoundly respectful of the client. Not only is it *their*

Figure 12.3. The cycle of events in therapy
(Copyright 1983, by Leslie Cameron-Bandler and Michael Lebeau, and reprinted by permission.)

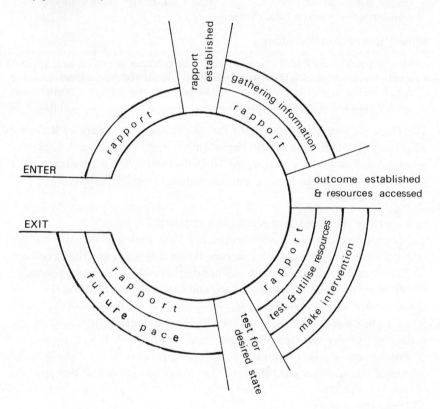

solution, but the change is made at an unconscious level. 'The special advantage of metaphor is that people respond without trying. Their conscious processes do not interfere' (Cameron-Bandler, 1985, p. 195).

The change process in therapy

The main thing to say about the change process in therapy *for the client* is that NLP believes change does not automatically involve pain. As John Grinder (Bandler and Grinder, 1979) said at one point:

> People have strange ideas about change . . . one of the weird things that's
> happened – and it's really an example of natural anchoring – is that pain and
> change have become associated. . . . That's ridiculous! There's no necessary
> relationship between pain and change.   (p. 177)

while Richard Bandler added:

> Most therapists intrinsically believe – at the unconscious as well as the conscious
> level – that change has to be slow and painful . . . [and] what you believe will come
> out. It will be in your tone of voice, in your body movement, in the hesitation as
> you lean foward to . . . work with someone.   (pp. 177–8)

The change process in therapy *for the practitioner* is a matter of knowing
what to do, when, and more importantly, how. And Figure 12.3 is a
procedural flow-chart which some NLP therapists use to organize their
perceptions and behaviours (Cameron-Bandler, 1983).

The phases are:

1. Enter the relationship and establish rapport.
2. Maintain rapport and begin gathering information about the client's
   structure and problem, their outcome or desired state, and their ecology.
3. Access and anchor resources – either deliberately, or opportunistically.
4. Maintain rapport, utilize resources, and make the intervention (i.e., use
   one of the NLP techniques).
5. Test your work – that is, does the client behaviourally demonstrate the
   outcome or desired state right here and now?
6. *Future pace* – this is a jargon word for the process of ensuring that the
   change transfers forward through time, and outside of the therapy session.
7. Close the session.

Thus the NLP practitioner must be able, at one and the same time, to:
establish and maintain rapport, take in and process information about
representation systems, track sequences or strategies, listen for and question Meta-Model language patterns, and follow the recommendations for a
well-formed outcome – while keeping in mind that in front of him or her is a
unique and valuable and, in many ways, accomplished human being.

And, there is no way that these six or seven tasks can all be done
consciously. So a large part of NLP Practitioner training is devoted to
practising and acquiring the skills involved to the point where they can be
done without thinking, and those precious 7 ± 2 chunks of attention can be
devoted entirely to the client.

However, it is because the NLP therapist uses multiple-level skills, and
because therapy is at the level of *structure*, that major change can be
accomplished in one or two sessions. And typically, an NLP therapist will

not expect to see a client for more than four or five sessions in all. As with brief or strategic therapy, the aim is to get the change in as short a time and as elegant a fashion as possible.

It also needs to be stressed that the flow-chart in Figure 12.3 need not be followed blindly or doggedly or by rote, and the art of therapy is to have this format – or one like it – in your head, and yet still be able to 'go with the client'. The aim of NLP as therapy is to have the model fit the client, and not the other way round.

CASE EXAMPLE

Although some people might consider the problem presented here as relatively minor, it could – if left unchanged – have far-reaching effects on the health of the client and the well-being of her family. So this case is worth thinking about as 'an ounce of prevention' as well as being a demonstration of NLP in action.

The client, whose name is Mary, is married, in her mid-thirties, has three children, and lives near London on an old farm. She runs management training courses, provides 'goal-setting' consultations, and has other business interests. She carries a Filofax-type diary, and has obviously been on a time-management course. She is ten minutes late for the session, and arrives flushed and slightly breathless.

After saying hello, and inviting her to sit down, the therapist (Eric) engages Mary in fairly casual conversation, ostensibly about the traffic, how she got here, did she have any trouble finding the consultation room, and so on. In the process, the therapist notes Mary's preferred rep system, how she sequences events in time, and which Meta-Model patterns she uses. He also takes in the signs that suggest Mary's internal state, and which indicate she is not in a useful place to begin work.

He establishes rapport by means of the behaviours detailed earlier, particularly matching breathing. As a test, he shifts in his seat, and when Mary makes a similar shift – which indicates rapport has been established – he begins to slow down his rate of breathing. Mary responds by slowing down her rate of breathing, and as she does so, she enters a more therapeutically useful state. The process so far has taken about four to five minutes.

Eric: So, Mary, what brings you here today?

Mary: Well, as I told you on the phone, I get a lot of things done and I keep up to schedule, but by the end of the day I'm tired and irritable, and I feel all strung up inside. I want to feel tired but

relaxed when I've finished. I want to feel as if I'm in control.
(*This is a good start: Mary has already stated what she wants in positive terms, indicated how she would know she had it, and recognized herself as the initiator of change.*)

Eric: So you get 'strung up' . . . How do you do that? I mean, how does your day go?

Mary: I have to plan what to do. I can't just go and do things, otherwise I get into a terrible muddle.

Eric: But how do you 'plan what do do'?

Mary: (*Eyes up and left, and then begins to act it with her hands*) Well, I write out a list, and. . . .

Eric: I see. Do you write it out then, or do you start some of it the night before?

Mary: (*Eyes up and left, and then hands busy again*) I think about some of the things the night before, but the main thing is when I draw up a list in the morning. That's my 'things to do'.
(*Mary's lead system is visual, but most of her rep system words are kinesthetic. In addition, before she says anything meaningful, Mary's whole posture 'starts' as if she were about to get up and run. That is, she 'thinks' in terms of doing.*)

Eric: Well, I can make a picture of that – but how does the rest of your day go? Can you run through it for me?

Mary: OK. I start at the top of the list and work down – I make a point of putting my 'things to do' in order. . . .

Eric: And how do you know it's time to be hassled?

Mary: (*Thinks*) I usually feel OK in the morning, then about mid-day as I look at the list, I'm aware of growing tension. . . .

Eric: Do you do anything about that? That mid-day growing tension?

Mary: No. I've learned to put it to one side . . . and . . . (*she pauses, movement or 'thinking' interrupted, as it were*).

Eric: You were in mid-afternoon.

Mary: Oh yes. Umm, I just carry on and get the list done . . . and then I find I'm strung up.

Eric: Uhuh. And what will happen if you don't change this pattern?

Mary: I can see myself getting ill. I can feel what happens to me already, and I don't think it's good for me.
(*One guess about Mary's structure is this: as soon as she finishes doing one task, she makes a picture of the next task, and then feels compelled to engage in that. It is not only a major strategy for her, but in some contexts is quite an achievement.*)

Eric: OK (*pause*). Mary, I'm not happy about taking away your drive to get things done, or what motivates you. And it strikes me that the things you do in the day are *all* important to you – is that right? For example, would you feel better if you only did, say, six out of the seven 'things to do'?

Mary: Possibly. (*However, her non-verbal messages say 'I'm not so sure' – i.e. she is incongruent.*)

Eric: Well, supposing you only did five things in a day? Or four?

Mary: Mmm, not really. The income I produce is important to us. And if I did less, I would feel. . . . It wouldn't be right.

(*In fact, Mary's most important response was immediate and non-verbal. 'You will always get an answer . . . if you have the sensory acuity.'*)

Eric: Would you be happier to get the same amount done as you do at the moment, but be in a better state at the end of it?

Mary: If that's possible.

(*The well-formed outcome conditions have all been met – in particular, the ecology of the present state has been preserved.*)

Eric: OK, I think I see where we're going. Has there ever been a time when you moved at speed and performed excellently, and you had all the time in the world, and you felt good about it?

(*The resources needed are usually within the client's history.*)

Mary: (*Eyes up and right, then flicking to up and left several times, and then defocused – a typical 'search' sequence.*) Yes . . . skiing.

Eric: And that was a good time for you?

Mary: (*Breaks into a smile*) Oh *yes*.

Eric: Good. OK, now I want you to look at that picture as if it's really happening now . . . can you see it?

(*Mary nods.*)

OK, as you look at that picture, is it coloured or black and white?

Mary: It's coloured.

Eric: And what happens if you increase the colour . . . in terms of your feelings?

Mary: Not much.

Eric: And if you make it more pastel . . . or even black and white?

Mary: Mmm. It's a bit less exciting.

Eric: OK, this picture is it moving or is it still?

(*From the outside minimal cues, the therapist already has the answer – for example, the prediction here is that this is a moving, 3D, focused picture. It is, however, important to check.*)

Mary: Moving.

Eric: And what happens if you speed it up?

Mary: I like it . . .
Eric: And if you slow it down?
Mary: It doesn't make any difference.
Eric: OK, is it 3D or is it more 'flattened' – like a picture on the wall?
Mary: It's 3D.
Eric: And what happens if you 'flatten' it?
Mary: Oh, it feels all wrong . . . dull.
Eric: OK, make it back like the way it started . . . now is it focused or is
          it blurred?
Mary: It's focused. Very sharp . . . the air is like . . . it's so crisp you can
          touch it (*she brings finger and thumb together in the air to
          demonstrate*).
Eric: What happens if you make it more blurred?
Mary: Ugh. It just becomes . . . I don't like it.
Eric: OK, bring it back. Just a couple more of these. Is it big or is it
          small?
          (*The prediction is natural size*).
Mary: I'm there. It's life size.
Eric: And what happens if you make it smaller?
Mary: Hmm. I find that difficult. I prefer it bigger.
Eric: OK, back to the way it was. Now is it panoramic, that is, does it
          go from the horizon over here (*indicates*) to the horizon over
          here (*indicates*)? Or is it more limited . . . maybe with a frame
          . . . or a 'fluffy' edge?
Mary: It's panoramic.
Eric: And what happens if you put a frame round it?
Mary: It stops . . . it just becomes a still picture. Oh, and it shifts, it's
          further away.
Eric: OK, thank you for all that information. Now, if we turn to how
          you get 'strung up'. . . .
          (*A similar process is gone through with the first moments of the
          problem state – looking at a page of 'things to do' – to find the
          'critical' submodalities, that is, the ones that produce the greatest
          variance in kinesthetic reaction. To save space, they are: the
          degree of depth, the degree of focus, and whether the picture is
          panoramic or a vignette.*)
Eric: OK, I want you to do the following: I'm going to give you the
          steps first, and then I only want you to run through it when
          you've understood it. Is that OK?
          (*Mary nods.*)
          OK, I want you to hold your hands out in front of you like this

(*demonstrates, both palms facing towards self*), and on your left hand put a picture of the way you draw up your list, and on your right hand see yourself proceeding effortlessly through the day – the way you would skiing down hill. Got that? It's important that on this right hand you're *in* the picture – you see yourself in it, OK?

(*This is a 'personalized' version of the swish pattern.*)

Now I want you to begin with this picture (*indicates LH*) panoramic and focused and 3D, and have this picture (*indicates RH*) start blurred and flat and with a frame round it. Now here's the important bit: I want you to make this picture (*LH*) flatter and blurrier, and shrink it to a small frame *at the same time* as you make this picture (*RH*) more 3D and more focused, and as it gets nearer, 'snap' it into panoramic. Can you do that?

Mary: Sure.

(*Mary runs through the sequence, while the therapist monitors her external cues to see if the new state has the same 'look' as the skiing earlier. When she's finished, she stops and looks at the therapist.*)

Eric: OK, now I'd like you to do that again, with the same two starting pictures as before, but this time do it a little bit quicker.

(*She does so.*)

OK, now re-orient to this room . . . and then go back and do it at least three times.

(*She does so.*)

That's right . . . make sure you take a little break between each time, that's very important . . . OK, how does that feel?

Mary: Very strange . . . it's delightful.

Eric: So what happens if you think of your list now?

(*Mary defocuses, and then her face shows the 'skiing' response.*)

OK. Well, Mary, I think we're done. But there are just a few things to make sure we cover. Thinking ahead now, when is your next busiest day? And can you imagine what will happen when you plan for it?

(*Mary shows the 'skiing' response.*)

And how about another one three months from now?

(*Ditto: this is future pacing.*)

OK, that's it.

Mary: Thank you.

Eric: You're welcome. . . . Is that an original Filofax, or is it one of the other versions? (*He picks it up and flicks through it.*) Can you buy these sheets separately, or do you have to buy the whole lot?

Mary: With this one you have to buy the complete set. But it's worth it. I
            find it tremendously useful.

Eric: Uhuh. And which one is the day-planner?
            (*This is a covert piece of questioning. Since Mary uses the planner
            every day, the therapist watches out of the corner of his eye to see if
            Mary maintains the new response as she thinks of, and looks at,
            her diary.*)
            OK . . . I'll be glad to know how you get on, so feel free to get in
            touch if you need to, or better still, send me a postcard – if you
            have the time.

REFERENCES

Aldrich, C. A. and Aldrich, M. M. (1947) *Babies Are Human Beings: An Interpretation of Growth*, Macmillan, New York.

Ashby, W. R. (1956) *An Introduction to Cybernetics*, Chapman and Hall, London.

Bandler, R. (1985) *Using Your Brain – for a Change*, Real People Press, Moab UT.

Bandler, R. and Grinder, J. (1975a) *The Structure of Magic — A Book about
Language and Therapy*, Science & Behavior Books, Palo Alto CA.

Bandler, R. and Grinder, J. (1975b) *Patterns of the Hypnotic Techniques of Milton
H. Erickson, MD*, Meta Publications, Cupertino CA.

Bandler, R. and Grinder, J. (1979) *Frogs into Princes*, Real People Press, Moab UT.

Bandler, R. and Grinder, J. (1982) *Reframing: NLP and the Transformation of
Meaning*, Real People Press, Moab UT.

Bandler, R., Grinder, J. and Satir, V. (1976) *Changing with Families*, Science &
Behavior Books, Palo Alto CA.

Bateson, G. (1972) *Steps to an Ecology of Mind*, Ballantine Books, New York.

Bateson, G. (1979) *Mind and Nature*, E. P. Dutton, New York.

Brockman W. P. (1980) Empathy Revisited: The Effect of Representational System
Matching on Certain Counselling Process and Outcome Variables, PhD disserta-
tion, The College of William and Mary, Williamsburg VA; *Dissertation Abstracts
International* (1981) Vol. 41, No. 8, p. 3421A.

Cameron-Bandler, L. (1978) *They Lived Happily Ever After*, Meta Publications,
Cupertino CA. Revised and reprinted as:

Cameron-Bandler, L. (1983) *Lasting Feelings: The Applications of Neuro-Linguistic
Programming to the Process of Change* (3-hour video tape), FuturePace, San
Rafael CA.

Cameron-Bandler, L. (1985) *Solutions — Practical and Effective Antidotes for Sexual
and Relationship Problems*, FuturePace, San Rafael CA.

Cameron-Bandler, L., Gordon, D. and Lebeau, M. (1985) *The EMPRINT Method:
A Guide to Reproducing Competence*, FuturePace, San Rafael CA.

Dilts, R. B. (1977) Individual baseline EEG patterns and NLP representational
systems, reprinted in R. B. Dilts (1983) *Roots of Neuro-Linguistic Programming:
A Reference Guide to the Technology of NLP*, Meta Publications, Cupertino CA.

Dilts, R. B., Grinder, J., Bandler, R., Cameron-Bandler, L. and DeLozier, J. (1979) *Neuro-Linguistic Programming*, Vol. I, Meta Publications, Cupertino. CA.

Dolan, Y. M. (1985) *A Path with a Heart*, Brunner/Mazel, New York.

Egan, G. (1975) *The Skilled Helper*, Brooks/Cole Publishing Company, Monterey CA.

Falzett, W. C. (1979) Matched versus Unmatched Primary Representational Systems and their Relationship to Perceived Trustworthiness in a Counseling Analogue, PhD dissertation, Marquette University, Milwaukee WI; *Dissertation Abstracts International* (1980), Vol. 41, No. 1, p. 105A; reprinted in *Journal of Counseling Psychology* (1981) Vol. 28, pp. 305–8.

Galin, D. and Ornstein, R. (1974) Individual differences in cognitive style – reflective eye movements, *Neuropsychologica*, Vol. 12, pp. 376–97.

Gordon, D. (1978) *Therapeutic Metaphors: Helping Others through the Looking Glass*, Meta Publications, Cupertino CA.

Grinder, J. and Bandler, R. (1976) *The Structure of Magic II*, Science & Behavior Books, Palo Alto CA.

Grinder, J. and Bandler, R. (1981) *Trance-formations: NLP and the Structure of Hypnosis*, Real People Press, Moab UT.

Grinder, J., DeLozier, J. and Bandler, R. (1977) *Patterns of the Hypnotic Techniques of Milton H. Erickson, MD*, Vol II, Meta Publications, Cupertino CA.

Haley, J. (ed.) (1969) *Advanced Techniques of Hypnosis and Psychotherapy: Selected Papers of Milton H. Erickson*, Grune & Stratton, New York.

Hammer, A. L. (1983) Matching perceptual predicates: effect on perceived empathy in a counselling analogue, *Journal of Counseling Psychology*, Vol. 30, pp. 172–9.

Kinsbourne, M. (1972) Eye and head turning indicates cerebral laterization, *Science*, Vol. 179, pp. 539–41.

Kocel, K., Galin, D., Ornstein, R. and Merrin, E. (1972) Lateral eye movements and cognitive mode, *Psychonomic Science*, Vol. 27, No. 4, pp. 223–4.

Lankton, S. R. (1980) *Practical Magic: A Translation of Basic Neuro-Linguistic Programming into Clinical Psychotherapy*, Meta Publications, Cupertino CA.

Lankton, S. R. and Lankton, C. H. (1983) *The Answer Within: A Clinical Framework of Ericksonian Hypnotherapy*, Brunner/Mazel, New York.

Lewis, B. A. and Pucelik, R. F. (1982) *Magic Demystified: A Pragmatic Guide to Communication and Change*, Metamorphous Press, Lake Oswego OR.

Maurer, R. E. (1982) The Effect of Postural Congruence on Client Perception of Counsellor Empathy, PhD dissertation; *Dissertation Abstracts International*, Vol. 43, No. 2, p. 529B.

McCormick, D. W. (1975) Primary representational systems and Satir coping styles, unpublished paper, the University of California at Santa Cruz.

Miller, G. A. (1956) The magic number seven plus or minus two – some limits on our capacity for processing information, *Psychological Review*, Vol. 63, pp. 81–97.

Miller, G. A. Galanter, E. and Pribram, K. (1960) *Plans and the Structure of Behavior*, Holt, Rinehart and Winston, New York.

Ornstein, R. (1972) *The Psychology of Consciousness*, W. H. Freeman, New York.

Ornstein, R. (1973) *The Nature of Human Consciousness*, W. H. Freeman, New York.

Owens, L. F. (1977) An Investigation of Eye Movements and Representational Systems, PhD dissertation, Ball State University; *Dissertation Abstracts International* (1978) Vol. 32, No. 10, p. 4992B.

Pantin, H. M. (1982) *The Relationship between Subjects' Predominant Sensory Predicate Use, their Preferred Representational System, and Self-Reported Attitudes towards Similar versus Different Therapist – Patient Dyads*, PhD dissertation, University of Miami, Coral Gables FL; *Dissertation Abstracts International* (1983) Vol. 43, No. 7, p. 235B.

Rossi, E. L. (ed.) (1983) *Healing in Hypnosis: by Milton H. Erickson*, Irvington Publishers, New York.

Rowan, J. (1983) *The Reality Game*, Routledge & Kegan Paul, London.

Russell, B. (1905) On denoting, *Mind*, Vol. 14, pp. 479–93; reprinted in: D. Lackey (ed.) (1973) *Essays in Analysis: by Bertrand Russell*, George Allen and Unwin, London.

Satir, V. (1967) *Conjoint Family Therapy*, Science & Behavior Books, Palo Alto CA.

Schmedlen, G.W. (1981) *The Impact of Sensory Modality Matching on the Establishment of Rapport in Psychotherapy*, PhD dissertation, Kent State University; *Dissertation Abstracts International*, Vol. 42, No. 5, p. 2080B.

Sperry, R. W., Gazzaniga, M. S. and Bogen, J. E. (1969) Interhemisphere relationships: the neocortical commisures: syndromes of hemisphere disconnection, reprinted in P. J. Vinken and G. W. Bruyn (eds.) *Handbook of Clinical Neurology*, North-Holland Publishing, Amsterdam.

Stevens, B. and Rogers, C. R. (eds.) (1967) *Person to Person*, Real People Press, Moab UT.

Thomason, T. C., Arbuckle, T. and Cody, D. (1980) Test of the eye-movement hypothesis of neuro-linguistic programming, *Perceptual and Motor Skills*, Vol. 51, p. 230.

Watkins, J. (1978) *The Therapeutic Self*, Human Sciences Press, New York.

Watzlawick, P., Weakland, J. and Fisch, R. (1974) *Change: Principles of Problem Formulation and Problem Resolution*, W. W. Norton, New York.

Suggested further reading

Carroll, J. E. (ed.) (1951) *Language, Thought and Reality: Selected Writings of Benjamin Lee Whorf*, MIT Press, Cambridge MA.

Dimond, S. and Beaumont, K. (1974) *Hemisphere Function in the Human Brain*, Wiley, New York.

Jackson, D. D. (1968) *Therapy, Communication and Change*. Science & Behavior Books, Palo Alto CA.

Perls, F. S. (1973) *The Gestalt Approach: Eye-witness to Therapy*, Science & Behavior Books, Palo Alto CA.

Watzlawick, P., Beavin, J., and Jackson, D. (1967). *Pragmatics of Human Communication*, W. W. Norton, New York.

There are now over 90 scientific articles in print covering research into NLP, with more on the way. A detailed bibliography is being maintained by Donald W. McCormick, and is available from:

NLP Proficiency Associates
PO Box 7818
Santa Cruz, CA, 95061
USA

Please enclose an international money order for $7 to cover cost and postage. Regular updates are available from:

Donald W. McCormick, PhD
3720½ Centinela Avenue
Los Angeles, CA, 90066
USA

CHAPTER 13

INNOVATIVE THERAPY IN BRITAIN: CONCLUSION

John Rowan and Windy Dryden

OVERVIEW

It is hard to look round the psychotherapy scene in Britain today without a
sense of confusion and even perhaps cynicism. There is such a proliferation
of therapies and labels and methods, some with very high-flying blurbs, and
some with very expensive entrance fees, that one might be pardoned for the
kind of reaction which one student felt when saying:

> If you're a Freudian, it's all down to sex, or Jung says it's all the collective
> unconscious, Adler it's power, Klein it's the breast, Lowen it's your body, Ellis
> it's your mind and Kelly it's your computer. So you pays your money and your
> analyst fits you into his system.

However, in recent years there has been a big shake-out of all these things,
because of the difficult economic situation, which has meant a mood of
contraction and retreat rather than the expansion and advance which were
so characteristic of the late 1960s and early 1970s. Humanistic psychology in
particular has 'cleaned up its act' through the formation of the AHPP – a
body which takes care of technical and ethical standards in the humanistic
field, and acts as a disciplinary body for all humanistic practitioners who join
it. And the AHP has recently brought out a booklet which outlines very
succinctly the scope and limits of the field of humanistic psychotherapy.

  With these contrasting aspects of the situation in our minds, what are we to say about the specific psychotherapies in this book?

Primal integration can be said to be the Rolls-Royce of psychotherapy, because it includes everything a client might need. It has fewer gaps and untrodden paths than any other approach in the book. But for that very reason it may not be suitable for the novice client. It may be too much too soon for the client who has done very little therapy before. It is ideal for the person who has been in therapy for five years or more and is beginning to get impatient at the rate of progress. If we think of the whole process of psychotherapy as a course with two phases, primal integration is a phase two therapy. Phase one is when the client is gradually discovering through personal experience that there is such a thing as the psychodynamic unconscious and childhood trauma. Phase two is when the client heals the splits which have appeared through that process, and goes on to deal with the more fundamental splits which lie deeper in the psyche. This is doing work at the level of what Michael Balint called 'the basic fault'.

Feminist therapy is a curious label in a way, because it means an attitude towards the whole field, rather than a particular technique or theory. So there can be analytic feminist therapists, humanistic feminist therapists, and no doubt cognitive/behavioural feminist therapists, though we have not met any of the latter. But it seems to be an attitude which can in principle spread to any of the other specific psychotherapies in this or any other book. In fact, it is important that it should, because it is basically saying that in the past psychotherapy, like every other field, has been biased against the female. In fact, those male therapists who claimed to cultivate and understand the female were often no better in this respect than those who said nothing about the matter. So if this balance could be redressed, it would be of benefit to all psychotherapists and their clients, of whatever persuasion.

Encounter can be said to be the fullest and most complete approach to group work. It is prepared to go into every area of therapy and life in order to do its work, and is enormously flexible because of that. Just because of that, of course, it is very demanding of the group leader, who has to be exceptionally well-trained and to have done a lot of work on himself or herself, just not to have his or her buttons pushed by the group members. It is a paradoxical approach, because while on the one hand it is very open and democratic and egalitarian, it does on the other hand give great power and authority to the leader. One of the old school of encounter leaders used to be nicknamed 'the drill sergeant', because he introduced so many structured exercises. But in recent years the trend has been for the leader to be much less charismatic and pushy, and much more laid-back and willing to listen.

Co-counselling is a marvellous and politically very interesting approach, which has a great deal to offer. It is horrifying to us when we pick up an enormous tome on self-help groups and therapies, with every approach you can think of in it, and co-counselling gets missed out. Presumably this is because it has not been adopted by the kind of people who write academic papers, and so there is not much literature about it, but this is a feeble excuse to ignore something so widespread and important. It is a matter of great pain to us, also, that the original school (Re-evaluation Counselling) launched by Harvey Jackins has always stayed isolated from the mainstream of humanistic psychotherapy and counselling. By keeping so pure and independent, it has missed out on a whole network of connections which could have increased its effectiveness manyfold. There are, of course, drawbacks to co-counselling, simply because it is so well-designed to be safe for the novice. It is very easy for a pair of co-counsellors, or even a whole local community, to get into a cosy collusive way of working where nothing very deep or challenging ever gets done. Co-counselling communities are notorious for getting too sweet and sugary all too easily. The incessant smiles and hugs, so warm and delightful at first, can come to seem like a fixed convention just as remote from reality as the put-downs they replaced, and very off-putting to the outsider. But co-counselling was very good for me (JR), and fulfilled an important role in my own development, so it certainly can perform very well.

Psychodrama is one of the most approachable of the group methods. It is hard to go to a psychodrama group and not come away feeling 'I could do that!' But in fact it is much harder than it looks. There was one incident at a conference where a psychodrama leader, who was supposed to be highly trained and experienced, completely lost control of one situation in his group, and had to be rescued by a visiting leader who happened to be sitting in. As in all group work, the group leader (the director in this case) has to be very responsive to what is actually going on in the group – not what is supposed to be going on. Psychodrama is one of the best developed group methods in the field, but it is not as often written about as it should be.

Bioenergetics is another of those therapies which we would regard as 'phase two'. It gets people into very deep material very quickly, and is not for the novice or for the faint-hearted. In the film *W.R. Mysteries of the Organism*, some of the scenes show Lowen at work in his New York studio, and it is clear that there is a lot of screaming going on. In fact, when Janov wrote his book *The Primal Scream*, many people pointed out at the time that there tends to be a lot of screaming in all the Reichian and neo-Reichian approaches. It is for this reason that bioenergetics is one of the approaches which tends most of all to get growth centres thrown out of their premises, because the neighbours cannot stand the noise. This is particularly true when bioenergetics is used as a group method, as it often is. In a big room with 50 people who all seem to be screaming at once, the noise can be deafening. But done in a one-to-one way, in the manner suggested in this book, it is not so much of a problem.

Biosynthesis is the most complete of the body therapies. It has been patiently honed and put together by David Boadella, who is one of the master therapists of our time. It is very expert-oriented, and requires a great deal from the therapist because of this. But it seems to offer a really well worked-out body therapy which we are sure will be developed further in the future.

Biodynamic therapy is one of those approaches which is closely controlled and monitored by one person. Gerda Boyesen is a brilliant therapist and a very delightful person to meet, but she does not seem to have any way of really trusting people to go out and do biodynamic therapy. She seems to feel that even her own family members do not always get it right. This seems a pity, as it means that her work will die when she does. Perhaps the publication of this chapter will encourage her to spread out more and allow her methods to diffuse into the population of therapists more generally.

Psychosynthesis is one of those approaches, like gestalt therapy, which people plagiarize and lift things from unmercifully. Everybody seems to think that he or she can do guided fantasy, just because he or she once went to a psychosynthesis workshop, or even a workshop somewhat removed from the original. Certainly many of us in the 1970s came across many of the ideas before realizing that this was where they had come from in the first place. The important idea of subpersonalities, for example, comes from psychosynthesis, and is now used by all and sundry. But in its original form it is a very powerful and wide-ranging discipline, which in principle at least can cover the whole gamut of psychotherapy. In practice, however, all the emphasis tends to be on the higher self and the superconscious, no doubt because that is the missing area in most other therapies. It is still a pity, however, because psychosynthesis in its original form seems to have promise of being a very gentle approach (not many screams in most psychosynthesis work) which can still take people anywhere they need to go.

While transpersonal psychotherapy can be thought of as a pale derivative of psychosynthesis, the present chapter shows that it is much more than that, and has quite different origins. There are in fact a number of ways of carrying out transpersonal approaches, and the one given in this book owes much to the personal stature of Ian Gordon-Brown and his co-workers over the years. Some people may feel that it is a little technique-oriented, but the authors have created something which is very effective and intellectually defensible, and it is good to have this chapter now available and in print, so that this work can be made known to others who may use it and take it further.

Neuro-linguistic programming is one of those American approaches with all the apparatus of certification, levels of training and so forth. It is brash and manipulative, and very unlikeable so far as many British people are concerned, partly because of its cavalier attitude to other forms of therapy or counselling. It is certainly better for specific nameable and measurable problems, rather than for deep personal difficulties. But it does contain some very sharp thinking about the whole process of communication within psychotherapy, and it can only be ignored at the peril of overlooking something important. It is particularly strong in the area of observation – of noticing what the client is doing. And it shows how to use that observation to make better interventions, more accurate and more pointed. We have certainly learned much from it about how to gain rapport with a difficult client, and even if this were all, it would be useful. But there is much more to it than that, and well worth knowing.

All these approaches may come across as a little technique-oriented, but in fact the person of the therapist is always very important, even in NLP. As has often been pointed out, it is always necessary in psychotherapy to go by the actual person doing the therapy, not by the label on the door.

THEMES AND ISSUES

What emerges from all this about psychotherapy? As we read through all the material, certain important themes and issues seem to us to come out almost between the lines, hardly mentioned directly at all in some cases, but very important and not to be overlooked or forgotten. Let us look at some of them here.

Manipulation

The first of these is the subject of manipulation. Psychotherapy offers a very particular type of relationship, no matter whether it be individual or group therapy. It is a type of relationship where it is possible for the therapist to dominate the scene in a very active expert-oriented way, or to hold back and be more passive, or to be very loving and holding, or to be a cool or warm facilitator, or to take up many other roles. But no matter what approach or style of therapy may be involved, the therapist may be more or less manipulative, in the sense of using the situation set up to get goodies of one kind of another at the expense of the client.

This can be done in very obvious ways, or can be quite subtle. But as soon as we start listening with the fourth ear, we start to hear the tone of it. As one of the authors says in Ernst and Goodison (1981):

> Yet [my analyst] was obviously a kind man, he never told me what to do, or what I should think, or laid interpretations on me. He was not oppressive in the blatant ways that feminist writers on therapy have documented. He didn't try to seduce me, tell me I should use make-up or dress differently, accuse me of being incapable of real love because I didn't have orgasms. I have no doubt that overt oppression of women does go on in therapy [references given] but I think what happened to me is equally common and perhaps more difficult to particularise. The oppression lay in *who he was*, the questions *he didn't ask* and the material *I didn't present*. It lay in the way I felt when I arrived at his house on my bicycle and he drew up in his large car; the sense I had that he must see his wife and family and home as normal and my household as a sign of my abnormality. To be cured would be to be capable of living like him.   (p. 308)

However, it also seems to be true that certain therapies lend themselves to manipulation much more than others. Any therapy which places a big distance between the therapist and the client will be more likely to offer chances for manipulation than any therapy which minimizes that distance. Thus in this book the therapies which seem least likely to lead to manipulation are encounter, psychodrama, co-counselling, feminist therapy, primal integration, bioenergetics and biosynthesis, in that order. The others seem to us to lay themselves open to manipulation much more easily, which is not to say that the authors here represented do this at all.

And this seems to be related to the question of whether therapy is political or not. There is clearly a liberatory potential of some kind present and on offer in psychotherapy, but does it lead to political involvement or action? If we look at this historically, it does seem that political involvement, as Kahn (1973) suggests, lies much more with those mentioned above than with the others. He put forward seven variables which could be used to describe various kinds of group work, as follows:

1. Passive leader versus active directive leader.
2. Focus on group versus focus on individual.
3. Talk encouraged and action discouraged versus action encouraged and talk discouraged.
4. Psychotherapy versus goals other than therapeutic.
5. Cognitive emphasis versus affective emphasis.
6. Informed by pro-establishment values versus a socially radical orientation.
7. Encouraging members to go home and adjust to their environment versus encouraging them to rebel against it.

Encounter and Reichian-based groups scored the maximum number of points on the last two of these, going for the second of the two alternatives in each case. This account seems to be borne out in our own British experience.

It was encounter leaders who were instrumental in starting up the process which led to the formation of the Red Therapy group in the 1970s. Moreno was notoriously involved in political activities and social engagement of one kind and another, and psychodrama's interest in action brings it very directly in contact with the real world, once the group session is over. Co-counselling has always had a deep interest in the politics of liberation and the interests of minority groups, and has done a great deal in this area. Feminism of course is very directly political in all its implications. Primal integration people have always been extremely active socially, though not always in the same directions as one another. And of course Reich, the man who more than any other is behind all the body therapies, was one of the most socially concerned and politically active people in the history of psychotherapy. This theme seems to me (JR) extremely important.

One chapter in a recent book on psychotherapy (Rowan, 1983a) is called 'Listening with the Fourth Ear', and is all about how therapists can do better justice to the political and social aspects of their work. It says there that mental disturbance is systematically created by the conditions in which we live. This is what Alice Miller (1985) means when she says that she does not cast the blame on to the parents, because she sees them, too, as victims of their childhood and of the child-rearing ideology that shaped it. The patriarchal culture surrounds us all.

All therapy is implicitly political. Everything we do in therapy always has implications for the way we lead our lives as citizens and social individuals. But many forms of therapy are apparently not aware of this and do not acknowledge it. Thus they run the risk of lending themselves to social manipulation without even knowing it. Any form of therapy which allows direct confrontation of the therapist by the client will tend to be at the non-manipulative end of this continuum. Any form of therapy which allows group relationships between individuals to arise and be expressed will not allow manipulation so readily. Any form of therapy which puts the therapist in a privileged and unchallengeable position will be more likely to be at the manipulative end. The NLP people sometimes quite happily admit this: 'Yes', they say, 'we do get the client to do what we think is best. That is why we have to be so carefully trained and so good at what we do.'

So this seems to us a very important dimension to consider. Anyone who has a social and political conscience would do well to take into account this dimension when deciding what to recommend and what to develop for the future.

Activity and engagement

Another dimension has to do with the extent to which the therapy is active and encourages the direct engagement of the client with the therapist. It is obviously possible for a therapy to be at one end of this continuum and have an emphasis on honesty, egalitarian involvement, political involvement, wide range of techniques, body orientation, emphasis on catharsis and the ability to reach many people; or to be at the other end and have an emphasis on a warm, comforting atmosphere, a deep mystique, a spiritual message and a very quiet, individual orientation.

The point about reaching many people is interesting here. It is obviously good to reach more people, since most people are far more limited than they need to be, and psychotherapy would help them to take off the masks and be themselves a good deal more. But it often seems to be the case that reaching more people dilutes the essence of psychotherapy, and makes it more showy at the expense of real working through of a problem right to the end. Perhaps there is a case for reaching fewer people but working with them in greater depth. But there are political implications here again.

By reaching more people – perhaps through groups or large events – perhaps we can start a process which people can then continue in their own way. Perhaps to be showy is no bad thing if it turns people on to their own potential, and tells them how to begin. On the other hand, perhaps such people would then be so seduced by the showiness, by the brash effects, that they would stay with the foothills rather than climbing the mountains which are really necessary to deal with. There is some suggestion in our own experience that co-counselling, which in itself is a massive and far-reaching approach, capable of very deep working, can often be used by people merely to do trivial things which are not really very challenging to them at all. This is also possible with a trained therapist, but the therapist is more likely to confront and challenge and stimulate and suggest alternatives.

On the other hand, the therapist who works in quiet depth may be hiding from social engagement and from the political implications of his or her work. This is not to be overlooked or unremarked. There is something obscene about someone who purports to be liberating people from the shackles of their neurosis if all he or she is doing is to be putting people back into the shackles prepared by society for them. Historically the active therapies have had a good record of going for change rather than adjustment, and it seems important to encourage this to continue into the future.

Therapy and spirituality

A third issue which seems to emerge is the question of therapy and spirituality. It has become clearer and clearer over the past ten years or so that spirituality is not something which is dying out, but a deep and essential part of being human, which needs to be done justice to and treated very carefully. In this book some of the chapters are explicit about that, but several other chapters mention it and touch on it in various ways. A recent book by Frances Vaughan (1986) deals with it in some depth and detail.

This is a different kind of spirituality from that with which we are familiar from our childhood experience of religion. It is essentially an experiential approach we are talking about here – an approach which takes our own personal experience as primary. Wilber (1983) makes the distinction between legitimate religion and authentic religion. Authentic religion comes from our own personal experience of spirituality; legitimate religion attempts to translate that into something which people can be given as a set of rules or precepts or stories or visions. In between the two come conversion experiences – coming from a powerful mass emotion engendered by a charismatic speaker – which may be more or less legitimate or more or less authentic depending on the prior position of the person being converted.

Authentic spirituality often comes through personal experiences in psychotherapy, particularly deep cathartic experiences, but also visionary experiences of one kind or another. The person, let us say for example, has a peak experience, which as Horne (1978) suggests, is actually a basic form of mystical experience – what he calls casual extraverted mysticism. If this is treated in the right way by the therapist, the person may be encouraged to see this as an indication of a spiritual birthright which can grow and become more important with the passing of time and the cultivation of more and deeper experiences in the same area. This is discussed (Rowan, 1983b) at greater length elsewhere.

Wilber (1986) suggests that the psychotherapists of the future may have to consider nine different levels of work, rather than the one, two or three which they now deal with. A great deal of this extra burden has to do with levels of spiritual development in the transpersonal realms. Unless therapists can deal with these higher levels, they will inevitably distort and misjudge and be unable to tackle the problems which people bring to them which refer to these levels.

Therapist blocking

And this raises in a new form a problem which rears its ugly head over and over again in psychotherapy – the way in which the therapist can block the client.

Why this happens is very simple. It is hard for a therapist to deal with something in the client which the therapist has not yet dealt with in his or her own therapy.

A good example of this is to be found in Malan (1979) where in Chapter 15 he deals with a case history where there are clear signs of umbilical affect – in other words, the patient is remembering life in the womb, and traumatic experiences which happened there. It is all about tubes and starvation and all the rest of the phenomena which Lake (1980) describes so well. But because Malan himself has never been into this area in his own therapy, and because there is no place for this in his own theory, he is compelled to falsify it. He says that the experiences link firmly with *feeding at the breast* (his italics), and that 'any reference to an umbilical cord cannot be anything other than psychological anachronism!'

This is only a particularly vivid example of an issue which recurs again and again in psychotherapy. Some therapists are psychologically open, and can and do learn from their clients about events which did not occur in their own therapy. Some do not.

In the past this has mainly been true about early experience. The experience of birth, for example, is crucially important for many clients, and the traumas resulting from it affect their lives in many ways, as Grof (1985) more than anyone else has spelled out in detail. But most therapists of all persuasions have never been into this experience in their own work on themselves; and so when the client brings it up, he or she gets pretty short shrift. Such a client may then fall into the hands of the Rebirthers, which as Albery (1985) makes clear, is not a good idea. But now we can see that the same is true at the other end of the scale.

Not only have most therapists not been through their own (probably psychotic) material in the womb and through the birth process, but they have not been through their own (probably mystical) material in the transpersonal level of development. And so they are going to falsify this, too. If a client brings up such material, he or she is going to be diverted into some other channel – one which the therapist is more familiar with.

And we are getting more and more sophisticated now in the extent to which we can distinguish between psychotic or neurotic material and mystical material. No longer can we be content with romantic statements such as 'The schizophrenic and the mystic are both in the same sea: it is just that the schizophrenic is drowning and the mystic is swimming.' Rather do we say with Lukoff (1985) that is is possible to distinguish seven possible diagnoses, ranging from the psychotic at one end to the mystical at the other.

We ask basic questions such as – Is the person suffering from a standard psychiatric complaint? Is there overlap with mystical experiences? Is a positive outcome likely? Is there a low risk of damage or danger? If the answer to all these is Yes, the person is suffering from mystical experience with psychotic features, and needs to be treated by transpersonal psychotherapy and not committed to a hospital. If the answer to any of these questions is No, other things are suggested. We cannot go into the details here. But this is sufficient to indicate that we can start to be very specific about what is going on in any individual case.

Now obviously this has very big implications for the future training of psychotherapists. Training courses are going to have to cover the birth and prebirth material at one end, and the spiritual material at the other end; or as Wilber (1986) puts it, the prepersonal and the transpersonal. It is not hard to do this at an intellectual level, but the rest of the person needs to be involved too, in individual and group therapy. And of course this raises immense problems as to how the teachers are to be taught or retaught, but that is best discussed in another volume.

EDITORIAL EPILOGUE

Windy Dryden

I should make it clear from the outset that I am not an advocate of innovative therapy. My role as editor here was to read the chapters presented in the book from the position of someone knowledgeable about the general field of psychotherapy but without the detailed knowledge of the approaches covered in this volume that my co-editor, John Rowan, has.

Before training as a counsellor in 1974, I was quite active in the field of humanistic therapy as a participant in numerous therapeutic groups. I participated in many encounter groups, co-counselled for a while, explored therapeutic massage and experimented with some of the body approaches which existed at that time. Although all these approaches claimed to deal with the 'whole person', I considered at that time that certain important aspects of my personhood were not being addressed. Returning to this field some 13 years later I find that I still have similar reservations and I would like briefly to discuss them here.

While the approaches discussed in this book focus on affect, the body and on spiritual issues I still consider that they de-emphasize both the cognitive and behavioural domains of human existence. In the early 1970s, anything that smacked of *cognition* (by this term I mean not only the ways in which we interpret and evaluate experience but also the fundamental attitudes and philosophies we bring to our experiences) was dismissed as intellectualizing. While this situation is less prevalent among the innovative therapies today than it was then, I still consider that these approaches de-emphasize the attitudinal or philosophic element of human functioning. Two exceptions are those feminist therapists that have a cognitive-behavioural outlook and surprisingly encounter as presented in this volume by Mike Wibberley. NLP does focus on cognitive activity but does not address the philosophical basis of cognition.

Also somewhat neglected in the innovative therapies is the behavioural domain of human functioning. First, clients sometimes have deficits in important behavioural skills (such as assertion, social skills, study skills, etc.) which can usefully be overcome partly by rigorous skills training in therapy sessions. Second, clients often need to act differently in the world to effect lasting changes and they may need concrete behavioural assistance to transfer their therapeutic learning to their everyday lives. While some feminist therapists do in fact include assertion training in their therapeutic approach (see Chapter 3) most other approaches as discussed in this book tend not to emphasize the need to provide clients with specific help in the behavioural domain. There is sufficient evidence from the research literature on psychotherapy to show that behavioural interventions have a definite place in any integrated approach to therapy.

I have used two phrases in the preceding sentence which I would like to focus on: 'research literature' and 'integrated approach to therapy'. While it is not readily apparent from the chapters in this book, practitioners of innovative approaches to psychotherapy have a somewhat negative attitude towards the research literature in psychotherapy, particularly that which deals with therapeutic outcomes (e.g. Rowan and Walford, 1987). I think there are three reasons for this. First, they view the logico-empirical scientific method that underpins much of this research literature as being elementaristic, where humans are split up into constituent parts and the whole person is thus neglected. Innovative therapists are loath to take an elementaristic view of the person. Second, much of this research deals with quantitative data and neglects qualitative data. Innovative therapists are basically against reducing human experience to quantitative units preferring to deal with the richness of subjective data. Finally, innovative therapists see the context of logico-empirical research with its emphasis on prediction and control as one which is characterized by a dehumanizing encounter between 'researcher' and 'subject' which is anathema to the humanistic tradition that underpins many of the approaches in this book.

I have argued elsewhere (Dryden, 1980) that all research traditions have their flaws but all have their place in dealing with different aspects of human experience. Furthermore I argue that if we find consistent results from the 'dominant' research tradition (based on the canons of logico-empiricism) and from the new paradigm of research as discussed in Reason and Rowan (1981) which employs humanistic research methods, than we can be more confident that our findings are robust than if our findings stem only from one tradition. Interestingly, Rowan and Walford (1987) come to a similar conclusion when they say: 'There is more than one type of useful result, more than one research tradition, and more than one way of studying human beings' (p. 24). Thus, innovative therapists could benefit from researching their methods using both research traditions. To date they have been reluctant to do this particularly within the dominant research tradition, although I have listed above certain reasons why this may be so.

My second phrase, 'integrated approach to therapy', points to an important current trend on the psychotherapy scene. A growing body of therapists are becoming interested in exploring what different approaches to therapy have to offer in the search for an integrative approach to our field. Here I think more traditional therapists (psychoanalytic, behavioural and cognitive) have much to learn from a dialogue with their innovative colleagues, particularly in the areas of dealing with affect, the role of catharsis, social factors in psychotherapy, the importance of the body and the place of spiritual issues in human disturbance. But the dialogue will have to be two-way. Innovative therapists also have much to learn from their traditional colleagues particularly, as I have said, in the areas of the role of cognitive and behavioural factors in psychopathology and its treatment. Whether such dialogue will take place in Britain remains to be seen. It rests, to some extent, on the willingness of all therapists to struggle towards employing an acceptable common language and respecting others' different 'ways of knowing' and 'visions of reality' (Messer and Winokur, 1984). The task is a daunting one but one which is worth persisting with if we are to avoid the ever increasing proliferation of different therapeutic schools.

John Rowan

There seem to be three points made by Windy Dryden in the preceding argument. One is that the approaches in this book tend to avoid the cognitive and the behavioural; another is that therapists of the kinds represented in this book tend to fight shy of research on their methods; and the third is that such therapists tend to keep their boundaries raised instead of trying to communicate in any meaningful way with therapists of other persuasions.

As for the cognitive and the behavioural, I do not think that innovative therapists (if we can take the ones in this book as representative) avoid them in general. One of the things I have always liked very much about psychosynthesis, for example, is that the client will perhaps go through some amazing semimystical experience of contacting his or her higher self or whatever, and have the most extraordinary emotional reactions to this; and then, when the client is more composed again, the guide will say something like: 'That's all very well, but what does it really mean in terms of what you will do on Monday morning?' In similar vein, the NLP people talk of 'future-pacing' as a way of making the therapeutic gains really effective in everyday life.

But what such therapists do not do is to try to use the cognitive and the behavioural as the therapy itself. And this is because they feel that this is not the right level to work to obtain real deep changes in the personality. On the whole, although there will be exceptions, people do not come to innovative therapists for simple lacks in social skills or for a lack of general ability to understand what they are doing. They very often come because they have had some therapy before, but it has not done them much good; or they may come because there is nothing particularly wrong with them – they just feel there must be more to life. The kind of therapies outlined in this book challenge people powerfully at fundamental levels, and there tend to be very strong emotional reactions to this; if such reactions do not come, the person is often holding them back, and resorting to the cognitive and the behavioural in order to do so.

In therapy there is always a choice for the therapist as to whether to patch up the person for the moment in accordance with the existing personal and cultural norms, or to go in for real deep change, which may mean challenging old personal norms and even existing social norms. Many of the cognitive and behavioural therapies have taken the former option; most of the innovative therapists go for the latter. And I think this is because the innovative ones have a much more acute sense of the harm which is being perpetrated through the normal process of socialization. Social and cultural norms are not keys to a solution; they are part of the problem.

In other words, innovative therapists often do not want to act in similar ways to those psychotherapists working in Nazi Germany who might have worked with people to help them to adjust to the system, or to those working in South Africa at present to help them to adjust to apartheid. They are aiming at change, not adjustment. And in this work it often seems more productive to go beneath the surface and work there in the darkness which has not been in such direct contact with the system. As feminists never tire of pointing out, our language has become seriously and damagingly infected by the assumptions of a patriarchal culture, with its top-down norms and its male-oriented ideology. By moving into the preverbal and the transverbal we stand a better chance of undermining the mystifications of language.

To the extent that cognition is trapped within the conventions of a patriarchal system, it is not innocent, not clean, not unbiased. We cannot take for granted that it will serve our purposes. And that brings us straight on to the second point at issue – the subject of research and research methods. Many people do not realize how great is the gulf at present between researchers and practitioners. It is very rare indeed for practitioners to read research or to get much out of research studies. And researchers are very often remote from actual practice, and even sometimes think it is a virtue to know nothing about psychotherapy from the inside.

And this is the essential point about research as ordinarily practised. It is always from outside. As soon as the researcher is reduced to an outsider, the research subject is reduced to an object. And instead of real meaningfulness being pursued, it is statistical significance which is pursued. It has often been pointed out that statistical significance and actual importance are not the same thing, and that they may even be antithetical. Earnest orthodox researchers like Beutler *et al.* (1986) say things like this:

> Collectively, these findings suggest that while similar gender matchings may exert a statistically significant effect on psychotherapy process, research methodologies must be rather rigorous and well defined in order to allow this relatively modest effect to emerge as outcome differences.

In other words, the effect is so tiny that we need a microscope in order to see it.

The contortions which conventional researchers (what I prefer to call old paradigm researchers) get up to in pursuing their dream of prediction and control are sometimes tragically extraordinary. A recent large volume on process research (Greenberg and Pinsof, 1986) makes the excellent and totally valid point that process research and outcome research are mutually necessary. Outcome research which does not pay sufficient attention to process does not know what it is talking about:

> Basing outcome research on ascribed or alleged orientations without actual verification is equivalent to giving blue and green pills to patients in a drug study without knowing the content of the pills.

Similarly, process research which pays no attention to outcome is inadequate and one-sided in its complementary way:

> For instance, to know that certain behaviour therapists convey high levels of warmth and support to their patients during desensitization is interesting, particularly in regard to most behaviour therapists' disregard of relationship issues, but ultimately such a finding is irrelevant unless it is linked to some kind of patient

outcome. The critical question is did their high level of warmth and support make any kind of meaningful difference?

Well, that all makes sense and leads in to the rest of the book, with its detailed examinations of many different systems of measuring or describing the process of psychotherapy. But 720 pages later, Greenberg is saying this:

> A study of the relationship between the three variables therapist intervention (T), client process (C) and outcome (O), however, poses a difficult 'three-variable' problem for traditional experimental designs. Although it is possible to study the relationship between any two in both correlational and experimental designs, the task of relating all three at the same time is difficult . . . unless T is shown to cause C and cause O at the same time, the nature of the *direction* of the causal relationship between T and C always remains in doubt and one never knows whether it is T or C which leads to O. [To research this problem adequately] appears beyond the capabilities of current research procedures.

So after all the work has been done, and all the research surveyed, all that the authors can do in the end is to throw up their hands, and say in effect – let the next generation do it.

Now this kind of research has been going on for over a hundred years now and the old paradigm is wearing thin and running out of excuses. The point is that the old paradigm of research cannot, even in principle, give us the kind of knowledge we need to understand and explain what happens in psychotherapy. We have to move to a new paradigm of research which does not even attempt to talk about variables, but which talks instead about people, and to people, and with people. This is not the place to go into all that, which has been fully described and discussed elsewhere (Reason and Rowan, 1981; Lincoln and Guba, 1985; Mahrer, 1985).

So that brings us to the third issue – the subject of an integrated psychotherapy. Psychotherapists are notoriously narrow and unsympathetic to other traditions, and it seems hard to change this. Perhaps two groups are particularly likely to keep their boundaries raised and be unwilling to compromise in any way.

The first group is the orthodox and established camp of those who have been trained long ago and have achieved status and dominance in the profession. They seem to look down on others as not quite measuring up to the rigours of their extensive and expensive training and their broad and deep experience.

The second group is the innovators, by which I mean here those who have actually invented some new approach – people like Reich, Moreno, Jackins, Janov, Lowen, Boyesen, Perls and so on. Such people typically turn into staunch defenders of their own organization against all comers, and mistrust any attempt to combine or add techniques or theoretical insights with their own approach.

So this leaves the not-so-well-established non-innovators as the people who are most likely to favour integration. Such people very often follow an eclectic path. If it is true, as many studies testify, that the micro activities of therapists of many different persuasions do not differ very much from one another, and if it is true, again as often shown, that the search for the one most effective therapy is a wild goose chase, then an eclectic approach would make the most sense for many therapists. Thorne (1967) argues in favour of an integrative approach which actually has a very firm and consistent theroretical base, but which allows for great variety in the actual techniques to be used in a given session. Dryden (1984) too argues in the same direction. As can be seen in the present volume, my own approach is integrative in the sense of including techniques from all four of Jung's categories of thinking, feeling, sensing and intuiting.

But I think there are limits to this process, because of the model outlined in the Introduction. Therapies which are doing different things on different levels and aiming at different versions of the self are complementary rather than compatible. If I did too much work at the mental-ego level I would feel I was holding people back rather than encouraging them to grow. If I did too much work at the subtle level I would feel I was turning into a spiritual guide rather than a psychotherapist. So I want to concentrate most of my efforts into the centaur level where I think the real work of my kind of psychother-apy is carried on. I will take side-trips into the other levels, but I want to come back to home base most of the time.

So I feel that there is most scope for co-operation and mutual information within each level, rather than between levels. This kind of integration could certainly be very helpful, and I am sure it will take place more and more in the coming years.

Acknowledgement

We would like to thank Joyce Watson of the Centre for Personal Construct Psychology for assistance in helping us to clarify the issues discussed in this chapter.

REFERENCES

Albery, N. (1985) *How To Feel Reborn?* Regeneration Press, London.
Beutler, L. E. *et al.* (1986) Therapist variables in psychotherapy process and

outcome, in S. L. Garfield and A. E. Bergin (eds.) *Handbook of Psychotherapy and Behaviour Change* (3rd edn), Wiley, New York.

Dryden, W. (ed.) (1980) The relevance of research in counselling and psychotherapy for the counselling practitioner, *British Journal of Guidance and Counselling*, Vol. 8, pp. 224–32.

Dryden, W. (1984) *Individual Therapy in Britain*, Harper & Row, London.

Ernst, S. and Goodison, L. (1981) *In Our Own Hands*, The Women's Press, London.

Greenberg, L. S. and Pinsof, W. M. (eds.) (1986) *The Psychotherapeutic Process: A Research Handbook*, Guilford Press, New York.

Grof, S. (1985) *Beyond the Brain*, State University of New York Press, Albany.

Horne, J. R. (1978) *Beyond Mysticism*, Wilfrid Laurier University Press, Waterloo.

Kahn, M. (1973) The return of the repressed, in E. Aronson (ed.) *Readings about the Social Animal*, W. H. Freeman, San Francisco.

Lake, F. (1980) *Constricted Confusion*, Clinical Theology Association, Oxford.

Lincoln, Y. S. and Guba, E. G. (1985) *Naturalistic Inquiry*, Sage, Beverly Hills CA.

Lukoff, D. (1985) The diagnosis of mystical experiences with psychotic features, *Journal of Transpersonal Psychology*, Vol. 17, No. 2, pp. 155–81.

Mahrer, A. R. (1985) *Psychotherapeutic Change*, W. W. Norton, New York.

Malan, D. H. (1979) *Individual Psychotherapy and the Science of Psychodynamics*, Butterworths, London.

Messer, S. B. and Winokur, M. (1984) Ways of knowing and visions of reality in psychoanalytic therapy and behavior therapy, in H. Arkowitz and S. B. Messer (eds.) *Psychoanalytic Therapy and Behavior Therapy*, Plenum, New York.

Miller, A. (1985) *Thou Shalt Not Be Aware*, Pluto Press, London.

Reason, P. and Rowan, J. (1981) *Human Inquiry: A Sourcebook of New Paradigm Research*, Wiley, Chichester.

Rowan, J. (1983a) *The Reality Game*, Routledge & Kegan Paul, London.

Rowan, J. (1983b) The real self and mystical experiences, *Journal of Humanistic Psychology*, Vol. 23, No. 2, pp. 9–27.

Rowan, J. and Walford, G. (1987) Counselling research: an ideological study, *Counselling Psychology Review*, Vol. 2, No. 1, pp. 16–24.

Thorne, F. C. (1967) *Integrative Psychology*, Clinical Publishing, Brandon.

Vaughan, F. (1986) *The Inward Arc*, Shambhala, Boston.

Wilber, K. (1983) *A Sociable God*, McGraw-Hill, New York.

Wilber, K. (1986) the spectrum of development, and The spectrum of psychopathology, in K. Wilber *et al.* (eds.) *Transformations of Consciousness*, Shambhala, Boston.

NAME INDEX

SUBJECT INDEX

Index compiled by Peva Keane